# Historical Perspectives on the Education of Black Children

# Historical Perspectives on the Education of Black Children

HARRY MORGAN

PRAEGER

Westport, Connecticut
London

**Library of Congress Cataloging-in-Publication Data**

Morgan, Harry.
   Historical perspectives on the education of Black children / Harry
Morgan.
      p.   cm.
   Includes bibliographical references and index.
   ISBN 0–275–95071–9 (alk. paper)
      1. Afro-American children—Education—Social aspects—
History—19th century.   2. Afro-American children—Education—
Social aspects—History—20th century.   I. Title.
   LC2741.M67   1995
   371.97'96'073—dc20          94–42843

British Library Cataloguing in Publication Data is available.

Library of Congress Catalog Card Number: 94–42843
ISBN: 0–275–95071–9

First published in 1995

Praeger Publishers, 88 Post Road West, Westport, CT 06881
An imprint of Greenwood Publishing Group, Inc.

Printed in the United States of America

The paper used in this book complies with the
Permanent Paper Standard issued by the National
Information Standards Organization (Z39.48–1984).

10 9 8 7 6 5 4 3 2

**Copyright Acknowledgments**

The author and the publisher gratefully acknowledge permission to use
the following excerpts:

*The Souls of Black Folk* by W.E.B. Du Bois. Copyright © 1970 by Washington Square Press. Reprinted by permission of Pocket Books, a division of Simon & Schuster, Inc.

Reprinted by permission of the publishers from *White Teacher* by Vivian
Gussin Paley, Cambridge, Mass.: Harvard University Press, Copyright
© 1979, 1989 by the President and Fellows of Harvard College.

*The Autobiography of W.E.B. Du Bois* by W.E.B. Du Bois. New York:
International Publishers, 1971. Reprinted with permission of the publisher.

*To Harding and Martin*
*You Are Always On My Mind*

# Contents

# Illustrations

# Acknowledgements

This book could not have been completed without the help of friends, colleagues, and my students, who assisted in various ways to assure the quality and quantity of this work. I gratefully acknowledge the contributions of the many people who provided their knowledge, wisdom, and labor in different ways. This group includes, but is not limited to, Janet Baty, James K. Baum, Priscilla Bennett, Thomas Carrere, Claire Dennis, Harry Dennis, Dorothy Dickerson, Judith Manthei, Jeanne Mueller, George Rolle, Alice Scales, Connie Lisa Selman, Margaret Short, Verl Short, Tim Tribiano, Galyn Vesey, Casse Bianca Ward, and Geri Williams.

# Historical Perspectives on the Education of Black Children

# Introduction

This book will describe historical perspectives related to the education of Black children through their heritage, their family and community, and institutions of learning. The author will discuss the complex interactions between Blacks and Whites and the roles enacted by philosophers, theorists, and practitioners in this process.

The Black experience in the United States has been the topic of a great many creative and scholarly works in the form of literature, television, theater, and movie presentations. These media events have focused upon Black urban life, the southern experience, northern migration, slavery, poverty, civil rights, and many other issues that are now well known. Seldom, however, has the focus been upon Black children and their attempts to make meaning of their existence. In their coming of age, their acquisition of knowledge through formal and informal experiences provides the foundation for self-esteem, wisdom, and maturity. As these qualities emerge, Black children tend to sense that all experiences are not merely simple daily rituals, but that some are more important than others, and they know intuitively some to be ingredients essential in giving meaning to *their* lives.

We now know, for example, that all children develop an awareness of racial color differences by the age of three and that by the time they reach kindergarten they understand these conditions to be permanent. We also know that when given the opportunity, our children are watching and listening for new information.

From this early age Black children find a special meaning in the concept of role model because role modeling is fundamental to their acquisition of a sense of who they are. This knowledge must be integrated with what they already know—mostly from observing the actions of others.

Only within our recent past have Black children been provided opportunities to observe Black adults in so many highly valued social roles. During the period of slavery in the United States, most Black children made meaning of their lives through experiences that offered little more than a life of labor; and this labor was primarily for the benefit of those with whom they could not identify. During their early childhood some Black children were permitted to be playmates of White children on the plantation, and some were even taught school subjects by mothers of those White children— often in direct defiance of laws that forbade such activity.

By the time Black children reached the age of seven, their White playmates would go off to school, or White parents would decide that their children were too old to be friends with slave children. These close but fragile childhood relationships had to conform to the world of slave and slave owner—an adjustment that must have been tearful for Black and White children alike. White children would enter the common rites of passage built into the social system for them. The Black child would once again ponder a private and reoccurring question: Who am I, a person, an animal, or something between the two?

The Black child's role models—field hands, maids, cooks, all responding to the demands of Whites—did not provide the meaning many Black children of slave families wanted to make of their lives. Children would observe that many adults in their families were given the same responsibilities as farm animals. These children grew out of early childhood knowing they could aspire only to a similar lifestyle. In growing up and working at making meaning of their lives, they observed that Whites were referred to with titles of respect, that complete obedience to them was expected. They also saw that Black children—and adults who looked like them—had only a first name regardless of age.

For the most part, over time many Blacks acquiesced to the subservient roles open to them as the ultimate meaning of their lives. But there were many Black activists, like Nat Turner and Denmark Vesey, who organized campaigns designed to free themselves and others like them from the system of slavery. These organized efforts created complex partnerships in which organizers would sometimes be aided by sympathetic Whites, yet at the same time be betrayed by Blacks in whom they placed their trust.

Despite the oppressive conditions of slavery in the United States, a relatively large population of plantation slaves could read, had specialized skills, and burned with enough determination to seize their own freedom. They were the runaways. Those who were successful achieved their freedom through clever planning that among other things, required a new name, the acquisition of proper papers, money, and transportation to a free state.

At the same time, many Blacks had already gained their freedom "legally" —some with the aide of sympathetic Whites, some on their own. There were also many Blacks who had never been slaves. By 1815 over 100,000 free Blacks resided in the southern states combined. For certain their children were watching.

The educated blacks of the late 1800s appeared to prefer the term *Negro.* Institutions that separated the races by labeling public facilities used the term *Colored. Black* was more often than not a derogatory label, especially among those who were dark skinned. The issue of identity was to emerge often and in every aspect of life for the now free people of color. In a country where Blacks were to be kept in their place, no label that inspired self-esteem or positive self-valuing would be accepted in public or official discourse.

In certain areas of the South, South Carolina and Virginia, for example, there were free Blacks who owned land and property and were considered wealthy for their time and place. There were a few Blacks who themselves owned Black slaves. They established their own churches and institutions of learning to ensure that their own children would become educated and capable of perpetuating their economic and social status. Among free Blacks of the 1800s, many would finance their own schools for children and adults. This self-help initiative would recruit both White and Black teachers. More often than not Black churches were used as venues; but they also used private homes of free Blacks, constructed their own buildings, and accepted offers from Whites who volunteered for Christian reasons. Their institutions were deliberately named *African* schools and *African* churches —with pride in their endeavors. Free Blacks were persistent in opening other meeting places whenever their facilities were destroyed or discovered in areas where laws had been enacted against them.

Before the end of 1863, Black children learned that slavery had now become illegal, and many among them watched as their parents agonized over whether to remain where they were or to abandon the plantation for a different place and a new start. A decision to leave would mean leaving behind a terrible but predictable pattern of existence. For mothers and fathers it would call forth the arduous task of finding a way to make a living in an unknown environment, knowing that others depended upon them to make a better meaning of their lives.

In 1863 President Abraham Lincoln issued the Emancipation Proclamation which changed the status of Africans. Slaves, previously defined as property, were now citizens. In 1868 the U. S. Congress implemented the Fourteenth Amendment to the Constitution, establishing *equal protection* for all citizens. In 1870 Congress approved the Fifteenth Amendment, guaranteeing all citizens the right to vote. Africans had become African Americans.

In 1875 Congress passed a civil rights bill that prohibited discrimination in public accommodations in the nation. However, in 1883 the Supreme Court declared the Civil Rights Act of 1875 unconstitutional. By 1896 the Supreme Court upheld the doctrine of "separate but equal" in *Plessy v.*

*Ferguson,* creating an opportunity for all states to discriminate against Black citizens in every institution in the nation.

Through various experiences, such as listening to dinnertime conversations, Black children would learn that they were *Colored citizens of the United States.* As a group they would be referred to as *Freedmen.* They were also aware that these labels might not be permanent because sometimes they were called *Negro,* or derogatorily called Nigger—the latter being occasionally paired with *Black.*

The subject of racial identity had not emerged in any serious fashion among the Black literate classes until late in the 1800s. The names of churches and schools were still proudly prefaced with the word *African.* It was the voice and writings of William Edward Burghardt Du Bois in the 1890s that focused upon the philosophical and pragmatic issues facing Black Americans. Educated at Harvard and at the University of Berlin, Du Bois debated Booker Taliaferro Washington about the role of Blacks, as individuals and as a group, in a society dominated by Whites. Also literate, Washington articulated his theory of self-help so well that he put under his control practically all White corporate and most individual financial contributions for organizations promoting the interest of people of color.

In 1899 Du Bois initiated the first Pan African Congress to maintain a social and political connection with what he considered to be the basic heritage of Black people. Washington remarked that his interest in Africa was no greater than his interest in any other foreign country. Black children watched and listened as these two Black men, whose views were respected among both Blacks and Whites, brought national attention to the state of race relations in the United States.

Washington's message was simple: Blacks could help themselves, in the process showing Whites they were both capable and willing to pursue hard work. Du Bois agreed with the need for Black enterprise, but he balked at the notion that Blacks had to prove their merit to Whites before Blacks could be recognized as full citizens. It was his view that human rights and political rights should be available to all citizens regardless of racial identification. Further, Du Bois argued that the White experience should not be assumed as an index against which Black people are to be valued.

The philosophical roots of John Locke would emerge in the *empirical* principles of Booker T. Washington and would confront their natural counterpart in Du Bois's philosophy of Rousseauesque *romanticism.* Du Bois's fervor for unequivocal civil and political equality would be the agenda for meetings, conferences, and study groups involving both races. The most notable conference was held in Niagara Falls, New York, and later became known as the Niagara movement. By 1910 this group of Black and White activists and scholars formed the permanent organization that is now known as the National Association for the Advancement of Colored People (NAACP). And the children were watching and listening.

The NAACP used the courts and public opinion to press for the political and economic equalities commonly granted to whites. Through the 1950s —50 years after the formation of the NAACP—the words *Negro* and *Colored* still remained acceptable labels and were often preferred in private as well as public matters.

The 1960s were to become a decade of great social change, primarily through Black and White youth acting upon their discontent. They emerged from this tumultuous period with *Black* replacing *Colored* and *Negro* as the preferred term of identity for a group now made up of many different social and political voices—yet, all aimed at a single generic cause. In this new social environment, *Negro* and *Colored* were even used somewhat negatively.

We now know that the long drive for equality has produced civil rights for all through the efforts of individuals, organizations, and people in government who have worked to ensure fair political and occupational access. This work toward equality is conducted in a social context that promotes the acceptance of a belief that African heritage is embedded in all Black Americans—as Du Bois had suggested almost 100 years ago.

As we move toward the year 2000, among Black Americans, *African American* has become the commonly preferred label of racial identity in public discourse, in government and court documents, in schools and centers of higher learning. It is preferred by residents in the Black community, most of whom now willingly embrace the positive value of their African heritage. African Americans in positions of influencing public opinion through various media tell us that this is the *final* identity label for Black Americans. The future might tell a different story—and our children will be watching. Chapter I, "The Early Philosophers," serves several purposes for the reader. It establishes an important framework of thought for the remainder of the book. It dispels the myth that the history of Black people originated with the slave trade. American scholars tend to dwell on this period of Black history because as a country we have never resolved the guilt associated with the genocide of Native Americans and the forced bondage of Africans. The first chapter is also informative for the educator and the informed public. The role of Aesop's fables in our literary and social interactions is probably common knowledge, but the fact that this role represents a Black philosopher's contribution to our lives is probably less well known. Chapter I also attempts to establish a connection between the early philosophers, among them Aesop, and current teaching practices and learning activities. The ideas of these philosophers have come to influence us through the work of early theorists like Sigmund Freud, Erik Erikson, B.F. Skinner, and Jean Piaget.

Chapter II, "Early Theorists and Practitioners," describes the various theories prevailing in colleges, universities, and other teacher-training institutions today. When adults are cast in the role of teacher, their work is a reflection of the theory and philosophy of thinkers and researchers whose work they studied in education, philosophy, and sociology courses. The theories taught in today's institutions of higher education are more often than not those of Skinner, Freud, Erikson, and Piaget, as well as Maria Montessori. These theorists were influenced by earlier philosophers like Plato, John A. Comenius, Jean Jacques Rousseau, John Locke, or the more recent John Dewey.

Practitioners are consumers of knowledge and wisdom available in educational literature. Our current literature on the teaching and learning environment from research studies, speeches, and proceedings from learned societies is generally available from any college or university library, or from state and federal offices of education dating back to 1929. Books and related documents from earlier periods are also available. Very few methods of teaching, strategies for presenting information, or new programs in education have not been tried before. A number of older methods were abandoned, but they continue to return under new labels, and the new crop of educators who do not know history well present them as new ideas. Some of these "new ideas" are merely old methods that long ago fell out of vogue and are now repackaged with a modern vocabulary and a bit of tinkering here and there. Practice in any field of human service has evolved from a theory, or a combination of theory and past practice, with a mix of the practitioner's own ideas.

Chapter III, "The Slavery Period," puts into perspective Black self-help in education during the period of slavery, and it examines the roles played by various White groups in attempting either to abolish slavery, or reinforce its existence. At times Blacks met in small, clandestine groups to share their knowledge, occasionally teaching each other to read. Young slaves like Frederick Douglass, who was taught to read by his White mistress, exploited their skill by teaching eager Black field hands to read. There were also free Blacks who established their own schools, and there were leaders like Thomas Jefferson who supported the teaching of reading to slaves so that they might learn to embrace Christianity through reading the Bible.

The work of Quakers, a Christian group that came to the Americas from Europe in pursuit of religious freedom, was critical to abolitionist efforts. The Quakers committed time and money, frequently putting their own safety in jeopardy, to provide free schools for Blacks even when few facilities were available for White children. Their work often provided an environment for self-help that encouraged and sometimes enabled Blacks to develop their own schools. There were also individual White benefactors who founded schools in anticipation of a free Black society that would need education to enable Blacks to assume roles of citizenship alongside Whites.

The Quaker schools for Blacks, and the founding of the Manumission Society to prevent the kidnapping of northern Blacks for enslavement in the South, gave rise to a class of Black professionals and intellectuals who formed a substantial middle class in the Northeast. Many of these Blacks and their children were provided academic foundations in the Quaker schools that admitted them to the most prestigious colleges and universities in the United States. Some were like the famed Shakespearean actor Ira Aldridge, who was acclaimed in Europe, not America, because American audiences had yet to accept talented Blacks at the highest levels of their craft. Other graduates attended the African Free School in New York City, later to seek further education elsewhere, like James McCune Smith, who went on to obtain a medical degree in Glasgow, Scotland. He returned to his country of origin to become the first Black pharmacist in New York City as well as director of the first orphanage for Black children. Others founded newspapers, and yet others became state and federal officials as well as college presidents.

Chapter IV, "Beyond the Slavery Period," describes the social and political atmosphere that existed immediately after slavery. The U.S. Congress commissioned the Freedmen's Bureau to provide for the assimilation of freed Blacks in the part of our country devastated by our national conflict between southern states and northern states. Congress did not appropriate sufficient resources for the mission, and the administration in charge of the Freedmen's Bureau requested the help of benevolent and philanthropic societies. The response was swift, and many professionals and ordinary citizens went from the North to help the Freedmen's Bureau with its southern mission. Black and White teachers from New York, New Jersey, and the New England states traveled South to set up schools for the newly freed slaves. Many of the volunteers were beaten, and a few were killed by roving White gangs bent upon upsetting any final resolution of the Civil War. This wave of White Northerners to the South in support of a Black cause was the forerunner of a similar group of northerners who responded to a call for help 100 years later, when northern Whites flocked to the side of the Reverend Martin Luther King Jr., during the 1960s civil rights movement. It was a time when Blacks had developed their own schools and were well represented in the population, when Black children attended integrated schools in many northern communities, where they were small in number.

Chapter V, "The Decades That Followed Slavery," intends to build a picture of the social and political context within which African American women and men worked to create for their people a place where they could benefit from the opportunities rightly available to all citizens. It presents biographical sketches, along with descriptions of the institutions for learning that African Americans founded and helped to develop. In the same context is detailed the impact that three extraordinary African Americans—Frederick Douglass, W.E.B. Du Bois, and Booker T. Washington—had upon African Americans from all classes and conditions from 1880 until 1950. The chapter examines their experiences as children growing up in different environments; it follows their growing into adulthood and reviews the significant contributions each has made to our country.

Chapter VI, "The Controversies Over African American Intelligence," describes how I.Q. seems to have a historical life of its own. It is remarkable that within the past 30 years or so a small group of brilliant scholars, with high positions in academic circles, would devote a significant part of their professional energy to discredit the intellectual integrity of Black children. Sir Cyril Burt, a famous British psychologist and journal editor, often called the "Father of Psychology," and Professor Arthur Jensen are probably the most well known researchers in the group that also includes William Shockley, professor of engineering at Stanford University, and Richard Herrnstein, of Harvard University. Through the 1960s Burt claimed that his studies of twins raised in different environments provided fundamental proof that intelligence was for the most part an inherited characteristic. He reported that his sample of identical twins reared in different environments displayed a remarkable similarity in their performance on I.Q. tests when each pair of twins was tested during the same intervals. Reports from Jensen, Herrnstein, and Shockley all cited the work associated with Burt's twin studies to bolster their own theories of Black inferiority and White superiority on I.Q. tests. A foundation called the Pioneer Fund, at one time having offices in New York City, has been reported as seeking to fund scientists who study Black negative/White positive racial differences. Herrnstein and Jensen, as well as others have received support from this fund. Leon Kamin was the first among a small number of researchers to criticize Burt's work long after it was being cited by persons knowledgeable in the field of psychology. After Burt's death an investigation of the records indicated that his studies were *faked*. He had convinced himself through personal knowledge that Blacks were inferior to Whites, and he concocted the data to prove his hypothesis.

Also in this chapter is a general discussion of differences in how learners process  information because of  subcultural differences in childrearing patterns and similar social variations. Some of these patterns have been studied, and a body of scientific information has emerged called *cognitive style theory*. This theory suggests that differences in performance under a variety of circumstances might be linked to styles of parenting. Observations of family life in an African village, for example, showed that infants raised by mothers there were precocious in developing motor skills like crawling, walking, and climbing. They tended to develop these skills earlier than did White European infants or African infants raised in urban areas of Africa. Similar findings were reported for African American babies. It is suggested that classroom environments that stress docility and quietness might be too restrictive for the socially active African American child from moderate-to low-income families. Such suggestions need further study before we know for sure that certain environmental preferences for processing information do indeed exist among some African American children.

Head Start, a childcare program designed to aid poor children in their quest for a better chance at success in the early grades, is discussed in Chapter VII. From its beginning very few thought the program would survive 25 years. It was begun by early childhood specialists and federal bureaucrats. Hundreds of professionals have passed through various levels of the program as teachers, social workers, nutritionists, administrators, and paraprofessional aides in various roles. Public schools and private childcare centers have borrowed their ideas and innovations. However, the program survives on memories. For budgets over the years have been cut, and funds intended for the program have been diverted to satisfy political interest, while most Head Start teachers work at or near the minimum wage. Given these conditions, the program's survival is remarkable.

The cultural and political context within which such programs are developed is related to social policy and our attitudes toward the poor. We are ambivalent about the possibility that a poor mother might abuse the federal/state-supported childcare and not seek employment, but we are also ambivalent about accepting children as a social responsibility, making it ultimately our government's responsibility to assure that children's needs are met. Head Start was a part of the 1960s fight on poverty; it is one of the few programs that remain. Why does it survive? Perhaps because it is the best way we know to avoid another generation's having to experience a Great Depression. Head Start represents a way of saving poor children from repeating a life of poverty as adults, a life similar to what they might be experiencing as children.

Highly useful materials and programs are available to educators, activists, advocates, and parents. All one needs to access them is the time and the inclination, and suggestions found in this chapter will enable one to select materials for the integration of African American information and materials into classroom studies and throughout our simple daily rituals.

# I

# The Early Philosophers

*Why, beautiful still finger are you black? And why are you pointing upward?*

—Angeline W. Grimke

We now know from the work of Louis Leakey (1903-1972), the British anthropologist born in Kenya—and from the studies of others who followed his work—that human civilization had its origin in Africa. We also know that parts of North Africa, like Egypt, were settled by Africans from the south who brought with them an established culture that included not only commerce but also the religious concept of monotheism—all this about 10,000 years before the flowering of the Greek and Roman civilizations. The African influence on Greek and Roman culture has been reported and documented by various scholars.

By the time Alexander the Great was sweeping the civilized world with conquest after conquest from Chaeronia to Gaza; from Babylon to Cabul; by the time the first Aryan conquerors were learning the rudiments of the war and government at the feet of philosophic Aristotle; and by the time Athens was laying down the foundations of modern European civilization, the earliest and greatest Ethiopian culture had already flourished and dominated the civilized world for over four centuries and a half. (Danquah, 1927, p. 3)

During this early period, thoughts about any formal structure for the education of children in large groups were centuries away. Primarily through oral directions and rituals, families and kinship groups were ascribed the responsibilities of teaching their young to enable them to assume a role in matters affecting the group's hunting, gathering, mating, and safety. The natural emergence of folk tales from the oral tradition of African culture of that time, however, set the stage for significant and lasting contributions to the children's literature of today.

It is highly unlikely that anyone in today's world has not heard of Aesop's fables. Hundreds of folk tales have been attributed to this African, who historians agree lived around 560 B.C. Scholars suggest that he was a slave from Phrygia, Anatolia. Phrygia was located in northern Anatolia, near what we now call Turkey. Several hundred years prior to Aesop's birth, Phyrgia had been a rich and powerful state. It is highly likely that residents of such an area would have had more than a few slaves. The language and customs were European and more related to Greek than African. The language of Phyrgia was not Anatolian but Indo-European and was written alphabetically. Aesop probably had access to a variety of dialects, including the language of Africans (hieroglyphics) and a language similar to that of the Greeks. He was described as having black skin and thick lips, which led to his name, Ethiop, which translated into "black." Aesop's most popular fables involve few events, mostly with animals carrying on a human conversation. Many other of his fables that are less known involve only humans, and yet other fables involve humans together with animals.

These fables were intended not to provide the world with a body of facts or descriptions of actual events but to advance a way of examining life and attitudes of mind. Embedded in Aesop's simple plots is simple wisdom; the fables contain messages concerning trust, honesty, cooperation, individual frailties, and human indulgences. Over the centuries Aesop's fables have appeared in many languages and continue in their popularity with every generation of children and adults. For many years the stories attributed to Aesop have found their way into literature available to adults and children in classroom texts, commercial storybooks, and movie and television dramatizations. In many social situations it has become common to express a moralistic judgment or a matter-of-fact assessment of an event through the use of an Aesop fable.

The following selections are from the most well known fables as well as from the less well known. They involve animals with animals as well as animals with humans.

## THE FOX AND THE GRAPES

One day a fox came upon lovely ripe grapes on a vine high above his reach. The fox jumped to retrieve the grapes but his attempt was far short. He failed several more times. Even a running leap was not successful. He sat down, and looking at the grapes he announced that they were probably sour anyway and not really worth getting (Jacobs & Heighway, 1966).

*Moral:* There are those who pretend not to want things that are beyond

Attic Red Figure Chous, "University of Pennsylvania Museum, Philadelphia (neg. #S4-69480)."

their reach.  Also, sometimes your grasp is shorter than your reach.

## THE HARE AND THE TORTOISE

One day a hare came upon a tortoise and thought that he could create some amusement for himself.  "How long does it take you to get where you are going?" taunted the hare.  The tortoise replied, "I usually reach my destination in a shorter time than you think."  The hare laughed, and this annoyed the tortoise, who challenged, "I will run a race with you and the fox can be the judge."  Soon thereafter the fox marked the distance and started the race.

The hare took off so swiftly that he was soon out of sight.  He thought the idea of a tortoise being swifter than a hare was so absurd that he sat down to take a nap in the shade.  The tortoise kept going at a steady pace and in time passed the place where the hare was napping.  By the time the hare discovered what had happened, the race was over and the tortoise had won (Grimm & Grimm, 1961).

*Moral:*  A steady commitment is often more important than speed. And, the race is not always won by the swiftest.

## THE BLACKAMOOR

Once upon a time a man bought an Ethiopian slave, who of course had black skin as Ethiopians usually do. The owner thought that his new slave was black because of neglect by the previous owner, so he set out to correct this condition.  He collected a supply of water and cleaning cloths and worked very hard at scrubbing away the blackness.  After a long period of toil, the slave remained as black as ever.  Because of the long period of naked exposure, the slave became severely ill and died (Vernon-Jones, 1992).

*Moral:*  Characteristics of others are not imperfections merely because they do not match your own.  Also, toiling to change things in your own image can cause great loss.

## THE LION AND THE MAN

On one particular day a lion and a man just happened to be traveling in the same direction. Soon the conversation started with the man boasting that men were actually more powerful than lions. The lion thought that this point of view was amusing and insisted that everyone knows that lions have superior strength and courage.

Their argument reached its loudest pitch when they came upon a statue that depicted a man on top of a lion holding him in submission. The man pointed to the statue as proof of his argument. The lion replied, "When lions make statues they also put themselves on top" (*The Aesop for Children*, Rand McNally, 1947).

*Moral:* There are at least two interpretations for all questions. And, the view that we have of ourselves cannot always be trusted.

Aesop developed the fable as a form for examining issues related to ethics, morality, justice, and the role of the philosopher in society. He promoted the idea that all living things have common interests in existence through shared experiences. He therefore thought it quite reasonable to have animals, humans, and other living things carrying on conversations.

The people of Aesop's time were bewildered by many natural events such as extreme weather variations, water occasionally turning to ice, the aging process and the constant change things seem to undergo. Accepting that everything changes diminishes the need to consider the ethical and moral behavior of the individual, except for self-interest. Through the fable Aesop demonstrated that *ideas* about essential things like honesty, compassion, virtue, and justice remain unchanging, but individual behavior can change as we make personal choices about our own role as a person among other living things.

William Caxton translated and illustrated a selection of Aesop's fables in 1484. In 1692 a special edition was published for children by Sir Robert L'Estrange. *The Aesop for Children* was published in 1919 by the Rand McNally Company. This edition was illustrated by Milo Winter and contained over 100 fables attributed to Aesop. A 1947 reprint is presently available from book sellers and in many libraries. Another notable Aesop edition was published in 1912 containing 214 story translations by Vernon Jones, along with illustrations by the noted Arthur Rackham. A facsimile of this early edition was published recently by Gramercy Books (a division of Random House). The original introduction that was written by G. K. Chesterton, and included in the reprint, is a superb commentary on Aesop and the fable as philosophical literature.

Aesop's fables were collected by a Greek political figure named Demetrius of Phaleron around 300 B.C. He titled the collection *Assemblies of Aesopic Tales*. Approximately 300 years later this collection was translated into Latin by a freed Greek slave named Phaedrus. Approximately 100 years after the Phaedrus translations Valerius Babrius, a well-known writer of his time, translated Aesop's fables into Greek. Thus, Aesop's philosophical thought was to surface over 200 years later in the paradoxes presented by the philosopher Heraclitus of Ephesus. He expressed the view that everything within the purview of our sensual experiences (auditory, olfactory, visual, etc.) never remains the same but undergoes constant change. About 100 years later Plato chose to take this line of reasoning to task. He reasoned that there were things in possession of permanent characteristics and presented supportive Socratic arguments in his *Forms and Ideas*.

It is well to remember that Aesop, whose belief in the consistency of ideas is mirrored by Plato, lived about 300 years before Aristotle, Plato, and Socrates. The Greek philosopher Pythagoras (560 B.C.-?), however, lived about the same time as Aesop. In his view, everything could be explained by numbers. Today's researchers in education theory and practice, whose studies are quantitative, often approach their work in the belief that anything that exists can be measured by using numbers much as Pythagoras did. The view that we can understand the world through numbers drew many followers to Pythagoras almost cultishly, and that makes it difficult to discern which of his ideas might have been initiated by a follower. Indeed, not all of Pythagoras's converts were committed to mathematics with such fervor as his.

Alcmaeon (530 B.C.-?), for example, applied his mathematical orientation to his studies of medicine. It was Alcmaeon who eventually influenced other Greek physicians to modify their reliance on superstition with an infusion of a more pragmatic approach to understanding disease and treatment. It has been reported that Alcmaeon dissected animals and discovered that the brain was responsible for intellectual activity. He also discovered the critical function of the optic nerve and the Eustachian tube. Not all work was successful for Alcmaeon, and he was never really completely free of superstition despite his mathematical approach.

Pythagoras and his followers invented the well-known Pythagorean Theorem. Practically every student in geometry has had to learn that the square of the hypotenuse of a right triangle is equal to the sum of squares of the other two sides. Pythagoras and his followers used religion, mathematics and mysticism to study the relationship between humans and their environment. Many of their ideas were penetrating, though their findings were sometimes incorrect, especially about the shape of the earth and the function of the planets. More important, though, was their systematic examination of phenomena that interested them; in that, they were ahead of others.

Other scholars have reported that Aesop in fact had an effect upon the thinking of Aristotle (384-322 B.C.), Plato (427-347 B.C.), and Socrates (470-399 B.C.). The writings of Plato, a student of Socrates, have been cited among the most influential philosophical works affecting Western thought. The strong oral tradition inherent in the fables of Aesop preceded what is now known as the Socratic Method. Namely, the putting forth of a series of questions as a means of exposing the logical conclusion—already known to the questioner—on the assumption that truth and reason are compatible. This approach is labeled the Socratic method because it was employed by Socrates.

From what is known, Socrates did not write. Plato's writing provided a role for a Socratic character, who had the wisdom to propose the appropriate question for the discourse at hand. Plato's most widely read philosophical work over the years was *The Republic* (circa 376 B.C.). In this writing Plato suggested that the well-being of young children should not be left to the often self-serving interests of their parents. This view, radical for its time, was accompanied by the idea that knowledgeable persons should be recruited by the state to act as teachers of those children who should be educated. For the ancient Greeks education in the formal sense was viewed not as a social responsibility but as the responsibility of the family and other relatives.

Among the brightest of scholars in Plato's Academy in Athens, Aristotle was known to challenge his teacher on many occasions. The Academy provided a forum for these intellectual encounters. Plato believed that mathematics was an appropriate basis for understanding reality, whereas Aristotle argued for a more empirical perspective. Sensory perception and observations of phenomena, he argued, provided a better understanding of the universe.

Aristotle spent most of his time trying to explain the stars and planets. He taught others that the heavens were perfect and permanent and could not be destroyed. Earth, in contrast, was thought of as changeable and imperfect. He divided earth into four elements: water, air, fire, and earth. His simple explanation, complex for his time, did not go unchallenged. Water, he suggested, always seeks its own level, fire burns upward, air fills in the space around us, and objects that are released always drop to the earth.

His observation that humans were at the top of a system that organized all living things in a hierarchy was correct. He was incorrect, however, when he disagreed with Pythagoras about the function of the heart and the brain. For Aristotle believed that the heart was the center of thought and that the brain served as a device to cool the blood. Despite what we know about the function of these organs today, we often repeat Aristotle's error when we say, "I thought with my heart and not my brain." It was Aristotle's emphasis on sensory experiences that conflicted with the views of Plato, who was more impressed with mathematical forms. Their views continue to be argued in scholarly debates to this day. In today's educational research community, for example, this perceived conflict of ideas is discussed in the context of *quantitative* versus *qualitative* investigations. We now know that in many ways both Aristotle and Plato were on a proper course in that scientific investigations require measurements and observations.

Aristotle was the most racist of the Greek philosophers, and his views on White superiority often go unmentioned. It was his view that Greeks were superior and among those people who had a right to enslave others. He suggested that climate and geography made some people predisposed to becoming slaves. The Greeks, according to Aristotle, had the intellect and superior position and therefore the right to enslave other races. But Plato's elitism did not lag far behind Aristotle's racism. Education, in the view of Plato, should be provided by the state. The curriculum should include literature, poetry, music, gymnastics, and military training. Plato also proposed that state-financed schools should provide academic services for children ages 6 to 18 (a system remarkably similar to our state-run primary and secondary schools). However, only children of the elite, of the ruling class, and the few others who had the potential for leadership roles in society would be accepted in the Platonic model of schooling.

Each philosopher, with his cult followers and students, appears to have had definable areas of exploration in attempting to understand and explain to others the nature of the relationship between humans and their environment. With some it was mathematics, whereas with others, such as Heraclitus, it was the elements (he studied fire as the primary element of change in the universe). Then there were those like Aristotle, Plato, and Socrates, who emphasized intellectual encounters in the oral tradition. Plato founded the Academy to institutionalize this form of scholarly inquiry.

The extent to which the particular contributions of early philosophers like Aesop, Pythagoras, Alcmaeon, Socrates, Plato, and Aristotle continue to influence our intellectual thought today is remarkable. Equally remarkable, however, is the extent to which historians have excluded Aesop—an African—from this very literature. In discussions about philosophical influences on Western thought, the foci continue to be Eurocentric, and Africans like Aesop are virtually ignored.

## PHILOSOPHICAL INFLUENCES ON EDUCATION

The widely read philosophical views of John A. Comenius (1592-1670) emphasized a role for the family in the growth and development of young children. In his book *School of Infancy*, published in 1630, Comenius compared the growing child to a small plant that needed the freedom to develop in an environment where nurturing parents are essential.

He thought that the period of birth through age six is critical and that during this early period, developmentally supportive experiences are essential for later life. This notion was at variance with the Platonic tradition that recommended state control of education of youth because the motives of parents are too self-serving.

Two philosophers, Locke and Rousseau, would become in their time well-known thinkers proposing different perspectives on teaching, learning, and child development. Although they lived during different times with very little chronological overlap, their philosophies regarding human experience have been contrasted in serious discussions among philosophers, theorists, and practitioners, even to the present.

Jean Jacques Rousseau (1712-1778), the French philosopher, held views of the human condition similar to those of Comenius and others labeled *romanticists.* Rousseau was bothered by the seemingly ever-increasing social rules limiting human experiences. It was his view that individuals from birth are innately good; that if given the freedom to experience, they would follow the principles of nature: "Everything should . . . be brought into harmony with . . . natural tendencies." John Locke (1623-1704), on the other hand, was among the philosophers called *empiricists.* They believed that the human organism from birth needed control and direction for the purpose of contributing to an accepted social order. If certain freedoms were granted, according to the empiricists, they should be planned and controlled. We will revisit these philosophic views at various intervals in this book to illustrate the impact they have had upon teaching and learning theory.

Rousseau's ideas were expressed in his book *Emile,* which described in intimate detail a relationship between a child and tutor. It became a controversial document in its day because of its direct challenge to the often stiff and distant relationships that were maintained between teachers (including tutors) and their pupils at that time. The basic theory Rousseau wanted to promote was exemplified in Emile's role as a learner. With the focus on the freedom of experience, Emile was provided great latitude to explore various elements in nature without unwarranted restrictions. This involved long walks with the tutor among natural environments. As questions were proposed by Emile, the ensuing discussions could take place among the examples that called forth the queries. Thus, natural environments enhanced the learner's readiness to acquire knowledge, and encounters could be dealt with at the appropriate maturation levels. "We know nothing of childhood; and with our mistaken notions the further we advance the more we go astray. The wisest writers devote themselves to what a man ought to know, without asking what a child is capable of learning" (Rousseau, 1979, p. 1).

The John Locke school of thought suggested that the human organism, beginning at birth, was passive and should have its experiences controlled primarily for the enhancement of a well-organized social order. He introduced the theory of *tabula rasa*—the view that infants come into the world as a "blank slate," totally receptive to environmental influences. The child's growth and development, therefore, should be planned by knowledgeable adults who would control the youngster's experiences. These "controls" are the planned events and activities to which the children would be exposed, thus enabling them to acquire the proper knowledge for their role in society and the world. This philosophy would serve as a model for the theories and practices of *behaviorism.* Practitioners in the fields of education and psychology were taught that their approach to work required the control of the individual's experiences within the context of their practice.

Locke's preoccupation with order and control for the good of the state was extended to justify slavery in the English colonies in America and elsewhere. The British policies of colonization and enslavement called for philosophical justification that was compatible with their Christian beliefs. Philosophers like Locke considered Africans and Native Americans heathens; therefore Christians had the obligation—and the right—to take their land and save it from waste, and to "civilize" the inhabitants by making them Christians. Rousseau and other romanticists, in contrast, expressed antislavery beliefs.

Prior to 1900, wherever there were formal gatherings for the purpose of teaching children, whether church, privately sponsored, or public venue, students were required to sit passively, at permanently fixed desks, with full attention directed toward the teacher. For John Locke had taught his followers that the proper environment for learning required a strict control of the learner's experiences. In such a setting, the learners need not be consulted about their perceived needs, nor should they participate in their own learning until directed to do so by the adult in control.

Romanticists argued that the learners were in the most strategic position to determine their needs, and if given the freedom to act upon their environment, by observing children's behaviors, adults could determine the appropriateness of adult teaching interventions. Piaget (who will be discussed later) in fact based his theories on observing children who were encouraged to interact with their environment.

Early in 1900 practitioners, theorists, and philosophers began to question the appropriateness of the controlled, didactic classroom for childhood learning. The philosopher John Dewey (1859-1952) would articulate this cause. Through his writings and public appearances he became one of the most widely known proponents of Rousseau's philosophy by identifying individual experience as essential for productive learning.

In reaction to the teacher-controlled classroom of the time, Dewey proposed a learning environment where social interaction was viewed as a major factor in the teaching-learning process. In such a model, experience would expand the number of ways in which learners could participate in their own learning. Like Friedrich Froebel years earlier, Dewey thought that desirable intellectual goals could be achieved through play. These goals included the acquisition of thinking skills, logical reasoning, and concept formation—all in the context of the child's freedom to encounter real experiences along with opportunities to interact with others.

## REFERENCES

The Aesop for children. (1947). Chicago: Rand McNally & Co.
Aldred, C. (1961).The Egyptians. New York: Praeger.

Celarier, J. L. (1966). *Plato's republic: Analytical notes and review.* New York: American R. D. M. Corporation.

Cross, R. C., & Woozley, A. D. (1964). *Plato's republic: A philosophical commentary.* New York: Macmillan & Company.

Danquah, J. B. (1927). Foreword. In S. Lapido (Ed.), *United West Africa (or Africa) at the bar of the family of nations* (pp. 3-5). London: African Publication Society.

Greenleaf, P. (1978). *Children through the ages: A history of childhood.* New York: Barnes & Noble.

Grimm, W. & Grimm, J. (1961). *Folk-lore and fable.* New York: P. F. Collier & Sons Corporation.

Grubb, W. N., & Lazerson, M. (1982). *Broken promises.* New York: Basic Books.

Jacobs, J., & Heighway, J. (1966). *The fables of Aesop.* Ann Arbor, Michigan: University Microfilms, Inc.

Locke, J. (1959). *An essay concerning human understanding.* New York: Dover. (Original work published 1690).

Pollack, L. A. (1983). *Forgotten children.* London: Cambridge University Press.

Rogers, J. A. (1972). *World's great men of color.* New York: Macmillan.

Rousseau, J. J. (1947). *The social contract.* (C. Frankel, Ed.). New York: Hafner Press. (Original work published 1762)

————. (1979). *Emile.* (A. Bloom Trans.). New York: Basic Books (original published in 1762).

Snowden, F. M. (1970). *Blacks in antiquity.* Cambridge, Massachusetts: Belknap.

Vernon-Jones, V. S. (1992). *Aesop's fables.* New York: Gramercy Books.

# II

# Early Theorists and Practitioners

*Children have two visions, the inner and the outer. Of the two the inner vision is brighter.*

—Sylvia Ashton-Warner

From what is now known, the first formally organized school for children under the age of six was started by a young Protestant minister, Jean-Frederic Oberlin (1740-1826) in 1767. Oberlin appointed Louise Scheppler to head the school and train others who worked in nearby villages. The idea of formal schooling for children younger than six was yet to be introduced in the United States by Margarethe Meyer Schurz (1832-1876), in Watertown, Wisconsin, in 1856. Mrs. Schurz, a German immigrant, taught classes for young children in German. Elizabeth Peabody (1804-1894), would become the first to establish a kindergarten to be taught in English.

Following the philosophy of Rousseau, Oberlin established freedom of experience as a model for his classrooms. At his own expense he established a school in rural France among poor and working-class families, many of whom did not speak standard French. One of his collaborators, Scheppler, set out to learn the new dialect in order to communicate with pupils in their own language. Oberlin's teaching-learning plan included a display of pictures labeled in standard French and in patois. Also, labels were affixed on common articles in the classroom (chair, table, etc.)—one label with the spelling from the pupils' patois, the other with the spelling from standard French. This remains common practice in the early childhood classrooms of today.

Oberlin's schools, called *knitting schools,* emphasized experience rather than direct instruction. The conductices, as teachers were called, would sit among a group of children, do their knitting, and introduce language experiences through fables related to the children's lives.

This method of teaching is currently finding a place in many classrooms as the *whole language* approach in which spelling, grammatical forms, and word recognition, are taught through literature (complete stories), in the whole context, as opposed to reducing words to the sounds (phonics) of each of their letters.

Sara Benezet had previously taught village children to knit, so the basic idea of the knitting format could have been introduced by her. This format provided opportunities for children to participate in their own learning. Many preschools today use this format; they hold morning meetings with the class to discuss the time, weather, and day of the week and to make plans for the school day.

The Oberlin school provided sensory experiences, art, and music, along with language development and activities designed to enhance math concepts. One of the most direct applications of Rousseau's philosophy was Frederich Froebel (1782-1852), a German educator who has been credited with creating the kindergarten movement in Germany. The word *kindergarten* can be translated from German to mean "children's garden." A maturation concept first introduced by Comenius and later discussed by Rousseau, this term suggested that the growth of a child could be compared to the growth of a small plant, which would need care and attention and the freedom to develop. Comenius emphasized that this should start at birth.

Froebel introduced the idea of play as an essential ingredient in early childhood experiences. To enhance these experiences Froebel designed colorful objects in various shapes and textures and presented them to children as *gifts.* Art was encouraged because it was thought to bring children to the esthetics of nature and broaden their appreciation of beauty and creativity. Music was also encouraged, and Froebel composed songs for children.

Elizabeth Peabody (1804-1894), inspired by Schurz, started a crusade to spread kindergarten programs all over the United States. She gave inspirational talks to women's organizations, at settlement houses, and schools, and to any child support group that would provide fund-raising opportunities. She would eventually establish a kindergarten in Massachusetts using the Froebel model. By 1873 the kindergarten had become a permanent part of the St. Louis school system. It was inevitable that the teacher-centered didactic models that had emerged from the philosophy of John Locke would be deemed inappropriate for the new classrooms for preschool and kindergarten children. However, there was not a common agreement on whether the learner's experiences should be controlled in a teacher-directed environment, or whether children should be encouraged to move about the classroom and engage in a variety of activities—some by choice, some at the teacher's suggestion.

Fannie Jackson Coppin, a Black woman born in slavery, perhaps the most well known among women of her time, established a reputation as an educator of distinction. Coppin's freedom was purchased by her aunt, who was impressed by young Fannie's intellect, and how quickly she seemed to learn. Young Fannie was sent by her aunt to live in Rhode Island with a family who would allow her to attend the nonsegregated schools there. Fannie did so well at the Rhode Island Normal School that she was accepted at the prestigious Oberlin College in Ohio. At Oberlin she majored in education, and became the first Black to student teach in the nearby community. She organized classes for other Blacks who had grown up in slavery, teaching reading, arithmetic, and music.

The first African American woman in the United States to graduate from a major college, after graduation, Coppin joined the teaching faculty of the Institute for Colored Youth in Philadelphia. Within five years, she became principal of the school. (The Institute for Colored Youth will be discussed in Chapter III). Coppin State College in Maryland was named in honor of this great practitioner of education.

Charlotte Forten Grimke (1837-1914) was born to a wealthy Black family in Philadelphia. After being tutored at home, she was sent to Salem, Massachusetts, to attend a nonsegregated school. Grimke graduated from Salem Normal School, today Salem State College. Her first job was teaching at Epes Grammar School in Salem, where she was the first African American in the state to teach in a desegregated setting. When the Freedmen's Bureau sent out the request for volunteer teachers, Grimke was among the many Black and White teachers to respond. She volunteered to work with recently freed slaves in the Sea Islands under tremendously difficult and hazardous conditions. After the Freedmen's Bureau completed its work, Grimke moved to Washington, D.C. and was employed in the U.S. Treasury Department. During her career, direct instruction was the primary method of teaching children. This approach to teaching and learning emerged from Bible-training classes for young people, where conformity and attentiveness were considered essential.

However, teachers at various levels were experimenting with new approaches to teaching and learning, and new ideas were being introduced about when learning begins for young children. On a lecture tour in 1913 and 1914, Maria Montessori (1870-1952) emphasized, "I must have the aid of mothers." With this statement Montessori introduced the idea that mothers were a child's first teachers, and that the early training done by mothers was not inferior to what is done in formal schooling. She insisted that the most critical period for child growth and learning was the time prior to formal schooling, the years from birth to age six. The Montessori method was introduced in the United States and offered an additional variation.

Maria Montessori was the first licensed female physician in Italy, where in

1907 she opened the Casa dei Bambini (House of Children) in a poor community in San Lorenzo. There she taught children skills for life. She designed special materials for sensory training in her classrooms. By the age of six, poor children, many of whom had been abandoned by their families, were taught social skills and etiquette. This was the first program ever developed with "disadvantaged" children in mind.

A severe critic of the Montessori method was W. H. Kilpatrick, who at this time was a professor at Teachers' College, a division of Columbia University. In the teaching field, Kilpatrick was very influential in that practically all White teachers in the nation, and even some Blacks as well, had been his students. Kilpatrick was also a supporter of John Dewey and usually interpreted Dewey's work for others. It was within this context that Dewey and Kilpatrick saw the Montessori method as a threat to the reforms they were putting into schools through their students. Montessori was at a great disadvantage because she could not speak English. She could not, therefore, openly debate her American critics.

Montessori was invited to the United States for the purpose of a lecture tour in 1913 and 1914. She was greeted by large audiences wherever she spoke, but for many in the audience her presentations were disappointing. She would describe an idea, speaking in Italian for 10 to 15 minutes; then her interpreter would speak for a few moments. It was obvious that she was saying much more than the interpreter was either willing or able to translate. She nonetheless remained an immensely popular educator while on tour in the United States. By 1915 over 100 schools in the nation were using the Montessori method, and Rhode Island officially adopted the method for its public school system in 1913.

Montessori emphasized the freedom of experience within a context of what she called sensory experiences. She theorized five intellectual stages of child maturation and development, and designed a set of experiences in which children were encouraged to participate. She encouraged self-exploration in a carefully designed learning environment with "sensory" learning materials. This approach was highly successful with the population of children who had been exposed to the discipline of survival in the streets of Italy.

Montessori insisted that a trained adult in the learning environment was needed to structure experiences to assure a degree of independence at each stage of development. Later she opened training centers for teachers who wanted to use the Montessori method in their approach to work. Over the years, rights to the name Montessori as designating a particular teaching and learning environment has entered the public domain. As a result, many programs with Montessori in their marquee are not in reality conducted in the method or spirit of Maria Montessori.

Her idea that disciplined experiences were required to promote intellectual freedom attracted a great deal of criticism from those like John

Dewey, who agreed more fully with the philosophy of Rousseau. Montessori theories were almost midpoint between those of Locke and Rousseau along a continuum of thought between freedom of experience and the control of experience. The role of the teacher in the Montessori method is one of intervener, as opposed to observer, who selectively becomes involved when the activities at hand appear to call for adult intervention.

John Dewey (1859-1952), the philosopher, was among Montessori's most severe critics. He had proposed a model of education that he called "Progressive Education." This approach would provide a classroom setting with materials for learners to explore and a teacher with whom learners could interact. The teacher would act as an informed facilitator similar to Oberlin's conductices in the knitting schools. Dewey did not object to Montessori materials, but he did not think it appropriate for them to be used for direct instruction, nor for their access and use to be restricted as in the Montessori classrooms.

A primary focus of Dewey's Progressive Education was the interaction among learners. In his view children learn as much from each other as from the adult in the classroom. Montessori did not discourage such pupil interaction, but it was not encouraged outside of utilitarian value. Despite these differences, Dewey invited Montessori to accommodate her approach to be more compatible with Progressive Education. Maria Montessori declined. John Dewey continued as one of the most prolific and widely known modern proponents of Rousseau's philosophy that freedom of experience is essential for child development and learning.

Like Froebel, Jean Piaget (1880-1961) thought that desirable intellectual goals could be experienced in early childhood through play. Under Froebelian influence, Piaget had a profound effect upon current early childhood classroom practices. His work, primarily through the observation of children, led him to conclude that children develop through a series of stages. In this he was in agreement with Montessori.

Trained as a biologist, Piaget was concerned with the maturation of the human organism. His writings detailing his observations influenced the entire world of childhood educators. His primary interest was the role of experience in the child's growth and development. It is important, thought Piaget, that growing children have the freedom to experience their environment to enable them to understand the world around them. Accordingly, it is the experiences children have that enable them to *assimilate* what they learn into what they already know. This assimilation takes place during the learner's interaction with the environment, whether that environment is made up of living or inanimate objects. Children can therefore participate in their own learning through solitary play, or play with others.

Experiences provide continuous opportunities for children to test their abilities and *accommodate* them to present environmental circumstances. Piaget defined four stages of development and described levels of assimilation and accommodation essential to the process of maturation and knowledge acquisition. From birth to approximately age two, infants learn through experiences that are highly personalized. Their interaction with objects that call for sensory perception influences motor skills and thought at a time when the infant does not understand that objects exist outside of its personal experiences.

Gradually, from age two to seven, the child undergoes experiences that enable it to form mental images through thought and language, but, can remain self-centered and unable to fully comprehend logical sequences of events. Between the ages of seven and eleven, Piaget theorized that experiences will begin to include the perspectives of other persons in terms of concrete actions and rules. Most of the children in this age group are unable to think in abstract terms. From the age of 12, children enter the formalized operations stage. They develop ideas about consequences, abstract issues, and events of the present and future. They begin thoughtful analyses of their experiences and ideas. It was not until the 1960s that Piaget's ideas were taken seriously by educators and psychologists in the United States. Prior to the 1960s the fields of learning theory and child development were dominated by adherents to the philosophy of John Locke and the theories of behaviorists. Another criticism of Piaget's work came from the research community, who viewed qualitative data collection with suspicion. Qualitative approaches to research—sometimes called ethnography—emerged from the 1970s with widespread acceptance among a significant number of researchers. The positive image of qualitative studies seemed to coincide with a more favorable review of Piaget's work.

Most of Piaget's ideas emerged from his encounters with children—including his own—in various environments. He posed questions to children of various ages, befriended them, and made careful documentation of their responses regarding logical reasoning, problem solving, and the knowledge they brought to the experience (i.e., previously learned information and how they used it), much in the spirit Rousseau described in *Emile.* From these observations he formulated a theory of stages of development that can be observed when children are actively involved in learning tasks and/or the common rituals of daily life. Parents among the informed public queried the feasibility of teaching their own children the Piagetian tasks identified as advanced levels, thus creating "gifted" children.

Annette Bardouille-Crema, Kathryn N. Black, and John Feldhusen of Purdue University studied over 200 Black children from families of different income groups. The children, of three age levels, were studied in relation to how well they performed selected age-related Piagetian tasks. The researchers reported that children from higher-income Black families performed better than children from lower-income families.

Piaget, Dewey, and Montessori are widespread in today's schooling for children of all ages. Montessori programs in 1990 were to be found in over 100 school districts, serving more than 600 classrooms. John Dewey's philosophy is embedded in teacher approaches in preschools, nursery schools, and various other settings. The child-centered approach, open education, humanistic education, whole language, integrated curriculum, and the contract plan—where teacher and student agree on the quantity and quality of an assignment to be carried out independently by the student—are all products of Dewey philosophy. Perhaps more preschool and early education programs are based in varying degrees upon the theories of Piaget than those of any other theorist.

Theories about learning and behavior that can be classified as *behaviorism* dominated practice in a variety of fields from the early 1900s through the 1950s. The influence of behaviorism remains in many current disciplines where professionals have concluded that the *control of experience* is best suited for behavior change in the individual. One can trace the development of this theory from the studies of Pavlov, Watson, and Skinner. Whereas Montessori, Piaget, and Dewey were influenced by Rousseau; Pavlov's, Watson's, and Skinner's theories have their roots in the *tabula rasa* philosophy of John Locke.

Ivan Petrovich Pavlov (1849-1936), a Russian psychologist, arrived at his discoveries while studying the gastrointestinal systems of dogs. He attended the University of St. Petersburg, where his concentration was animal psychology and medicine. Pavlov identified himself as a physiologist. He did not hold psychologists in high regard and he would not allow himself to be identified as such. For his discoveries he received the Nobel Prize in 1904.

Pavlov observed the salivation reflex in dogs when they were fed. He discovered that if he rang a bell at their scheduled feeding time, eventually they would salivate upon hearing the bell at that time, whether they were fed or not. From his observations Pavlov concluded that learning had occurred in the dogs because of their association between the bell and the feeding habits established by the researcher. The process of pairing an unconditioned stimulus (food) with the conditioned stimulus (bell) will elicit an unconditioned response (salivation). After conditioning, the conditioned stimulus (bell) will elicit the desired response. This became known as *classical conditioning*.

The psychologist credited with introducing behaviorism in the United States is John Broadus Watson (1878-1958). He completed his graduate work at the University of Chicago and received a professorship at Johns Hopkins University. He became well known for popularizing psychology through articles that he wrote for magazines, including *Collier's, Harper's,*

*Cosmopolitan,* and *Liberty.*

Watson was so influenced with the work of Pavlov that he rejected all theories of learning and behavior that involved subjectivity. It was his view that emotions could be controlled by classical conditioning and that all people were born with a few reflexes that were stimulated by reactions to anger, fear, and love. These reactions, he concluded, occur in response to certain stimuli. Loud noises and sudden loss of supper, for example, would elicit the response of fear.

He came under a great deal of criticism after conducting a classical conditioning experiment with an 11-month-old child. The experiment involved presenting the child with a white rat, at the same time creating an extremely loud noise to frightened the infant. The pairing of the white rat with the unpleasant noise soon made "Little Albert" fearful whenever the white rat appeared. Watson concluded that positive or negative emotion can be elicited through classical conditioning.

Applications of Watson's and Pavlov's work can be found in some of the reinforcement techniques applied by some teachers in today's classroom. Teachers on occasion will offer children a small gold star to be placed above their name on a list of all children in the class or on a written assignment that has been done well. The teacher wants the child to associate the star with good work. The teacher hopes that the desire to receive a star will then be paired with good academic performance—and will elicit that behavior in the future. Using such techniques, teachers also attempt to modify the unruly behavior of children who "act-up" through similar techniques. B. F. Skinner (1904-1992), obtained his Ph.D. from Harvard University. During his studies he became profoundly influenced by reading the work of Pavlov and Watson. Using their theories as a backdrop to his own work, Skinner spent five years conducting research to refine his own version of classical conditioning.

Skinner thought that classical conditioning was too limited in scope to provide a full explanation of learning and behavior. He thought that a severe limitation was that the desired behavior (in the form of the initial response) was elicited only when the stimulus was known. He reasoned that too many human responses are the result of unknown stimuli; and even when the stimulus is known, it cannot fully explain all changes in behavior at any given time.

Skinner is credited with establishing the theory of *operant conditioning.* In this context he experimented with small animals and birds and concluded that the *rate* and *quality* of emitted behavior could be controlled by the consequences of the observed behavior. One of his most well known experiments was conducted with a pigeon in a cage without food. In one part of the cage is a colored disc that would allow food to enter the cage when touched. When hungry, the pigeon will peck about the cage until it discovers that food enters the cage when pecking is done on the disc.

Skinner concluded that the pigeon *learned* that the most efficient way to satisfy hunger is to peck on the disc. This operant conditioning changes the pigeon's *behavior.* The frequency of the known behavior (pecking) was controlled by the consequences elicited by that behavior (food). When the consequences of the behavior were rewarding to the pigeon, the action was repeated under the same circumstances. Skinner called these consequences *reinforcers.* Reinforcers can be controlled in several ways—primarily negatively and positively. If a child is performing well in school and the teacher awards a gold star or verbal praise, the teacher hopes that this *positive reinforcement* will continue to elicit the desired behavior. When the child's behavior is not what the teacher wants, the teacher can ignore the child during such a performance; this would be *negative reinforcement.* Skinner's theories were advanced by others who were interested in children's past history of learning experiences.

Skinnerian theory implies that if experiences are controlled in an operant conditioning environment, then the ideas associated with stages of development (Piaget and Montessori), are irrelevant to learning and changes in behavior.

Teaching and learning environments, and teaching strategies employed in those environments, are structured according to the planner's acceptance of a particular behavior or learning theory. In most literature these terms are used interchangeably because an accepted definition of learning is, "a change in behavior due to experience." Theories about learning and behavior have their origin in the thoughtful work of early philosophers.

The most well known philosophers had large followings which makes it difficult to determine the precise origin of a particular idea. The many books written about the age of the philosophers have performed the highly useful task of delineating various lines of thought, using reason and historical markers to aid in pinpointing who said what, and when. However, giving credit to the actual source of an idea is not as important as the fact that today we have access to useful thought.

All practitioners in various areas of human services, especially teaching, have a particular theoretical framework built into their approach to work. Their acquisition of an approach could come from observations of their favorite grade school teacher, the theoretical assumptions of teaching staffs in their training, or a combination of a variety of experiences, including how they themselves were raised as children. Their approach could be *behavioristic,* where the professionals *control the experience* based upon their acquired knowledge of what they perceive as best for the learner (student) or client. The theoretical framework that drives the professional's work could also be centered on *freedom of experience* for the learner (student) or client. These two positions are the extreme ends of a continuum, and the professional usually works from a a self-developed theory that is somewhere along the continuum between these two extremes. In most classrooms and therapeutic settings, professionals will use their knowledge of the two extremes to formulate a suitable plan designed to satisfy individual and/or group needs that are unique to a particular setting. It often becomes a matter of selecting a basic approach, behavioristic or developmental with significant modifications being occasionally borrowed from the other approach(es).

It is most useful for professionals to have some degree of flexibility in their approach to work. Every student or client comes to the helping experience (classroom, etc.) with a history influenced by previous experiences unique to her or his time in history and by significant interventions like child-rearing practices.

Behaviorists would find the individual's background less relevant than would the developmentalist approaches. The developmentalist would encourage an interaction from which could be derived knowledge about the individual's present status given the person's history of experiences. Teachers sometimes refer to this as "starting with children from where they are." They caution against the use of grades and previous school records as sole instruments of assessment. It is also true that African American and Native American children come to school from families with historical experiences unlike those of White children. Where the early problems of European settlers have been resolved by laws and custom, African Americans and Native Americans come from families whose dinner table conversations reveal many unresolved issues. For example, our festive approach to Thanksgiving is not shared by all Native American families, nor do Native American children appreciate the "art" activity of constructing paper feather headbands to be used in a "whooping" march about the classroom. It is also true that White teachers have discovered that African American children are often embarrassed about the tone and/or information given when discussions of civil rights or slavery occur.

Behaviorists would suggest that we can determine in advance what we want a person to know or what is appropriate behavior regardless of the person's history. From this professional knowledge of what is needed on a case-by-case basis, an *operant* setting can be established to reach these goals.

The fundamental function of professional education is to provide the teacher with enough important information to formulate an approach to work based on a thoughtful assessment of the most appropriate means for advancing the learner's needs and interests.

# REFERENCES

Ashton-Warner, S. (1963). *Teacher.* New York: Simon & Shuster.

Bardouille-Crema, A. B., Black, K. N., & Feldhusen, J. (1986). Performance on Piagetian tasks of Black children of differing socioeconomic levels. *Developmental Psychology,* 22 (6), 841-844.

Blackstone, T. (1971). *A fair start: The provision of preschool education.* London: Penguin Press.

Deasey, D. (1978). *Education under six.* New York: St. Martin's Press.

Dennison, G. (1969). *The lives of children.* New York: Vintage.

Denton, D. (1974). *Existentialism & phenomenology in education.* New York: Teachers' College Press.

Dewey, J. (1899). *The school and society.* Chicago: Chicago University Press.

Donaldson, M. (1978). *Children's minds.* New York: Norton.

Froebel, F. (1889). *The education of man.* New York: Appleton. (Original published in 1826).

Gelman, R. (1979). Preschool thought. *American Psychologist,* 34, 900-905.

Jones, E. (1953-1957). *The life and work of Sigmund Freud.* 3 Volumes. New York: Basic Books.

Kagan, J., & Moss, H. (1962). *Birth to maturity: A study in psychological development.* New York: Wiley.

Kitchener, R. F. (1978). Epigenesis: The role of biological models in developmental psychology. *Human Development,* 21, 141-160.

Langer, J. (1969). *Theories of development.* New York: Holt, Rinehart & Winston.

Piaget, J. (1929). *The child's conception of the world.* New York: Harcourt, Brace & World.

———. (1950). *The psychology of intelligence.* New York: Harcourt, Brace & World.

Piaget, J., & Inhelder, B. (1958). *The growth of logical thinking from childhood to adolescence.* New York: Basic Books.

Prytula, R. E., Oster, G. D., & Davis, S. F. (1977). The "rat rabbit" problem: What did J. B. Watson really do? *Teaching of Psychology;* 4, 44-46

Purkey, W. W. & Novak, J. M. (1984). *Inviting school success.* Belmont, CA: Wadsworth.

Skinner, B. F. (1971). *Beyond freedom and dignity.* New York: Knopf.

———. (1953). *Science and behavior.* New York: Macmillan.

———. (1948). *Walden two.* New York: Macmillan.

Strachey, J. (1961). *The standard edition of the complete psychological works of Sigmund Freud.* Vol. 19. London: Hogarth Press.

Taylor, R. L., & Richards, S. B. (1991). Patterns of intellectual differences of Black, Hispanic, and White Children. *Psychology in the Schools,* 28 (1), 5-9.

Walsh, J. W. (1992). Us against them: A few thoughts on separateness. *Early Education and Development,* 3 (2), 89-91.

Watson, J. B. (1913). *Psychology as the behaviorist views it. Psychological Review.* 20, 157-158.

———. (1930). *Behaviorism.* Chicago: University of Chicago Press.

# III

# The Slavery Period

*Quakers almost as good as colored. . . . They call themselves friends and you can trust them every time.*

—Harriet Tubman

Starting at birth, infants pass through several complex stages of development. During each of these stages they are capable of interacting with others in their environment, and in the process they can become reciprocal in loving relationships with parents, siblings, and other caretakers. For parents, this can be viewed as a period of complete infant dependence and a bothersome interference, or it can be viewed as a time when they choose to work at loving and protecting their growing infant. Infants are physically and emotionally vulnerable. They were particularly vulnerable in colonial America, when infant mortality was high for all families—Black, Native American, and White. More likely than not, Black infants born into a plantation environment of slave parents would often die before their sixth birthday.

The slave traders were aware that a child under ten years of age would not be particularly useful on a plantation. Even after reaching that age, under the best circumstances, children could bring only half the price of an adult. Their separation from parents and other family members during the slave trade has been reported so exhaustively that it has become common knowledge even to the general public of our day.

Comprehensive investigations by Professor Herbert Gutman and his graduate students at the City College of New York reported some remarkable information about the tenacity of many Black families in well-established slave communities. Careful examination of legal documents, letters, diaries, and plantation records revealed that despite the ravages of slave existence, many Black men and women maintained devoted marriages, along with supportive kinship networks.

It has been reported by others that some slave women neglected their infants because they did not want them to be raised in a slave environment for the benefit of Whites. Some were said to have ignored or killed their young after having several of their older children sold. A Virginia slave woman in 1822, for example, was given a death sentence for killing her infant. The woman's defense was that she was an unwilling participant in the act that produced the child and would not have killed her newborn had the father not been a White man. A group of Whites petitioned the courts to spare the woman's life because the father was known to them as a "respectable married White man."

The education of Blacks in early America seemed to rest on three principles. The first and primary principal was to educate slaves for Bible reading, to make them Christian. The second principle—supported mostly by Quakers—informed that all people should be free and should support Christian efforts to abolish slavery. With slavery abolished, there would be a need for educated Blacks to protect their own interests. Another principle rested on a sense of fairness—fairness in that the character of the country emerged from a concept of individual freedom. Therefore, slavery should be abolished to enable Africans to take their rightful place among us. This "rightful place" implies civil rights, not necessarily equal status. John Jay, Harriet Beecher Stowe, Benjamin Franklin, and others supported this latter view by their words and their work, but Thomas Jefferson vacillated.

Most early efforts to educate Blacks were initiated by church authorities. Whereas the Baptists and Methodists were late in participating in this process, the Church of England was among the first, starting early on by organizing the Society for the Propagation of The Gospel in Foreign Parts to Christianize slaves in the colonies. In 1696 the Church of England sent to Maryland Thomas Bray, a member of the aforementioned society, to Maryland to promote the education and Christianization of Black slaves. By 1695 the Reverend Samuel Thomas was inviting Black children and adults to his parish in Goose Creek, South Carolina, to learn to read and write; many Blacks in his parish became well educated for their time and place. And in 1755 Hugh Bryan, an affluent Presbyterian, operated a school for slaves in Virginia.

As early as 1704 a school was opened for Black children in New York City. Elias Neau, who had come to the colonies from France, founded a school in Trinity Church. Instruction was first started in his home after the slaves had completed their daily work. By 1708 they moved to the church when the number of students increased to 200. Instruction was postponed when in 1712 a slave revolt planned and executed by Blacks killed nine Whites. Twenty-one Blacks were executed for their role in the plot, and six others took their own lives. The school was soon reopened after it became known that there was no connection between the school and the uprising. Only one of the school's students had participated. Being occupied as a student in the school was then perceived as a possible deterrent to African conspiracies.

The state of New York did, however, make conspiracy to murder a crime punishable by death. The 21 armed slaves involved in the revolt had met secretly in the center of the city. Their plan called for setting fire to the home of one of the slave owners as a distraction. Whites who came to help extinguish the blaze were then shot. The New York State Militia was called in as a show of force to other would-be plotters and eventually captured the slaves. Elias Neau died in 1722 but that did not end the work of the school. There would be a succession of eight ministers who would direct the work of the school until 1770.

By 1773 the Quakers in Rhode Island had opened a school for "Colored" children to teach reading and writing. A ministerial group from the Church of England provided the funds. In 1798 a school for "Colored" children was established in Boston with a White teacher, Elisher Sylvester, in charge. Seven years later, in 1780, New Jersey and Pennsylvania allowed Black and White children to attend the same schools. The Quakers were especially active in this trend as they opened schools for poor children and made no racial distinctions within this social class. They depended upon the good will and philanthropy of their membership to support the education of Black children on a local basis. Their work was encouraged in all the states, but they were more successful in the North than in the South.

The education of African American children during the late period of slavery, after 1800, was sporadic and unreliable for a variety of reasons. In northern cities where antislavery sentiment was strong, African American children were eligible for public schooling where it existed,  but these schools were seen as institutions for paupers.  Advocates for the rights of Blacks presumed that it was politically unsafe for children of African descent to be identified as financial burdens needing public funds.  Also, many northern Whites were against abolitionist movements for social and economic reasons.  Many viewed African Americans not as real citizens, but as *property*  to be supported by their owners. When the announced objectives were to enable slaves to read the Bible and be Christianized, however, Whites would invariably come forth with money, and facilities and would even volunteer their own time.

Abolitionists like John Jay and respected political activists like Thomas Jefferson  professed that they believed in the philosophy of equal access to education.  It was Jefferson's view, though, that slave owners should provide training in agriculture, construction, and skills related to industrial pursuits.  He was equivocal, however, about  the intellectual capacity of African Americans, even though he was aware of the work of men like Benjamin Banneker (1731-1804), Banneker was a Black scientist, writer, astronomer and inventor who constructed the first clock in America. He also published  an almanac that was highly  regarded, and he participated  in designing the architectural layout of Washington, D.C.

Banneker was taught basic reading and writing by Molly Welsh, his grandmother. Before coming to the colonies Molly had worked on a farm in Wessex County, England. She was charged with stealing milk from the farm, but she insisted that the pail had been kicked over by the cow she was milking. In England at that time stealing was a crime for which people could be put to death. She was found guilty, but the law at that time gave special consideration to people who could read, she was granted a pardon and required to leave England.

In those days, any convicted prisoners were transported to the "New World" and were required to repay the cost of their passage by working as an indentured servant for seven years. Upon their arrival, these "seven years passengers" were then offered for sale. The ship that transported Molly arrived in a Maryland port around 1683, and she was sold to a tobacco planter in that state. She worked the allotted seven years and later acquired a small area of land where she grew tobacco and gradually increased her savings.

As Molly Welsh's holdings grew, she purchased two African males to assist with the chores normally required on a tobacco farm. One of Molly's slaves was the captured son of an African chieftain and was unwilling to perform common labor. He said his name was Bannka, and Molly referred to him as a prince. She later married Bannka—despite laws forbidding marriages between Blacks and Whites at that time. Molly and Bannka had four daughters.

It has been suggested by historians that the geographical isolation of her farm enabled Molly to escaped the full force of racial restrictions. Her children were born free because their mother was White, but laws and practices at that time were restrictive as well as hazardous for free Blacks.

Molly had taught her daughters to read and write, which made their life even more threatened because these were skills that were possessed by very few outside of some wealthy Whites.

The family had to remain alert in all transactions so as not to offend wealthy and influential Whites. One of Molly's daughters, Mary, married Robert, an African who had been captured in Guinea and sold as a slave. Robert had converted to Christianity and was granted his freedom. Mary's last name had been spelled Banneky, and at marriage Robert took the same name. Robert and Mary became modestly well-off from farming tobacco, and they had a son named Benjamin. Robert was clever enough to place the name Benjamin on the deed of their property to prevent any legal entanglements after his death.

After being taught to read and write by his grandmother, young Benjamin attended an integrated school run by the Quakers and completed the equivalent of the eighth grade. Benjamin's quest for knowledge was not of significant interest to his parents, and he was required to carry out his share of the farm work. Benjamin was 28 when his father died. He remained with his mother for a time, teaching himself to play the flute and violin. Banneker maintained an interest in reading, even though he owned only a few books. It has been reported that he acquired his first book, the Bible, at age 32. During this time he cultivated a reputation for being knowledgeable and well read and Whites in the area would come to him for help in understanding official documents and for the writing of letters.

One of his White neighbors, George Ellicot, was a member of the Society of Friends. Ellicott befriended Banneker and loaned him books on occasion. Ellicott had many talents of his own, including a knowledge of astronomy, surveying, and drafting. It was through the books periodically brought to his attention by George Ellicott that Banneker taught himself to use mathematical tables, logarithms, and a projection of the eclipse of the sun. It was from this self-taught knowledge that Banneker was later able to publish his almanac.

George Ellicott's cousin, Andrew Ellicott, had been commissioned in a proclamation from President Washington, communicated through Thomas Jefferson, to survey the area that would later become the District of Columbia. Andrew requested the assistance of his cousin George, who he knew was a competent surveyor with an excellent knowledge of instruments used for this purpose. George was occupied with his own important matters at that time and recommended his neighbor and friend Benjamin Banneker. Flattered that Major Andrew Ellicott would consider him competent enough to be his assistant, Banneker worked on the project for a period of time and appeared to have been accepted as a qualified member of the staff and crew.

In reporting the work of the group, an area newspaper chided Thomas Jefferson about his reluctance to ascribe intellectual competence to people of color:

Some time last month arrived in this town Mr. Andrew Ellicott, a gentleman of superior astronomical abilities. He was employed by the President of the United States of America, to lay off a tract of land . . . for the use of Congress. He is attended by Benjamin Banneker, an Ethiopian, whose abilities, as a surveyor, and an astronomer, clearly prove that Mr. Jefferson's concluding that the race of men were void of mental endowments, was without foundation. (*Georgetown Weekly Ledger,* March 12, 1791)

It was the general view of Jefferson's slave owning associates—who were farmers and planters—that educating slaves was not good policy because expanding their general knowledge would create among them a greater desire for the same constitutional rights as those granted to themselves. They also pointed out that if education were provided, over their objections, it should be limited to the teaching of the fundamentals of the Christian religion. Religious instruction for African Americans was also the primary goal of Elias Neau and the organization he represented the Society for the Propagation of the Gospel in Foreign Parts, mentioned earlier. Neau, as a representative of the society, established the first school for African Americans in New York City in 1704. During this period the society continued to establish other schools for the religious education of African Americans in northern and southern communities.

It was necessary to teach the fundamentals of reading and writing in order for religious material to be read and understood. This rudimentary knowledge was easily generalized to other fields, and Blacks became more literate than many poor and recent immigrant Whites.

No religious group was more persistent about pursuing the rights of Africans in slavery than the Quakers, also known as the Society of Friends. The first religious group to move collectively against slavery, however, was the Mennonites, who issued the Germantown (Pennsylvania) Resolution Against Slavery February 18, 1688 at their monthly meeting held at the home of William Worrell. The Mennonites declared:

Some sell the children of these poor creatures to other men . . . consider well this thing, you who do it, if you would be done at this manner—and if it is done according to Christianity! We . . . are against this traffic of men.

As early as 1735 the Quakers were organizing schools for African slaves in the South and had taught many to read and write. There was substantial and well-organized opposition to the teaching of slaves to read and write in the southern states, but less so in the north. Quakers in the Northeast were much more successful than those in the South because of a more receptive abolitionist environment. They perceived of education as the empowerment necessary for African Americans to move from slave status to that of a free person. In 1775 the Society of Friends established the Society for the Relief of Free Negroes Unlawfully Held In Bondage, with Benjamin Franklin Its first president. Similar societies were formed in Delaware, Rhode Island, New York, New Jersey, Virginia, and Maryland. The memberships in these societies were made up mostly of White men and women prominent in their particular communities. One such community was Philadelphia, which became an important center of abolitionist activities and spread its influence throughout the Society of Friends.

In Philadelphia resided Anthony Benezet, a French Protestant who had come to the United States with his parents to escape religious persecution in France and England. He established himself as a teacher of the daughters of influential White families in Philadelphia. It was not long before he realized the relationship between his family's flight for religious freedom and the antislavery activity in the city. Benezet joined the Philadelphia Quakers and became an advocate for the abolition of slavery and for Black education.

From his experiences teaching Whites, Benezet insisted that Blacks were as teachable as any other people. In 1750 he opened a school for Blacks in his home—teaching mostly in the evenings—and encouraged his students to attend Quaker meetings. He operated the school in his home for 20 years. After his death, with funds he had bequeathed, a school was built in 1787 for Black children in Philadelphia. Additional funds were provided by the Quakers and by Thomas Sidney, a Black resident of Philadelphia.

Many members of the Society of Friends were dissatisfied with what they perceived as a slow pace toward abolishing slavery in the United States. In 1774 John Woolman of the Society of Friends published *Some Considerations on the Keeping of Negroes.* His writings recommended harsh consequences for Quakers who refused to free their own slaves. By 1775 Quakers who remained slave holders were not permitted to make financial contributions to the society. For those who persisted, it was recommended that they be expelled from The Society of Friends.

Through the aid of the *Underground Railroad,* the Black population in free states like New York, Pennsylvania, New Jersey, and the New England states was becoming larger and more diverse. There were those who had escaped to freedom in groups and as individuals with the aid of sympathetic Whites, and there were systems of safe houses set up for this purpose. There were many Black women who had come to antislavery activities early.

The increasing northern populations of Black adults and children were vulnerable to gangs of Whites who traveled north to capture them for a return to the plantation. There was little concern among these bounty hunters that in their vast net some who were seized were free Blacks who had either bought their freedom or had never been slaves. This was a matter of serious concern to the Quakers, however.

The Quakers formed the Manumission Society, first in Philadelphia, and later in New York in 1785, to protect Blacks from the slave bounty hunters. (The word *manumit* at that time was used interchangeably with abolition.) By this time, the Quakers were well-known abolitionists. The trustees of the *New York Society to Prevent the Manumission of Slaves* read like a Who's Who in New York at that time. Among them was Alexander Hamilton (1755-1804), an eloquent speaker, and one of the authors of the *Federalist Papers,* which *was* considered by scholars and historians to be one of the most insightful documents of that period. Some of these writings led to the Bill of Rights and portions of the U.S. Constitution. Hamilton also served as the first Secretary of the U.S. Treasury from 1789 to 1795. John Jay, an important contributor to the framing of the constitution and the first Chief Justice of the U.S. from 1789 to 1795, was also a trustee. Jay had supported anti-slavery organizations and various other schools for African Americans in New York. He expressed the view that slavery diminished the national character. Another trustee, George Clinton, served as a vice-president under two presidents after being a participant in the development of the U.S. Constitution. Others among the trustees were William Shotwell Lawrence Embree, Robert Bowne, Willet Seaman, John Keese, John Murray, Melancton Smith, Matthew Clarkson, James Duane, and James Cogswell.

Shortly thereafter, in 1787, the manumission group established the New York African Free School to empower Black children as educated citizens to protect themselves.

The first members of the board of trustees for the African Free School were:

| | |
|---|---|
| Melancton Smith | Lawrence Embree |
| Willet Seaman | James Cogswell |
| Jacob Seaman | Thomas Burling |
| Nathaniel Lawrence | John Bleeker |
| John Lawrence | John Murray |
| White Matlock | Matthew Clarkson |

The African Free School started with 40 pupils of various ages, most of them from slave parents. Cornelius Davis gave up a position teaching White children to be the school's first teacher. In 1791 a female teacher was hired and girls were admitted. By 1796 the school had its own building on Cliff Street in New York City, but this building was lost to a fire that was thought to have started in a nearby structure. The City contributed land for the construction of African Free School Number 1 at 245 William Street. African Free School Number 2 was erected in 1820 to accommodate 500 additional pupils.

In its early development, the school was opposed by many Whites in the city and the trustees were not as active as the teachers and administrators of the school would have liked. To increase interest and support, the school invited scholars and educators from around the world to observe its program. For these groups, special programs of poetry, prose and essay reading by pupils were presented.

This pragmatic mission of empowerment for free Blacks gave rise to a concentration on direct instruction in reading, writing, natural history, astronomy, arithmetic, navigation, and moral education. Joseph Lancaster had developed a unique approach to instruction, materials, and supplies in the teaching of poor children in England, and the Lancasterian system was adopted by the African Free School.

The African Free School gave to education some of our earliest examples of special classes for the gifted, called "Merit" classes, and the use of pupils to tutor younger pupils in lower grades. In later years the school expanded its curriculum to include globe use, composition, map making, and linear drawing.

NEW-YORK AFRICAN FREE-SCHOOL, No. 2
Engraved from a drawing taken by P. Reason, a pupil, aged 13 years

There were many famous graduates of the African Free School who went on to become leaders in the African-American and White communities. Ira Aldridge (1807-1867), known worldwide as "The Negro Tragedian," was one of their more well known graduates. Aldridge was recognized in Europe as one of the greatest interpreters of Shakespearean characters. A bronze plate was installed in his honor in the Memorial Theater at Stratford-upon-Avon. Another graduate, James McCune Smith, became the first Black pharmacist in New York City. He later graduated from the University of Glasgow in Scotland and became medical director of the Colored Orphan Asylum of New York City. He was a prolific writer and contributed many scholarly articles to abolitionist publications. Yet another graduate, Edward A. Jones, completed studies at Amherst College in Massachusetts in 1826, thus becoming the first African American to graduate from a college in the United States.

Another African Free School graduate, John B. Russwurm, graduated from Bowdoin College in Maine only eleven days later. Russwurm was the editor of the first African American newspaper, *Freedman's Journal*. He later became superintendent of schools in Liberia, and the governor of the Colony of Cape Palmas in southern Liberia. He remained in Liberia until his death in 1851.

Martin DeLaney (1812-1885), another graduate of the African Free School, was born to slave parents in Charleston, Virginia. The family escaped to Pennsylvania while Martin was still a child. Delany also attended the Oneida Institute in northern New York and the Canaan Academy in New Hampshire. He graduated from Harvard Medical School in 1852 and for a time practiced medicine in Pittsburgh, Pennsylvania where he participated with a group of physicians in halting a cholera epidemic. He never developed a large enough following to support his private practice in Pittsburgh.

DeLaney served as a medical officer in the Union army during the Civil War and was promoted to the rank of major. Prior to the war, he had led a study group to areas of West Africa with the intent of developing a plan for Blacks to return to their homeland. During the investigation, he negotiated treaties with several African chiefs who granted land for prospective returnees. While on the exploratory trip Dr. DeLaney made plans to grow and export cotton, but he was never able to complete the African colony project. DeLaney was a member of the British Association for the Promotion of Science, and editor of his own newspaper, *The Mystery*. In 1847, after closing his own newspaper, he joined Frederick Douglass to assist in the publication of *The North Star*. Because of his experience with government matters during the Civil War, he was recruited to work with the Freedmen's Bureau, a post-slavery federal agency to be described later. He published a highly respected political work in 1852, *The Condition, Elevation, Emigration and Destiny of the Colored People in the United*

**M. R. DeLANEY**

*States, Politically Considered.* In 1852, during his retirement near Wilber-force University, he wrote *Principles of Ethnology.*

Many New York African Free School graduates, such as Theodore S. Wright, who went on to graduate from Princeton Theological Seminary, and William Brown and William G. Smith, who graduated from Columbia College Medical School, did not distinguish themselves other than by being models of persistence and intelligence in the face of extreme obstacles for people of color.

As the school graduated increasing numbers of skilled and competent Blacks, White resistance grew among workers and employers. In 1839 Charles Andrew, a teacher in the male school, wrote:

A young man,17 years of age, who about two and a half years ago, left this school with a respectable education, and an irreproachable character, which he still retains, was taken as an apprentice to the Black Smith business. Depression of business rendered little or no opportunity of his obtaining a thorough knowledge of the trade, his father made arrangements with his master to release him, with a view of the lad serving his time out else where. Every place that appeared suitable to his object, was closed against him because he was black. A friend in Philadelphia agreed to take him; but when his friend came to make it known to his Factory, he found an insurmountable difficulty in his way viz. The unwillingness of the workmen to pursue their business in company with poor Isaac because he was darker than they. (Andrew, 1830, p. 118)

In 1829 there were 700 pupils registered at the African Free School, but the average daily attendance was only 300. After questioning some of his students, Andrew discovered that, students who completed studies for a skilled trade often had no more success at getting placed in a respectable occupation than did Black children who had not attended school.

Andrew also knew that the problem was more complex than a community response to occupational prospects after graduation. Two boys wrote a short play for presentation to a school audience. The skit involved a morning conversation between them as they met for school. The spoken parts revealed that one student was often late and gave the excuse that his mother was always late with his breakfast.

His friend replied:

Well, I love to be obedient to my parents, and know it to be my duty; but I really think, that if I could not get my breakfast on time for early school, I should run off without it; for, half an hour's study over my sum or any other part of my exercise at school, is of more consequence to me than even my breakfast. (Andrew, 1830, p. 136)

Andrew suspected that this dramatization might reflect common occurr-

**DR. JAMES McCUNE SMITH**

ences in the homes of pupils. He also realized that parents and other adults in Black families needed to support the work of the school and encourage their children to attend. His perspective on such an experience  was clear:

The reasons to be assigned for the neglect of privileges thus offered, may be similar in some respects to those which are found to exist among the uninformed in all communities, viz. an incapacity to appreciate the benefits of an education, of which they themselves have never been partakers. (Andrew, 1830, p. 115)

By 1835 The New York African Free School had become a part of the New York City school system. Not all pre-emancipation schooling for people of color was concentrated in the North.  Free Blacks in several parts of the South were active in promoting their own educational interests.   In Charleston, South Carolina, the Brown Fellowship Society held its first meetings in 1790 to seek funds from its members and other sympathizers for the construction of schools for Black children. A few years later, the Charleston Humane and Friendly Society, the Unity and Friendship Society, and the Minor's Moralist Society would organize with these same purposes in mind.  From funds supplied by the wealthy Brown Fellowship Society in 1810, the Minor's Moralist Society was successful in providing a commendable academic foundation for several children from free Black families. Present-day critics who cite a lack of self-help among people of color make their judgments because they do not know this history. This self-help activity was halted by strict legislation enacted against Blacks organizing for any purpose after the revolutionary activity of Cato, Nat Turner, and Denmark Vesey.

Charleston had served as an entry point for slave trade for many years, and by 1820 it had become the sixth largest city in the nation. The city had also been the scene of the first major slave revolt. The uprising of 1739 was led by a slave named Cato.  The group attacked an arsenal about 18 miles west of Charleston in Stono, killed two guards, and made off with guns and ammunition.  It was reported that they marched to the beat of two drummers and killed 30 Whites who had attempted to stop them. Headed south to Florida, the marchers were captured in South Carolina by a group of armed Whites organized to hunt them, but 12 to 15 slaves were reported to have escaped.

These small schools for Blacks were always met with White suspicion as centers of smoldering subversion. The only "subversive" activity was education, however. Daniel Alexander Payne (1811-1893), for example, was one of the students supported by the Minor's Moralist Society.  After schooling in early grades, he obtained borrowed books that included the Bible and became self-taught in Greek, Latin, French, and mathematics. For a while he was apprenticed to a carpenter in Charleston, and he soon became competent enough to maintain his own business.  Payne started with the ministry after a few years as a carpenter. In 1829 Caesar Wright, a free Black in Charleston, hired Payne to tutor his children in their home. It was not long after that when requests came from other Blacks, and Payne opened a school for the children of free Blacks—in the home of Wright—charging fifty cents a month. By 1834, laws prohibiting Blacks from meeting without the presence of a White person were passed in South Carolina.

In 1810 Herbert H. Hughes, a White teacher, was hired by Christopher McPherson to open a school for free Blacks and those who could get permission from their owners. McPherson himself was a free Black who was a zealous Christian of some means. The school opened with more than two dozen students who were charged $1.25 a month. Classes started after the work day and continued until 9:30 in the evening. The curriculum was unusual for a Black school of that period because it did not feature vocational or industrial skills. The academic areas were much like those of the African Free School in New York City. Astronomy, geography, arithmetic, and grammar were included in the curriculum. McPherson and Hughes were so pleased with the progress of their pupils that they solicited the community for other students. Indeed, McPherson was so exuberant that he had come upon the idea of a school for Blacks in the first place that he wanted to make it known to the rest of the country. He placed an advertisement in a major Richmond newspaper soliciting students, recommending that other communities in the nation open their own schools for Blacks.

The White residents of Richmond who had not objected to the school's original opening, were now annoyed that state-wide and possibly national attention could be drawn to this enterprise. A group of Richmond Whites asked the newspaper's editor to deny advertisement space to McPherson's school, arguing that it was improper and politically harmful for such a school to exist in their city. The editor gave in to the demands of the complaining citizens. This act of censorship angered Herbert Hughes, the White teacher, who promptly paid for his own advertisement in the same newspaper to support the school and its mission.

Hughes's statements supporting the education of Black people brought on police harassment and court action. McPherson, the free Black who had opened and financed the school, was ultimately brought before the court and committed to the Williamsburg Lunatic Asylum.

The 1800s saw several other examples of self-help among Blacks. Many Black benefactors stepped forth to support the education of other Blacks. For example, in 1829 a group of Black sisters of the Catholic Church, who had previously served in the West Indies opened the Saint Frances Academy in Baltimore, Maryland. Nancy Allison, a free Black woman, and Louis Bode, a Black Haitian, donated $15,000 and $30,000 respectively to the school. Yet another example is that of Daniel Alexander Payne, the self-educated business man cited earlier.

The reputation of Payne's school spread throughout the state, even though reports suggested that officially he never had more than 12 students at any one time. Whites objected to Payne's school for fear it would stimulate an interest in freedom.

Seven years prior to Daniel Payne's opening a school for Black children in Charleston, South Carolina Denmark Vesey and several White sympathizers in the same city had conspired to burn the city of Charleston, but were betrayed by a house slave. Vesey was a free Black who had devised such an elaborate plan to burn the city of Charleston that it has been cited as an inspiration for John Brown. A detailed account of the trials is currently held in the archives at Harvard University. Among those arrested were 131 Blacks and four Whites. In 1822 Vesey and 35 others were hanged, and 43 were transported for the conspiracy.

An organized challenge to Black servitude would also be launched by Nat Turner in 1831 in Virginia. Turner staged a revolt in Southampton County, Virginia. During the hostilities 60 Whites were killed and Turner was captured and hanged. This insurrection along with other less well known but similar acts of defiance among slaves and free Blacks created a very cautious White pro-slavery population. Strict laws would follow to curtail gatherings and the education of Blacks as a means of preventing future insurrections.

With his school closed by law, Payne left Charleston in 1835 for Philadelphia and soon after enrolled in the Lutheran Theological Seminary in Gettysburg, Pennsylvania. He completed his studies at the seminary in 1837 and was ordained an elder.

Active in Philadelphia as a teacher of Black children in various settings, Payne was also a preacher in several African Methodist churches in the area. He was appointed to several churches in Washington, D.C., and Baltimore, each appointment an advancement of importance. By 1852 he was ordained a bishop in the African Methodist Church.

Bishop Payne would focus upon education and encourage others in the African Methodist Church to do so. He was impressed with people of color who pursued their own education and supported scholarship among their own people. In this regard he participated in the purchase of Wilberforce University as a site for his educational expansion for Black higher education. The buildings and grounds were secured through indebtedness that was promptly paid off in the contracted time.

Wilberforce University had been a project of the Cincinnati Conference of the Methodist Episcopal Church to establish a center of higher education to prepare Blacks for teaching and the ministry. After collecting $13,000 in contributions toward the project, Reverend John Wright, the assigned agent, purchased land at Tawawa Springs, Ohio.

In 1856 Wilberforce University was incorporated as an institution of higher education. Its student body was composed primarily of Blacks whose fathers were White plantation owners in the South. With the outbreak of the Civil War, the mulatto student body would hardly return to an institution located in a state at war with the confederacy. Thus the year following the Civil War the school had too few students to remain open.

During that time the African branch of the Methodist Episcopal (the AME), organized the Union Seminary for Black students in Columbus, Ohio. Their primary mission was vocational education. The AME had turned down an offer to accept the responsibilities of the declining Wilberforce University following previous requests from the parent body, but after negotiations a no-down-payment agreement was reached. This made Wilberforce University the first institution of higher education to be under the complete control of Blacks. In 1863, Payne became president of Wilberforce University, which continues to be recognized as a major contributor in providing the Black community with learned ministers and educators.

Payne became the first Black president of a predominantly Black university in the United States as well as the first Black to address the entire Methodist family of churches in 1881 in London, England. His primary interest was in religious education, but he perceived of this as applicable to general areas of knowledge acquisition. In his view, the skills developed in religious education are fundamentally the same as those in other disciplines. Among his various writings he published a book entitled *Domestic Education and the History of the A. M. E. Church.*

When in 1865 the teachers and students of Wilberforce were attending a celebration of the Emancipation, the university's main building was set on fire causing considerable damage. However, the building was soon rebuilt using donations and the proceeds of a modest insurance policy.

The year that Daniel Payne was forced by law to close his small school for Black children in the home of Caesar Wright in Charleston, Prudence Crandall, a Quaker in Connecticut, would admit a young Black woman—Sarah Harris—to her established school for White girls. Much to her surprise, many citizens of this liberal northern community objected by threatening to take their daughters out of school if Crandall persisted. In her defiance, she advertised in the *Liberator,* a Boston newspaper, for other women of color to apply to her boarding school. Prudence Crandall had hired a young Black woman to help around her house, and the Black woman's fiance was a regular reader of an abolitionist newspaper published in Boston by William Lloyd Garrison, the well-known abolitionist. *The Liberator* was used by Garrison and his followers to inform the general public about the conditions of slavery and encourage readers to fight against it. A copy of the paper was brought to Crandall's attention by Mrs. Charles Harris, her Black family helper. The newspaper enlightened Crandall, and motivated her to become an advocate for the betterment of Blacks.

The community was divided over the issue of recruiting young Black women to attend a school in their midst and to share these facilities with their daughters, but an influential group led by Andrew T. Judson was against this new school policy. Judson believed that Blacks were slaves because they were inferior to Whites; and that if they were encouraged to pursue academic studies their failure would be certain.

Reverend Samuel May supported Crandall and suggested in an argument with Judson that Greek culture had borrowed from the learned works of Africans centuries earlier. Further, with such an illustrious heritage, Africans who were brought to the colonies should be expected to do well academically. Judson was not impressed.

Gradually Crandall acquired a few other young Black women as students. This was promptly followed by town boycotts by merchants, vandalism and destruction to the school building and the harassment of Crandall's students. At the same time, Judson and his followers were influential enough to have the state pass a law against anyone establishing a school, boarding house, or any other enterprise to educate Blacks from outside of the state without the consent of the local civil authority. In 1833 Prudence Crandall was arrested and jailed after refusing to allow anyone to pay her bond. At the moment of her departure into the cell, the Reverend May remarked that this would be recorded as one of the saddest days in our nation's history. At the first trial, held August 23, 1833, Judge Joseph Eaton suggested during the proceedings that the state law was probably unconstitutional, and the jury could not agree on a verdict.

The second trial was held July 22, 1834. Calvin Goddard and W. W. Ellsworth argued for the defense, whereas A. T. Judson and C. F. Cleveland argued for the constitutionality of the state law under which Crandall was charged. For a second time, the jury failed to render a verdict charging that there were defects in the information provided them by Judson and Cleveland. Each trial was followed by vandalism to the school and a general rejection of Crandall and Reverend May by their neighbors. A short time after the second trial Prudence Crandall closed the school and moved away.

The theme of domestic education would be taken up by S. S. Jocelyn, a White minister in New Haven, Connecticut. The idea for the establishment of schools for Black students that would concentrate on vocational arts was proposed by Jocelyn at the First Annual Negro Convention in Philadelphia in 1827. The next two conferences—in Philadelphia and New York—would call forth plans for the founding of colleges and high schools for Black youth. Funds were donated for the schools, with the first one planned for New Haven. However, Jocelyn and his followers could not overcome local opposition and the schools were never built.

Charles Avery, a wealthy White minister in Philadelphia, donated a part of his $300,000 estate to establish Avery College in Allegheny City in

Pennsylvania. The funds were designated to be used for the education of Blacks in Philadelphia and for missionary work in Africa to teach Christianity and education. Avery University was incorporated in 1849 and open to all Black students regardless of their religious affiliation. Henry Highland Garnet, a graduate of the African Free School in New York City, served as president for three years.

In 1853 the Synod of the Presbytery of Pennsylvania authorized funds for the founding of Ashmun Institute for the purpose of classical, theological and scientific studies "for the colored youth of the male sex." By 1856 the Ashmun Institute was opened with the mission to prepare educated young men for work in Africa and the United States. The school's name was later changed, and it exists today as Lincoln University.

The idea of vocational training, rather than academic scholarship, would survive in the Northeast, and by 1848, The Negro Industrial Training School would open in Philadelphia. A few years later various other schools for Black children, including public schools, study groups, scholarly clubs, and similar educational endeavors, were organized and funded by Black citizens. By 1860, there were over 2,000 people were involved in various learning activities.

Organized activities promoting Black education in the Northeast prompted the Massachusetts state legislature in 1855 to enact a law that prevented segregation in the state's public schools. Blacks and Whites had been attending the same classrooms in Wilmington, Delaware, since 1841 without segregation.

The concept of vocational and industrial education was supported by the Quakers through the founding of the Institute for Colored Youth in Philadelphia in 1832. A White philanthropist, Richard Humphries, bequeathed upon his death $10,000 to establish a school for the descendants of African families. By 1839 the construction was completed and Black youth were taught vocational skills like shoemaking and farming. This being successful, another Quaker, Jonathan Zale, contributed $18,000 to assist the school in changing its focus from industrial to a more academic curriculum, primarily for evening students.

By 1852 the institute was converted to an academically oriented day school with a building in Philadelphia on Lombard Street. Joseph Dawson and other White Quakers periodically provided funds to enable the school to continue its work. This academic institution was operated as a day school and continued to be known as The Institute For Colored Youth. With its new academic orientation, a new director for the school was recruited from New York. Charles L. Reason, a graduate of the African Free School, had already achieved a reputation among his people as a scholar. Among Reason's classmates at the Mulberry Street location of the African Free School had been, Ira Aldridge, James McCune Smith, Patrick Reason, George T. Downing, Samuel Ringgold, and Henry Highland Garnet.

Reason's parents had come to New York City from Haiti during a time when their homeland was experiencing Black uprisings against slavery. Charles was encouraged by his parents, who were educated, and a part of the Haitian Creole population from which the mother of John James Audubon— the well known botanist—also came.

As a youth, Reason had been such an exceptional student in languages and mathematics that by the age of 14 he was employed as a part-time instructor in his New York City school. This modest position would enable him to pay a tutor to advance his skills in mathematics. Prior to accepting the position at the institute, Reason had been professor of mathematics at New York Central College in Cortland County, in northern New York state.

During the 1850s graduates from the institute gained a great deal of recognition as young scholars, with knowledge surpassing that acquired by students of the many schools being organized for Blacks. Both males and females were attracted to the school, and it became necessary to expand facilities to prepare young Black scholars as teachers and ministers. As graduates pursued their missions, these two disciplines, teaching and preaching, would share many commonalities with ever-interchanging roles.

By 1856 Reason had returned to New York City, where he became chairman of grammar school curriculum in the city schools and a member of the board of directors of the New York City Teachers Association. He also became well known among his colleagues for published works of poetry.

While an educator in the New York City schools, Reason became interested in religious studies and attempted to enter a theology program through St. Phillip's Church. This program was a prerequisite for admission to the Theological Seminary of the Protestant Episcopal Church. Despite his completing the prerequisites with honors, along with his exemplary background in grade school and higher education, he was denied admission to the seminary by the Bishop of the diocese.

Reason lodged a complaint, a compromised was offered: He would be allowed to sit in classes at the seminary, with his presence acknowledged, but he would not receive traditional credit for the attendance. Reason declined the offer, and because he was not supported by the members of his congregation—that of St. Phillip's Church—he severed ties with the group. But Reason was not alone. Other Black scholars who had attempted to enter the Episcopal ministry in New York and New Jersey had also been denied. Reason worked in Philadelphia, however, left a legacy of higher education for Black youth, who were now able to prepare for more than a vocational trade.

Northern cities like New York were experiencing a steady influx of African Americans, who through various means had escaped from slavery. Isabella Baumfree (1797-1883), an active Black abolitionist, risked her safety many times by escorting Black families from southern states to New York and beyond. Among a group of Black women active in the abolitionist move-

**SAMUEL RINGGOLD WARD**

ment, she was especially effective because she guided adults *with their children* to safety. A resident of northern New York, she had been freed from slavery along with many other Blacks when New York state passed the Emancipation Act of 1827. Baumfree was more well known as *Sojourner Truth*—a name she said was given to her in a vision from God. She was well known among White abolitionists and could call on friends like Harriet Beecher Stowe—the author of *Uncle Tom's Cabin*—for assistance in her movement.

Acclaimed as an orator, Sojourner Truth traveled across the country giving talks to large crowds of adults and children. Her philosophical messages were replete with abolitionist and religious fervor. During the Civil War she went into military camps distributing gifts and encouragement to Union soldiers. Abraham Lincoln is said to have met with her in appreciation for her work in uplifting military morale. She was not only a lecturer but also a singer and writer. She described her work in *Narrative*, published in 1875.

Harriet Ross Tubman (1820-1913) received worldwide recognition for her work with the Underground Railroad escorting escaping slaves as far north as Canada. Growing up on a plantation in Dorchester, Maryland, she experienced the cruelties associated with being a Black child on a plantation. These memories instilled in her a missionary zeal to dedicate her life to helping others like her to gain their freedom. Her work involved secret communications to and from those who wished her assistance, and she engaged in detailed planning to carry out the mission. She was so successful that at one time a $40,000 reward was offered for her capture.

Tubman enlisted the help of White abolitionist sympathizers like Horace Mann, Susan B. Anthony (a women's-right-to-vote activist), and Ralph Waldo Emerson, philosopher and poet. The Underground Railroad was not really a railroad, but a way of describing a carefully selected route and a system of safe houses and resting places along routes selected by Tubman and her followers for safety and ease of travel. White sympathizers allowed their barns and often their homes as a resting place for Blacks fleeing from their plantations.

Tubman favored revolutionary action and supported John Brown, whose attack on slavery, carried out with a group of 13 Whites and 5 Blacks, was halted by his defeat at Harper's Ferry, Virginia. Tubman had helped Brown recruit soldiers for the raid at Harper's Ferry and was deeply affected when the effort failed and people she knew and respected were killed.

As a women's rights activist she joined Susan B. Anthony, a leader in the women's suffrage movement, as a speaker at antislavery meetings to promote equal rights for Blacks and women. On many occasions Anthony invited Tubman to use her home as a temporary shelter along the Underground Railroad. Tubman's work as a humanitarian was known in many parts of the world, and late in life she received a medal from Queen Victoria of

England. Since Tubman's death, renovations on several old homes along the famed underground railroad routes have revealed concealed rooms that were unknown to the new owners.

Abolitionist activities appealed to the consciousness of liberal Whites in the Northeast, and the Quakers continued their relentless efforts toward schooling for all who would pursue Christianity. Philadelphia, New York, and the New England states were experiencing an increase in their Black population through the work of Black abolitionists like Tubman and Truth and their use of passageways created by Whites who allowed their property to be used as safe havens.

The complex relationship between individuals and events brought large numbers of Black families to the Northeast. They wanted a better life for themselves and a better future for their children. When the slightest opportunity for schooling presented itself, Black children would be willing to walk great distances to learn to read and write.

In isolated areas where there were few Blacks, Black children were allowed to attend established schools attended solely by White children. A school was opened in the home of a Black resident of Boston, Primus Hall. After two years of operation in the Hall's home, a group of citizens petitioned the Boston School Committee for a school building for Black children of the city. Their proposal was rejected by the committee.

After eight years in the home of Primus Hall, the school was provided space in the African Meeting House in Boston. It was the persistence of Black and White citizens on the project that many believe led in 1820 to the establishment of the first school for "Colored" children authorized by the Boston School Committee—22 years after the first opening of the school for Black children in the home of Primus Hall. During that period several Black teachers served the school, including John B. Russwurm, a graduate of the New York African Free School and Bowdoin College in Maine.

In southern states Quaker efforts were considered successful even if schools were open one or two days a week. Instruction often took place in already available sites, more often than not in churches. In 1820 the North Carolina Manumission Society opened a Sunday school to teach Black males and females to read and write.

Slave holders supported this effort, since the studies were linked to Christianity, and the students would be taught only rudimentary single-syllable reading and writing skills for Bible study. The school was closed when the slave holders realized that Blacks were actually learning more than they had agreed upon.

As the Quakers pressed their mission for the education of slaves and free Blacks, they kept the issue before the state legislatures, religious conventions and conferences, and other official gatherings. This relentless-

**JOHN B. RUSSWURM**

ness led to a number of opportunities for Blacks. One of the more unique outcomes was the decision by two wealthy White residents of Granville, North Carolina, to finance the education of John Chavis, a free Black, to enable him to attend Princeton University. It was reported that the benefactors were conducting an experiment to see if a Black could successfully complete the academic rigors of a major university. Chavis's knowledgeability had already been acknowledged by Whites in his town who had been paying him to tutor them.

Having completed his studies at Princeton Chavis was recognized as a Latin and Greek scholar. Unlike other other Black university graduates of that time, Chavis was to find few scholarly occupations open to him except for preaching and teaching.

He ministered to many congregations in Virginia and in 1805 returned to North Carolina to serve several congregations there. When in 1831 North Carolina enacted a law that prevented Blacks from preaching, he returned to his earlier occupation—teaching White persons for a fee. His White students would later become judges, senators, and even a governor.

Education for Black children during the slavery period was a remarkable interplay between self-help, perseverance, Black and White philanthropy, and religious zealousness. The voyage from Africa to the colonies was completed under egregious conditions and created a screening system under which only the strongest could survive.

Seldom did African women survive pregnancy, childbirth, and the voyage, for example. For the most part, the children of slavery were born on American plantations, and to free Blacks in various parts of the nation.

If they did reach the age of six Black children in general had few opportunities for organized, consistent schooling. Black families who were free, well employed, and residing in geographic areas like Charleston, Philadelphia, or in New York, New Jersey, or the New England states, had access to education that was often superior to what was generally available to the average White family. Such opportunity was not available to plantation families. Frederick Douglass was taught as a child to read and write by the plantation owner's wife. Other Black children too young to work in the fields, learned through the sharing of books and schoolwork with White children of the plantation owner. Such examples were few, however; because most plantation children did not learn to read and write until they were adult, and often they taught themselves.

Philanthropy by Blacks and Whites was a significant factor in the education of Blacks. So was the contribution and support provided by religious groups. For purposes of proselytizing, and because some, like the Quakers, believed in a doctrine of fairness, various religious organizations financed construction, paid teacher salaries, and purchased materials. They enabled learning to take place in a variety of settings. A single teacher would meet with a few dozen children in an already existing shelter for a few days a week—and a few months out of the year. Some Black families with their children would occasionally meet at their Sunday place of worship on the plantation and with the guidance of the preacher (or convener) share what they had learned with those who knew less.

Learning would also take place in a well-organized teaching-learning environment in a well-constructed facility built for that purpose. For free Blacks the church was the regular meeting site, and that became both their venue for education and their place of worship. Ministers who had been educated in seminary theology were well prepared for their role as teacher and/or preacher, since these were among the few professional careers open to highly educated Blacks, who tended to alternate between the two.

By 1860, AME and Baptist churches in several northern and border states had well-established opportunities for childhood education. A Sunday school, summer Bible school, and day school were a regular part of their church activities. In Baltimore, both the AME and the Baptist organizations also established prestigious secondary schools. They were reported to have courses of study equal to those of the best academies in the nation. At the same time, Black families in Baltimore were being assessed $500 annually in taxes to support schools their children were not allowed to attend.

The proclamation that ended slavery had the side effect of ending the Black's legacy of having their own schools by choice. The transition to desegregated schooling would be gradual and take a variety of different forms. First, Blacks and Whites who had been responsible for establishing an alternative educational system were unwilling to give it up so easily for the traditional tax-supported system. They believed that the system they and their supporters had developed had a long and successful history, and that it was maintained by citizens and professionals sympathetic to the general condition of being Black in our nation. Most of all, to accept traditional schooling would be to risk their children's failure among a group of uncaring teachers in an institution that had previously rejected them. This argument would be revisited during the 1960s and the 1990s, when racial integration threatened to merge traditional Black colleges with their in-state White counterparts.

By 1835 the administration of the African Free Schools in New York City would be transferred to the board of education, and all children would attend schools according to their area of residence. This transfer was resisted by some parents because African Free Schools had been successful in teaching their children and providing them with an academic background that enabled them to pursue advanced studies in prestigious institutions. At the same time, other Blacks expressed the sentiment that they were entitled to attend an organized citywide system because they were required to pay taxes for its support.

In the Northeast in states like New York, Pennsylvania, and New Jersey, the transition was not difficult because in certain areas of the states schools were usually attended by both Blacks and Whites. The state legislatures, nonetheless, saw a need to mandate segregation. In New York state, in 1900 for example, under Governor Theodore Roosevelt an act was passed barring discrimination in schools. This would serve to change a similar legislative act of 1823 that allowed for the establishment of schools exclusively for the "Colored Race."

By 1870 public schooling that grouped children in grades one through twelve by the age of pupils was introduced by William T. Harris, who later became the U.S. commissioner of education. As superintendent of the public schools of St. Louis, Missouri, Harris also organized the first kindergarten for public school children in 1873. Harris had been encouraged and motivated in this direction by Susan Blow, also White, who was a part of an active movement for kindergartens. When provided the opportunity, she gave talks in churches and in settlement houses for immigrants and the urban poor. Through her contacts with missionary societies and the Women's Temperance Union, such organizations were promoting kindergartens all over the nation.

By 1882 the state of Pennsylvania removed laws requiring separation by race in public schooling. Despite this, several communities, including Delaware County retained some segregated schools for Black and White children. There was little Black opposition to this segregation because it provided jobs for Black professionals at a time when Whites would not consent to Blacks' teaching Whites in public schools, and it provided what some Black parents thought was a sympathetic environment for their children.

Prior to the Civil War Mississippi had virtually no public schools for either Black or White children. The federal government had granted certain lands to the state of Mississippi for the proceeds to be used for the development of public schools. More than a million dollars was embezzled from the fund, leaving few resources for schools. The first record of public schools in Mississippi occurred with the coming of federal troops after the Civil War. When the town of Corinth, Mississippi, was captured in 1862, a school was established by northern troops. In March 1865 Joseph Warren, a chaplain in a Black army unit, was appointed superintendent of schools by the Freedmen's Bureau.

Before the end of 1865 Warren had established a total of 30 schools in four counties, employing 60 teachers to educate more than 4,000 registered Black pupils. The teachers were all brought in from the North because southern White teachers refused to teach Black children, and few Blacks in Mississippi had any schooling at all. The minimum academic requirement for teachers in Mississippi, until 1930, was completion of the seventh grade.

The Mississippi constitution of 1868 directed the state legislature to devise a system of uniform education for children 5 to 21 years of age. On July 4,1870, the state legislature in Mississippi passed a law to uniformly regulate education in the state. The system was organized at the state level and attracted a great deal of opposition because the law specified that both Blacks and Whites should receive the benefits of public education. An African American publication in the 1920s reported the following:

The new system went into operation in October, 1870 and mob law ensued. In Monroe county, the Ku Klux Klan attempted to break up the schools; in Lowndes county, several teachers were whipped and schools broken up; in Noxubie, three or four school houses were burned and the county superintendent ordered to resign; every school house in Winston except one was burned and in Chickasaw county, a young Irishman who taught a Negro school was severely whipped. Similar outrages took place in other counties. Nevertheless the results of the first year of public schools in Mississippi showed that three thousand schools had been opened with an attendance of 66,257 pupils at a total cost of $869,766. (*Crisis*, December 1926, p. 91)

After Abraham Lincoln signed the Emancipation Proclamation, and as early as the fall of 1864, White male gangs with blackened faces would permeate the southern landscape as night riders. In some communities they were called the "Black Cavalry," and sometimes they were labeled "Negro Shooters." They were members of the local and national Ku Klux Klan, or potential recruits. Their assaults against citizens in the night included intimidations through warnings, beatings, and murder. These acts were designed to discourage Blacks from owning property, voting, or attending school. By 1968 the Klan had received national notoriety and its membership soared. The Klan's crimes against Black citizens were ignored by criminal justice officials who themselves often members of a local chapter and participated in the same activities. The Klan destroyed local schools where Blacks were attending, intimidated White teachers who came from the North to work in Black schools, and burned down school buildings built for Blacks. Whereas Whites from the North were seldom beaten unless they were men, Black teachers and Black students were beaten and even murdered.

Federal troops were not useful against such gangs because they were tired of war and did not want to interrupt what they considered a normal pattern of southern living. Many writers would have us believe that the hatred involved in Klan activities was the work of the uneducated and backwoods "redneck" southerners. This was probably true, but it was also true that law enforcement personnel, local authorities, judges, and persons in authority not only participated in the Klan's murderous activities but used their own offices to protect their criminal activities. In the most egregious acts of lawlessness, the federal troops and their officers were paid bribes to ignore the constitutional guarantees for Black citizens.

For many White teachers from the North, the fear tactics employed by the Klan served to confirm the horror stories circulated through the North about southern night riders and hate groups, yet they were not scared off. This confirmation provided them with a stronger resolve as it defined the importance of their moral commitment. Since White women were rarely abused physically by the hooded Klan during this period, and White men seldom murdered, many stayed while the more fearful returned to their northern communities.

The separation of the races in educational settings would present an alternating pattern as one traveled from state to state. Since the Emancipation Proclamation outlawing slavery, Blacks and Whites interacted in many formal and informal situations, and this continued as long as Blacks demonstrated that regardless of their education, knowledge or skill, they were of a lower caste than any White with whom they interacted. By 1890, however, in many parts of the nation Jim Crow laws were enacted state by state to harden racial restrictions and legislate the caste system that had earlier been custom.

These Jim Crow laws were designed to keep Blacks "in their place" by reducing any threat of defiance or "uppity" behavior. They worked most of the time, particularly in the South. During their encounters with Whites, Black women and men would more often than not, behave servilely, moving with a slight downward body shift or shuffle, and glancing away to avoid eye contact. White men and women would use take-charge language and assume the upper hand in all encounters. And the children—both Black and White—would be watching; learning the roles that would take them safely into adulthood.

## REFERENCES

Andrew, C. C. (1830). *The history of the New York African Free School.* New York: Negro Universities Press (reprint, 1969).

Bedini, Silvio, A. B. (1971). *The life of Benjamin Banneker.* New York: Charles Scribner's Sons.

Berlin, I. (1976). *Slaves without masters.* New York: Vintage Books.

Bond, H. M. (1966).*The education of the Negro in the American social order.* New York: Octagon Books.

Fuller, E. (1971). *Prudence Crandall: An account of racism in nineteenth-century Connecticut.* Middletown. CT: Wesleyan University Press.

Marshall, M., & Stock, M. (1969). *Ira Aldridge: The Negro tragedian.* London: Feffer & Simons, Inc.

McMillen, N. R. (1989). *Dark journey.* Chicago: University of Illinois Press.

Woodson, C. G. (1919). *The education of the Negro prior to 1861.* New York: Arno Press and *The New York Times* (reprint 1968).

Woodward, C. V. (1955). *The strange career of Jim Crow.* New York: Oxford University Press.

**IRA ALDRIDGE AS "OTHELLO"**

# IV

# Beyond the Slavery Period

*The Law on the side of freedom is of great advantage only where there is power to make that law respected.*
—Frederick Douglass

In 1863 Abraham Lincoln signed the Emancipation Proclamation, legally freeing all persons previously held as slaves. Two years later the Thirteenth Amendment was ratified and Congress created the Freedmen's Bureau (U.S. Bureau of Refugees, Freedmen, and Abandoned Lands). In 1904 W. E. B. Du Bois wrote this retrospective observation on the establishment of that federal agency.

Thus did the United States government definitely assume charge of the emancipated Negro as the ward of the nation. It was a tremendous undertaking. Here at a stroke of the pen was erected a government of millions of men—and not ordinary men either, but black men emasculated by a peculiarly complete system of slavery, centuries old; and now, suddenly, violently, they come into a new birthright, at a time of war and passion, in the midst of the stricken and embittered population of their former masters. (Du Bois, 1970, p. 18)

Looking back at that post-slavery adjustment period, Du Bois also thought that White teachers from his New England who went South in response to the Freedmen's Bureau's cry for help to teach Black children had done " the finest thing in American history."

In a very short time the Freedmen's Bureau became overwhelmed with the enormous task of overseeing the assimilation of a previously slave population of almost five million children and adults. Through a nationwide system of educational enterprises for Blacks that preceded emancipation, approximately 10% of Blacks had some vocational and/or academic training. Of that group of educated Blacks, 75% were already classified as free

Blacks. It is from this class of free Blacks, and from northern Whites that the Freedmen's Bureau would seek professional assistance. The Bureau also solicited the assistance of Northern benevolent societies and national church boards. The tasks for the Freedmen's Bureau was enormous in that before the war little or no public education systems existed in the South, and even the few that did exist were suspended during the Civil War.

Among the first to respond was a group that organized specifically for the purpose of assisting the bureau, the New England Freedmen's Association. This organization emerged from a small endeavor that first sent three White teachers to Hilton Head, South Carolina. The bureau's federal agent on the Sea Islands at the time was Edward L. Pierce, formerly of Boston. Pierce appealed to two White religious leaders in Boston, Reverend Edward Everett Hale and Reverend J. M. Manning, for help with the educational needs of Black children in the area. They selected three White teachers, who arrived at Hilton Head February of 1862.

The work of the Boston group soon expanded, and as the three teachers were arriving in South Carolina, back in Boston formal meetings were being held to establish the Boston Educational Commission as a project of the New England Freedmen's Aid Society. As the new commission organized for its approach to work, it declared that its mission would include religious as well as intellectual improvement of persons who were released from slavery. The combination of education and religion in schooling for all children in the United States would prove almost impossible to disentangle in the future.

In less than a month the Boston Education Commission and its parent, The New England Freedmen's Aid Society, had organized a group of 321 teachers and experts in agriculture, who left New York by boat for their mission in the Sea Islands.

Pierce and his group of volunteers were at first somewhat disoriented by this new territory so completely different from the cities to which they were accustomed. In several instances they were greeted by deserted plantations with Black children, women, and men in a state of aimlessness—and that seemed to make matters worse. The volunteers took to their tasks immediately by moving into the plantation homes as their residences, organizing labor assignments, and opening schools. An administrator was assigned up to 500 Blacks on as many as five plantations to systematize community life that included wages for Black workers.

The first year was successful, and the society reported that Black families with whom they worked had demonstrated a strong desire to help themselves. By July 1862 the plantation administrators were transferred to the Freedmen's Bureau under the aegis of the Department of War, and they were no longer employed by the New England Freedmen's Aid Society.

The society continued to send workers South, and gradually only for educational assignments. During the first year it was apparent that teaching Black children would require supportive services. The Hilton Head group informed their sponsors of the conditions they faced in creating an environment conducive to education. In response to their appeal, 258 cases of clothing, valued at $20,000, was sent from Boston to the teachers in South Carolina.

At the 1863 annual meeting of the New England Freedmen's Aid Society, a report on their work in the Sea Islands drew tremendous praise. In the midst of their success they could report a Black population that had responded to their aid with a great work ethic and an unrelenting quest for education.

The same level of exuberance was demonstrated at its next annual meeting held April 1864. The society began to put most of its resources in schools and by 1866 they would join with the American Freedmen's and Union Commission to place almost all of their emphasis on education. A joint constitution was drawn up to guarantee that these newly developed schools would not deny services to any person because of race or color.

The society's work would take a downturn by 1867. No longer receiving free rations from the federal government's Freedmen's Bureau, the Hilton Head group was ordered to leave the confiscated plantation homes; they were unable to find suitable buildings for schools and faced a persistent undercurrent of violence that was emerging from the last vestiges of the Civil War. In the face of these obstacles, they continued to expand into other geographic areas. Wherever they carried their education programs, they encountered a relentless desire for education in Black families.

By 1868 the society had 182 teachers in 79 different schools in Maryland, Virginia, North and South Carolina, Georgia, and Washington, D.C. With a total enrollment of almost 10,000 children, many of the schools received enough local support to finance their own needs. Much of this support came from Black families and White individuals. On March 20, 1874, the New England Freedmen's Society held its last meeting and turned its work over to local support and southern organizations. After 12 years of work on this educational project, they considered their mission complete, especially in the face of diminishing interests from northern contributors.

The Philadelphia Freedmen's Relief Association was organized similarly to the Boston Education Society. The organization was chartered as the Port Royal Relief Committee and initially financed 16 schools and 38 teachers. By 1865 it was sponsoring schools in the Carolinas, Maryland, Virginia, the District of Columbia, Alabama, Mississippi, and Tennessee.

The following year the association opened a normal and industrial school in Washington, D.C. to educate Black teachers. Another Philadelphia organization, The Friends Association for the Aid and Elevation of the Freedmen, by 1868 supported over 700 pupils in 14 schools in Virginia and  South Carolina.

In 1866 the Baltimore Society for the Moral and Educational Improvement of the Colored People reported having received $20,000 from the city of Baltimore to match contributions of $23,000 from Black citizens of the city to support school programs. Contributions from the city continued for the next few  years for the purchase of furniture and books.

In 1864 a Black organization in Brooklyn, New York, The African Civilization Society   received support from the Freedmen's Bureau to open a residence for Black orphans.  That year  the organization also opened a school for Black children in Washington, D.C. By 1866 the society was sponsoring schools in Mississippi, Louisiana, Maryland, Virginia, and North and South Carolina. By 1868 the society was employing 129 teachers to instruct 8,000 pupils.

In 1865 the Presbyterian General Assembly appointed a committee to study how they could be helpful in Freedmen activities.  By 1866 they were placing teachers and missionaries in the field for the purpose of helping Black families. They concentrated their work in North Carolina, Tennessee, Alabama, Kansas,  and a few other Southern communities.They trained Black teachers and ministers, supplied clothing for children and built churches and schools. In the beginning stages of their work, the Presbyterians provided 55 missionaries in various states to direct the education of over 3,000 children in day schools.  Beginning in 1864, the United Presbyterians of Washington, D.C. financed five schools for Black children.

The American Missionary Society had established a reputation among religious and educational organizations for its commitment to educational endeavors.  In 1858, the group founded Berea College in Kentucky, which by 1869 had over 200 students,  two-thirds of them Black.

The missionary society's emphasis on higher education would lead to the founding of Fisk University in Tennessee in 1866, Talladega College in Alabama in 1867, Hampton Institute in Virginia in 1868, Atlanta University in Georgia in 1869, and Straight University  in New Orleans, also in 1869.  In 1931, Straight University and the University of New Orleans combined to become  the present day  Dillard University. Each institution would provide higher education necessary to fulfill religious, industrial, vocational, and academic roles of leadership in  Black communities.

Schools at all levels were needed in an environment where the quest for intellectual advancement  far exceeded the opportunities.  The institutions for higher learning for Blacks like normal schools, colleges, and universities, were an essential element in this process.   Graduates from these institutions would be needed as teachers and intellectual leaders in the graded schools.   For example, the New York Society had by 1866 established 125 normal, vocational, and graded schools; they required over 200 teachers for these schools located in the Carolinas and Virginia.

Likewise, the Western Freedmen's Aid Commission had 58 teachers in Mississippi, Louisiana, Arkansas, Illinois, and Kentucky.

In 1873, a state-wide conference was held in Louisville, Kentucky to "consider the educational interest of the Colored children of Kentucky." The grass-roots organizing that led to this conference could not have developed had it not been for Henry Fitzbutler, a Black physician, who was the leader in this effort. Most Blacks in the state were fearful of White retaliation in response to any efforts to increase the intellect of Black citizens. The mere idea of a state-wide effort in this regard left many of the Colored citizens "aghast, seeming to fear extermination if found participating." The fear was so pervasive, that Fitzbutler, the organizer, was the sole person willing to chair the conference. His activities on behalf of Blacks attracted a great deal of attention in the national African American press. He was cited as "perhaps the most remarkable man identified with the colored race." This press was also knowledgeable about the political climate surrounding the Black citizens of Louisville.

At that time the colored people of Louisville were peculiarly under the influence which followed the antebellum prejudices. There was an admitted guardianship, comprising perhaps of eight or ten men, who, dictated public affairs for the colored people in a manner agreeable to the prejudices of the white people, and but a few colored people sought businesses or notable positions without consulting these "intermediators." (Penn, 1891 p. 316)

A graduate of the University of Michigan Medical School in 1872, and the first Black physician in Kentucky, Fitzbutler established a profitable medical practice in Louisville. He used a considerable amount of his income on behalf of promoting the interests of African American children. The 1873 conference on the status of educational opportunity for Black children in Kentucky was held in the Louisville circuit court building and chaired by Fitzbutler. Several important resolutions were passed and follow-up activities were planned.

The resolutions passed in this convention demanded equal school privileges for colored schoolchildren in Kentucky, and became the basis of the agitation in and out of the legislature, which resulted in greatly improving the educational facilities in the state. Subsequently, he (Fitzbutler) was the chief opponent to the resolution advocating separate schools as the will of the colored people, and the last course for all. And he was a notable member of the State Educational Convention, which met in the State House, at Frankfurt, in 1883, taking such a part in the work as to attract the attention of all classes of citizens throughout the state. Here, too, he was not ashamed to advocate the cause of his race, being appointed on permanent organization. He succeeded in getting an able colored man appointed a member of an important committee. (Penn, 1891 p. 317)

Despite the good efforts of religious groups, of individual entreprenuers,

**HENRY FITZBUTLER, M. D.**

and neighborhood based societies and national philanthropies, of all Black children in the U.S. between the ages of 5 and 20—less than 10% were enrolled in a school in 1820. This was out of a total population for that age group of 1,958,237. In an environment where Black families were free to promote their own education through the aid of activists such as Fitzbutler, their churches, societies, and the public systems, the enrollment for this age group grew to 32% by 1890.

Practically all northern communities had a public school system that had admitted Black children since the mid-1880s, and by 1890 this trend was well established. Because of the tradition of establishing African schools, the practice of setting up separate systems had become the norm. After years of developing their own schools through their own efforts and with the aid of benevolent societies, Blacks in northern cities were now being faced with discrimination in public schools essentially organized for Whites.

Blacks argued that public schools should be equally accessible to all. Some cities—New York being the exception—had an uneven policy with some communities wanting White-only schools. So in 1820 separate schools for the races were established without legislative action. As late as 1850 Blacks were making legal challenges in the courts to remove segregated patterns in Boston.

In communities where a dual system could not be maintained for a variety of reasons, Blacks and Whites attended the same schools. Public schooling and desegregation would create a mix that drew opposition in communities where Blacks constituted more than a meager percentage of the population. In Ohio, for example, a law was passed in 1829 to exclude Black children from public schools, and Black homeowners were granted a school tax rebate. Philanthropic societies, private groups, and churches assumed the burden of financing schools for Black children.

In 1849, however, a state law was passed in Ohio to establish schools for Black children to be financed as all other public schools were. When the White-controlled school board of Cincinnati refused to act in four years, the Black citizens of Cincinnati were granted the power to elect their own board of trustees. But the White school board refused to release the state allocated funds. Blacks organized and threatened to send their children to the White schools, for which they had a legal right to do. When a Black father carried out the threat and sent his son to a White school, the White teacher of the class to which the child was assigned petitioned the school board to have the child expelled because he was the wrong color for her class. The White school board met to resolve the issue and voted 15 to 10 to expel the child from school. Two members of the White board resigned; soon after the school board responded by establishing four schools for Black children.

In other states the transition was often possible without confrontation; Iowa, for example, in 1857 passed a law eliminating restrictions to educational facilities because of skin color.  By 1874 in Chicago Black and White children were attending the same schools. As early as 1848 Blacks in Michigan could cast votes at school board meetings.  By 1910, out of a population of 3,677,860 Blacks between the ages of 5 and 20, more than 45% were attending school. Thus throughout the nation  a great many Black children were being educated at public expense by 1910.  Black families were  taxed for municipal services, just as were White families, and in that sense they were also contributors to the funds that were "public." Indeed, Black families were paying as much for the education of their children as their White counterparts—and in Southern communities they were paying more.   The quality of education for Black children as late as 1915, as described in a U.S. Government report, was abysmal; "Inadequacy and poverty are the outstanding characteristics of every type and grade of education for Negroes in the United States."

The investigator of this report was knowledgeable enough to understand the essential nature of early education.  A field agent representing an educational foundation, he included the following in his report;  (In) the Southern States . . .  salaries for teachers in colored schools . . .  is proportionately not more than one fourth of that spent on teachers in White schools.  In comparison with the needs of  the elementary school system, however, it is most inadequate." The report continues with a description of the condition of secondary education in southern states. "Over 50% of the colored teachers in public schools have an education less than the equivalent of six elementary grades."

The Civil War,  Reconstruction and the previous servitude of Blacks—to which southern Whites had become accustomed—made the establishment of  public schools in the South extremely difficult.  These conditions brought teachers from the North and philanthropic programs that supplemented school construction, supplies and training for teachers. A 1916 report on the condition of southern schools for children described the conditions of school buildings for Black children as "miserable  beyond all description." The investigator declared, "Most of the teachers are absolutely untrained.  I have found only one in which the highest class knew the multiplication table.  We must put more money into our Negro schools in order that they may have more decent buildings, more inspiring surroundings, better equipment, and longer school terms."

That same year, for the Haines Normal and Industrial School of Augusta Georgia it was reported that "the wise administration of the principal has won for the school the confidence of both white and colored people." The school founder and principal was Lucy Laney, a Black woman and a well-known educator.  The Haines School was opened in 1886 in a local church basement.  The response to the school was so great that in the third year over 200 children were enrolled. In 1995, the legacy of this remarkable African American woman persists in Augusta, Georgia as Lucy Laney High

School.

Lucy Laney (1854-1933) was born into slavery in Macon, Georgia. With assistance from the Presbyterian Mission Board and financial support from F. H. Haines, a White woman living in Milwaukee, Laney was able to provide educational services to more than 300 children. By 1915—almost 900 students—711 in elementary grades and 149 in secondary were enrolled. At that time the Haines school also employed 22 Black teachers—18 female and 4 male. The subjects offered included French, German, Greek, English, mathematics, Latin, physiology, chemistry, history and sociology. It was reported by the U.S. Department of Education in 1916 that "the teachers are well prepared and doing thorough work."

As a slave Lucy Laney was taught to read by a sister of the plantation owner. Her teacher was surprised that by the age of four Lucy read well. Laney was in the first class to graduate from Atlanta University and became a teacher in the public schools of Savannah, Georgia. She had been an active participant in activities supporting the Freedmen's Bureau by the Presbyterian Board of Missions.

When funds were not allocated by the Board of Missions for the school that they requested her to start, Laney started the school anyway. It was the common view among organized benefactors, like religious organizations, that Blacks should be recruited as teachers of institutions serving their people but they were not capable of running a school. White trustees of funding agencies were engaged in serious debates about whether Blacks, especially Black women, were competent enough to operate their own schools. After her school proved successful, Lucy Laney was eventually granted partial support from the Presbyterian Board of Missions, and because of the generous donations from her White Milwaukee benefactor, Laney named the school for her.

Northern benefactors also felt the urgency to provide educational opportunities for newly freed Blacks, and they were somewhat impatient with the pace of progress in training Black teachers to become school supervisors. The freedmen's Bureau was especially surprised that Black teachers, after working in the classroom for a period of time, expressed the desire to replace northerners as school administrators. Northern progressives were for a time reluctant to give up control over Black education in the southern states because control reflected their commitment. The civil rights campaigns of the 1960s that were yet to come would also attract northern liberals to the common struggle for Black civil rights in the South. After time they too had trouble resolving these same issues related to Black and/or White control of the movement.

Charitable foundations were among the first to respond to the educational needs of freedmen. In 1867 George Peabody pledged $1,000,000 to be used for the education of the most needy in the southern and southeastern states. He specified that the fund should be allocated without distinction as to race or religion. Substantial contributions were granted to schools where Black teachers were being trained. But there were those, like Reverend Barnes Sears, who were known not to carry out the Peabody policy for fund allocation. In several instances teachers in Black schools were paid only two-thirds the salaries of their White counterparts. This was in 1871, when Black and White teachers in the Peabody funding area were being paid the same salaries. Sears also preferred to appropriate money to Fisk University in Nashville, Tennessee, rather than racially desegregated Berea College in Kentucky.

The trustees of the Peabody Fund were also politically active. They petitioned members of Congress to defeat the Civil Rights Bill then being debated, and in 1883 the Supreme Court ruled that the Civil Rights Act of 1875 was unconstitutional. It was their position that the development of separate school systems would result in an equal opportunity along the lines of the "separate but equal" philosophy.

By 1880 the Peabody Fund turned its attention almost exclusively to the training of teachers. The Peabody Normal College for the training of White teachers was established. At the same time grants were being made to other White and Black teacher-training institutions. The first general agent for the new mission of the Peabody Fund was Jabez L. M. Curry, a well-known southern White. He had earned his reputation as an Alabama state legislator who was a strong supporter of education at public expense—an unusual position for a Southerner.

He was also known to speak out on the educational needs of Black citizens. Prominent Blacks were pleased to learn that he would direct the fund. Some time later the Peabody Fund was dissolved and $350,000 was transferred to the Slater Fund, in 1914, for the education of African Americans.

Curry became general agent for the Slater Fund and encouraged its mission to provide funds for private teacher training institutions and public schools that emphasized vocational education. The fund was started in 1882 with a contribution of $1,000,000 from John F. Slater of Norwich, Connecticut. Gibbs Curry came under the influence of Booker T. Washington, and for many years Black schools that emphasized industrial education received most of the Slater funds.

In 1910 James Hardy Dillard assumed the position of general agent of The Slater Fund and created a more thoughtful mission. Prior to the time Dillard assumed leadership of the fund, elementary school graduation in southern schools was enough to qualify one to teach in a Black school. It was Dillard's concern that no middle school grades existed to bridge the educational gap between elementary school and secondary schooling, which was done on college campuses at that time. Dillard was aware that there would be great opposition to the establishment of a high school for Blacks in the South, so he articulated his funding pattern to "extend elementary schooling." The first schools to be established by the Slater Fund under this plan was in Louisiana in 1911. By 1915 the plan had eased into existence eight schools teaching students at the secondary level. The Slater Fund was contributing $4,000 for salaries with the states allocating over $10,000 as matching funds.

Dillard's insight expanded many rural southern graded schools for Blacks to the secondary level, thus providing additional study for Blacks, who upon graduation, were moving into teaching positions in their own communities. By 1929, there were almost 400 such country training schools being aided by the Slater Fund, as well as public and other private sources. W. E. B. Du Bois received aid from the Slater Fund to help support his graduate work, but he thought that their policies were misguided. He suggested that the Sage Foundation had ignored Blacks, and the General Electric Board in its first years focused primarily on the education of Whites. When financial support was provided by these foundations, Black industrial schools were major recipients of their aid.

Probably the most well known benefactor of education for African Americans in the south was Julius Rosenwald, the CEO of Sears and Roebuck. In the early 1900s when benefactors were being sought for the Young Men's Christian Association expansion program in Chicago, Rosenwald was one of the patrons who was approached. Rosenwald—who was aware of the racist policies of the YMCA—informed them that when they decided to assist Black men he would consider making a contribution. Sometime later, Rosenwald was revisited and asked if he would contribute to the establishment of a YMCA for Black men and he pledged $25,000. Even as late as 1960 the Young Men's Christian Association maintained separate buildings for Blacks and Whites in many northern cities, including Philadelphia and New York. Booker T. Washington, upon hearing about Rosenwald's expressed convictions, invited him to visit Tuskegee Institute. Rosenwald was impressed and donated $5,000 to the school under the conditions that Washington could secure a matching grant from another donor. Washington took Rosenwald on a tour of the rural backwoods areas where Blacks were still living in primitive conditions, with few or no normal amenities. The first school built with the aid of Rosenwald funds was in Macon County, Alabama.

In labor and land Black citizens contributed $282, White citizens contributed $360, and $300 came from the Rosenwald Fund. After viewing these conditions, Washington and Rosenwald created a plan of matching state funds with Rosenwald contributions to improve educational access for African Americans in the South. The Rosenwald Fund administration was headquartered at Tuskegee Institute, where school building plans were drawn up for the construction of southern schools for Black children.

State officials and community governments were required to match the Rosenwald funds. The more educated Blacks in the South were against the Rosenwald school building program because they viewed it as a "second tax." The December 1926 issue of *Crisis,* a publication of the National Association for the Advancement of Colored People (NAACP), under the editorship of W. E. B. Du Bois, published the following comment by a Mississippi resident of the Black community:

The Negro finds even a greater discrimination, in the matter of school building; the Negro . . . is denied permission to vote such schools into being . . . and the white qualified elector votes one for himself and quits . . . but taxes the Negro to pay for the white man's school. . . . And in this way comes the Negro's second tax. . . . the "Rosenwald School," a liability to the Negro instead of an asset; since having already paid general tax to help build the white school, he must now take his own private funds. (*Crisis,* December 1926)

The fund was active from 1913 to 1932, and during that time more than 5,000 teachers' homes and buildings for school use, were built in 15 Southern states. The fund also contributed to the construction of libraries, repairs of existing schools, and the development of transportation facilities.

In 1932, at the end of the Rosenwald school building and related support, the value of school properties where Black children were in attendance was $37 per child, contrasted with a value of $157 per child for White students. In the southern states where the fund had been active, by 1932 the average expenditure for Black children was $12.57 per child, matched with $44.31 being spent for each White child. For the cost of construction, 65% came from tax funds, 15% from the Rosenwald Fund, 4% from Whites and 16% from Black citizens.

The Rosenwald Fund managers had expressed the fear that Southern communities were becoming too dependent upon the fund to supply the needs of Black schools. As noted in the *Crisis,* the fund managers suggested that their financial support might delay the southern states taking responsibility to provide equal schooling for all citizens.

By 1928 the managers of the Rosenwald Fund were turning their attention to the needs of Black colleges and universities. They assisted in establishing "university centers" in the District of Columbia, Atlanta, Nashville, and New Orleans. At the same time, they recognized an appalling lack of health services in the United States for Black families. The fund allocated over $800,000 to call attention to this problem and stimulate support from public and private institutions. The fund's goals in this regard were to upgrade 12 Black hospitals already in existence, improve their care facilities and professional training, provide grants for Black public health nurses in southern communities, and appoint Black physicians in training as health officers.

The fund also contributed to programs and projects outside of direct Black concerns. For example, a grant was provided the American Hospital Association to study and implement a radical idea for its time—"group hospitalization." Approximately $1 million was contributed by the Rosenwald Fund for demonstration projects.

Several years before Rosenwald established his funding plan for Black education, in 1905 Anna T. Jeanes, a Philadelphia Quaker had provided $200,000 for the purpose of educating Black children of the South. Her donation became known as the Jeanes Fund. She stipulated that the principal of Hampton Institute, Hollis B. Frissell, and the principal of Tuskegee Institute, Booker T. Washington, should be consulted as to which institutions should receive grants from her donation. By this time, Booker T. Washington was known to have so much influence over funds flowing to Black institutions that he was labeled the "Tuskegee Machine." He wielded such power that few would openly oppose his philosophy about the education of Blacks. It was reported that he secretly controlled some Black newspapers and could thus get wide circulation of his political views. Much later in life he purchased his own newspaper. A primary contributor to Tuskegee and programs recommended by Booker T. Washington was the Carnegie Corporation. Washington and Andrew Carnegie became friends after initial grants were also made to Tuskegee Institute. Major grants were also made to Hampton Institute, Washington's alma mater, with much smaller grants going to Black institutions for building projects.

At her death Anna Jeanes left a request that the money be used to help very small schools because she assumed that the larger schools had greater access to funds. A plan was devised—with M. L. Sorrell of Iberville, Louisiana, as the first teacher—to place an experienced teacher in a small school. This "Jeanes" teacher would serve as a model, and in her classroom she would demonstrate exemplary teaching techniques for teachers from local schools to observe. In Virginia in 1905 a Black educator, Virginia E. Randolph, was selected as the "Jeanes" demonstration teacher in Henrico County. The Jeanes Fund paid the demonstration teachers' salaries, and by 1911 over 125 "Jeanes" teachers were working throughout the South. It was reported in 1930 that this number was over 300.

Later in 1902, John D. Rockefeller established the General Education Board to fund higher education for African Americans. Before 1916 The General Education Board had supported courses in home economics and farming for Blacks, but by 1920 the U.S. government had assumed responsibility for these activities.

This was one of several funds not under the influence of Booker T. Washington. It was the general view of Washington that vocational and basic education was best for Blacks. Southern educators believed that African Americans were incapable of higher education and that funds were more realistically spent on rudimentary skills. The General Education Board continued to fund higher education for Blacks, and by 1930 the fund had granted over $20,000,000 to twelve Black institutions of higher education.

Also the result of individual philanthropy was the Phelps-Stokes Fund established in 1909 from $900,000 bequeathed by Caroline Phelps-Stokes in her will for the education of Blacks in Africa and the United States. The first grants from the fund provided support for research on Black problems by scholars from White institutions in the South. The fund also provided financial support for a major study directed by Thomas Jesse Jones that was completed in 1916. The report was conducted under the direction of the U.S. Department of the Interior, Bureau of Education. The most important contributions made by the fund gave the academic community a body of very important information about Blacks—data collected scientifically and systematically—to enable public policy makers and government officials to make informed decisions. In 1888 the Daniel Hand Fund  was established to aid institutions of higher education in the South.  Its funds were disseminated primarily through the American Missionary Association to colleges and universities under the Association's aegis.

In an effort to advance industrial, vocational, and agricultural education in the nation, the federal government, created the Morrill Fund. The fund was established by a congressional act in 1862 to provide land-grant schools for Whites.  A land grant institution of higher education was established in each state, and in 1890 the legislation establishing land-grant colleges for White youth was extended by an act of Congress to include Blacks.  The fund required that the states provide the resources for buildings and certain facilities.  The financial agreements in the Morrill Fund created a partnership in Black higher education between the federal government and the governments of each southern state to maintain separate systems for Black and White youth.

In anticipation of the grant's extension, several states had already funded some Black institutions.  In 1872 Alcorn Agricultural and Mechanical College (Alcorn A&M) opened under land-grant funds to Black and White students.  By 1877, however, Alcorn A&M had Black students only. Hampton Institute in Virginia and Claflin College in South Carolina had organized earlier and were provided Morrill and matching state resources to increase their student enrollment and teaching faculty. Knoxville College in Tennessee was also well organized at the time of the grant and used the funds to expand its academic offerings to include concentrations in vocational and industrial education.The Morrill Fund was also used to establish and/or expand agricultural and mechanical schools in Jefferson City, Missouri; Tallahassee, Florida; Frankfort, Kentucky; Greensboro, North Carolina; Savannah, Georgia; Normal, Alabama; Prairie View, Texas;  and Pine Bluff, Arkansas. Traditionally, southern schools for White children during the period of slavery had  practically all been private.  Public education, or "education at public expense" was not compatible with southern tradition, which viewed education as a family responsibility and not a social (public) responsibility. Southern traditionalists went on to suggest that schooling should be purchased by each family for the children who they chose to be educated. Education, they thought, was the same as other commodities that families purchase, like food and clothing. They were willing to support benevolent activities that helped the poor as long as the activities came from an institution separate from one to which paying families sent their children. Where it did exist in the South, schooling for the poor was too embarrassing even for the poor to attend.

Some southern cities underwent a reasonably facile transition from the Freedmen's schools for Black children, which were taught primarily by Whites from the North as well as by Southern Whites. This was especially true in Charleston, South Carolina. Even in Charleston, though, the legacy of the Freedmen's schools that invited integrated faculties could not sustain the trend toward separate schools for Black and White children. The separation of the races within the context of "separate but equal" would lead to a steady decline in schooling for Black children. This decline started with a differential salary schedule where teaching in Black schools paid less than teaching in White schools.

Also, White teachers in Black schools had more influence with state and local officials, and being members of the White community provided them with advocacy opportunities. Their points of view regarding schools for Blacks and other issues affecting education would be respected by other Whites. Black teachers moving into these same positions at almost one-third the salary of White teachers were grouped with their Black students in a lower caste—in the process becoming more and more isolated and powerless. This differential influence was not true in all places; Mississippi was one exception. Another was Alabama where two White teachers who established a school for Black girls in Montgomery were completely ostracized from the White community. The only church in town that would allow them to attend was the Black church.

Throughout the south schools for Blacks were seldom visited by their White superintendents and soon became dilapidated for lack of repairs. In addition, corrupt hiring practice involving teachers and administrators was so rampant that it became common knowledge even to Black families who were not in the mainstream of communication. To make matters worse, Black schools seldom received their share of supplies and materials because of discriminatory state and local funding in favor of White schools and the diverting of some of their meager resources to provide additional aid to schools for White children. In part, these circumstances gave rise to a period of entrepreneurship in education that witnessed an unprecedented establishment of private schools for Black youth throughout the South.

Institutions offering various levels of education from early elementary grades to college-level courses were established by benevolent societies, religious groups, Black and White individuals, and the state and federal government.  Many schools operated with support provided by a combination of benefactors.  An individual, for example, would open a school of modest proportions and then seek aid from a variety of sources, or a benevolent society could have founded a school that was later turned over to a community group of Black citizens.  The many variations gave rise to a number of institutions organized for purposes of exploitation.  In an environment new to the game of regulating services to the public, institutions with a staff of fewer than five teachers, offering only courses in elementary reading and writing, could be promoted with elaborate names for the purpose of raising funds—most of which would end up in private hands.  It was not unusual for a clever entrepreneur to start an institution that existed only in brochures that were sent to well known benevolent societies and individuals in northern states.  Sometimes the "founder" of the enterprise would tour the various philanthropic organizations, showing up at their meetings to espouse an endeavor that did not actually exist. Large sums of money were raised under these circumstances.

An outstanding example of such chicanery occurred in 1907, when the founder of Latta University, in Raleigh, North Carolina, constructed what could be described as a shack and went on a tour of the North to solicit funds for the "university."  At a time when Latta had one teacher and  few pupils, the founder and president published a 400-page booklet extolling the virtues of his institution as having 400 students and an elaborate campus. Before the scheme was discovered,  large sums of money had been received primarily from two northern women. It has been reported that an entrepreneur from Brunswick, Georgia, set out to raise money for the Naval and Industrial School for Colored Youth.  He managed to secure letters of support from several prominent individuals, and for seven years collected funds for his "project" throughout the North. In 1915 he was convicted of soliciting money under false pretenses. Another clever scheme was successful in securing large sums of money from a northern woman who was known to be sympathetic toward causes designed  to improve the conditions of southern Blacks.  The solicitor reported the support of two prominent women in the South; when these "benefactors" could not be found, he reported that they had lost their lives when the ship on which they were traveling met with a fatal mishap. Examples of such fraud in the development of schools were fortunately few in number compared to the many schools that were legitimate.

The legitimate schools that were not a part of a state or local public system reached their peak in number and size around 1900.  They started to decline after 1920 for several reasons,  primarily because of an improved public school system that by then had a larger population of Black professionals from which to recruit teachers.

The more respected institutions and those that became well known because of the work of their graduates remain even today. Those that are still in operation have for the most part been taken over by the state or by a philanthropic organization, and in many instances names have been changed. Lincoln University, for example was first chartered under the name of Ashmun Institute, as mentioned earlier. The school was chartered as an institute to teach theology and literary subjects to "Colored" youth and prepare them for religious work in Africa. It was not opened until 1857, and in 1866 the name was changed to Lincoln University by White Presbyterian ministers, who served as the board of trustees.

Another example is the Cheyney Training School for Teachers that started as an upper-grade secondary school to train Black teachers for schools in rural areas around Philadelphia, Pennsylvania. Teacher-training institutions at that level were called *normal schools,* and in the absence of specified national requirements, secondary school completion served as teacher-training preparation for many communities in the nation well past the 1920s. Cheyney was founded by the Quakers to provide vocational and agricultural training for Black youth in 1837. Cheyney was moved from Philadelphia to its present location in 1902.

By 1916 Cheyney Training School had 87 students—22 male and 65 female—with 22 from Pennsylvania. There were two divisions, *preparatory* and *normal*, with the preparatory division a prerequisite for the normal division, where teachers were trained for work in elementary schools.

In the 1920s Cheyney also served as one of the many institutions that provided a summer school for Black teachers from southern states. In several areas of study some field work was required, and the nearby Black community in Chester and West Chester, Pennsylvania, served as source for these experiences. In 1925 Cheyney became a state institution. Today the same institution—having undergone many changes over the years—has become Cheyney University in Cheyney, Pennsylvania. Its current emphasis remains teacher education. It is the oldest institution of Black higher education in the United States.

By the early 1900s the most well known Black abolitionist was Frederick Douglass, whose activism had gained the respect of the vast majority of African Americans at all levels. He was probably the most well known Black activist of the nineteenth century through his speeches for the civil rights of African Americans and for voting rights for women. Douglass was born into slavery, founded a newspaper that became famous, secured his own freedom, and helped President Lincoln recruit soldiers for the now famous 54th and 55th Massachusetts Black regiments. He served as a role model for many African American writers, teachers, liberals, and conservatives. In his later years he was asked by a young scholar for advice on how to secure equal rights for African Americans. Douglass replied, "Agitate, agitate, agitate!" Douglass had tremendous influence upon African Americans of his time, but especially upon Booker T. Washington and W. E. B. Du Bois and their followers. As Frederick Douglass reached his seventieth birthday, Booker T. Washington was in his fifties and William Du Bois in his early thirties earning a Ph.D. from Harvard University.

Each man saw himself as advancing the torch of Douglass, but each man would have a different interpretation of how it should be done. Their focus was always on education and employment, and they were in common agreement as to the value of each domain. Unfortunately, they were so philosophically opposed to each other's views that it was impossible for them to come together and work cooperatively on different fronts in the same war.

## THE PHILOSOPHIES OF WASHINGTON AND DU BOIS

Booker Taliaferro Washington (1856-1915), born into slavery in Hale's Ford, Virginia, became the most well known Black educator of his time. By his followers—he would be described as a moderate—the rest of the nation would consider him an extreme conservative. William Edward Burghardt Du Bois was born in Great Barrington, Massachusetts. By his followers he would be considered a liberal—the rest of the nation would think of Du Bois as a radical.

Washington was more well known because he was older, and he had a reputation for helping to establish an internationally known institution—Tuskegee Institute. Washington served as principal and later president of Tuskegee for 34 years. During his time at Tuskegee he pioneered out-reach programs in the rural South. He also developed programs to teach the isolated and unskilled rural Blacks how to get more out of their crops, the importance of sanitation, hygiene, and financial matters. He stressed that schools for African Americans should concentrate on vocational education and the skilled trades in demand at that time.

Thus Tuskegee students were first taught basic trades and crafts. The first students, for example, made their own brick from firing in a kiln, and as a part of their studies they constructed buildings for school use on the school grounds.

An act of the Alabama legislature established Tuskegee Normal and Industrial School in 1880. The state legislature also appropriated $2,000 to pay salaries. Booker T. Washington was hired as the school's first principal upon the recommendation of Samuel Chapman Armstrong, the founder of Hampton Institute. Booker T. Washington had been one of Armstrong's prized pupils. Armstrong had founded Hampton Normal and Agricultural Institute in 1868.

The American Missionary Association provided the funds to purchase the land, and temporary buildings were constructed from modified barracks that had been used as a hospital during the Civil War. The school was the rough equivalent of a high school of today. Armstrong had been an officer in a Black regiment during the Civil War, and he fashioned a curriculum that integrated vocational training with basic academic subjects. By 1915 Hampton enrolled 762 Black students and a few Native Americans. The Native American students received federal support that extended from 1878 to 1911. The school had 147 White teachers and 63 Blacks. Black students were taught that cooperation with local Whites was an essential aspect of their training. The courses of study included agriculture, business studies, household arts, mechanical trades, and teacher training. Students were enrolled at the elementary level and progressed to the secondary level in evening or day classes. The evening students were involved in a "work-study" program which put them at a work site during the day and in two 50-minute classes at night.

Hampton was considered a pioneer in vocational education for southern Blacks, and the institution's philosophy and theories attracted as many as 20,000 visitors a year, including missionaries, school administrators, educational leaders, and planners from around the world. Armstrong became a recognized leader in what became known as "racial education." For some time it was generally felt among Whites and some Black educators that Black students lacked the capability as a group to successfully encounter the rigors of an "academic" education.

These views were mixed with the idea that Blacks at that time needed training for work more than for anything else. Armstrong and his followers believed that a career in a trade would provide a good life for Blacks because they had recently emerged from bondage and therefore needed time to assimilate into a free society, and training Blacks for a trade would not be obtrusive to White citizens. He also suggested that the drudgery of slavery fostered in Blacks a dislike for labor. Institutions like Hampton, he thought, should pursue a mission of instilling in Black students the belief that labor in industry and trade was a dignified pursuit. He also attempted to convince business interests that vocationally trained Black workers from Hampton could triple their value to the general economy after they entered the workforce. Economists of the 1960s would label this phenomenon "human capital."

As an invited speaker at the annual meeting of the National Education Association (NEA) in 1872, Armstrong appealed for more training schools similar to the Hampton model. He alarmed some members of the association when he suggested that Blacks and Whites were equally capable of acquiring knowledge but that Whites had greater capability of assimilating that knowledge. In pleading for more facilities where Black teachers could be trained, he suggested that a continuous supply of teachers was needed because as Blacks reached adulthood their mental capacity diminishes.

Many professionals were influenced by Armstrong's industrial training philosophy, but William T. Harris was not. Harris, mentioned earlier as an education innovator, had introduced kindergartens at public expense in St. Louis and became the U.S. commissioner of education. At the First Mohawk Educational Conference in northern New York, he responded to the then well known Armstrong philosophy. Harris expressed the belief that vocational education was designed for basic employment. Teacher training, he suggested, required intellectual studies that would ultimately bring Black educators into academic relationships with White professionals.

Harris visited Atlanta University in 1895, two years before W. E. B. Du Bois arrived as a professor. He praised students for their achievements in industrial education, but he emphasized support for their intellectual curriculum, which included classical studies like Latin and Greek. He predicted that future society would need "brain workers", those who supervised laborers and those who designed machinery.

By 1915 Armstrong was replaced by H. B. Frissell as principal of Hampton. But Armstrong's prize pupil—Booker T. Washington—devoted his entire professional life to promoting the Armstrong philosophy at Tuskegee.

Tuskegee Normal and Industrial School opened July 4, 1881, with 30 pupils and 1 teacher in a building in poor condition. Washington raised enough money to purchase a nearby plantation also in need of many repairs. These buildings served as the first campus for Tuskegee Institute. Washington's model for the school was Hampton Institute. By 1916 Tuskegee was one of the largest institutions of its kind in the South. Day and evening courses were offered in Bible training, teacher training, mechanical trades, agriculture, and household arts. By 1916 there were 1,388 students enrolled in several areas of concentration. The elementary level stressed reading and English. The secondary level offered courses in algebra, geometry, ancient history, physics, modern history, commercial geography, economics, and bookkeeping. Other secondary courses were taught for half the year; these included Negro history, psychology, education, civics, botany, and practice teaching. At the teacher-training level students were assigned to the Children's House, a school with grades run cooperatively by Tuskegee and the county.

The mechanical trades department offered concentrations in 14 different trades. Mechanical drawing and architecture required four years of study; other trades required three. The trades included blacksmithing, masonry, plumbing, painting, tailoring, carpentry, electrical engineering, shoe and harness making, machinery, plumbing, painting, printing, tailoring, tinsmithing and wheelwrighting. There were 447 students in this division in 1915. The division of girls' industries, offered courses in sewing, cooking, tailoring, basketry, broom making, and dressmaking. In agriculture a four-year concentration for undergraduates and a two-year concentration for graduate students were offered. Here, courses were offered in farm management, garden crops, farm crops, drainage, soils, insects, botany, chemistry, and animal husbandry.

These courses were also taught at the graduate level. The Bible Training School was developed to enable local ministers to improve their performance. To obtain a diploma, the completion of eight elementary grades was required. Tuskegee also provided a three-year nurse-training concentration. The campus hospital employed a superintendent, two interns, a head nurse, a pharmacist, and a housekeeper.

Aware of the public relations value of print media, Washington developed several publications that were distributed to foundations, benefactors, alumnae and friends. The printed word carried the same respect as the ability to read, and so the school published on a regular basis *The Negro Farmer and Messenger,* a monthly; *The Southern Letter,* and a bimonthly called *The Tuskegee Student.*

These publications enabled Washington to remain in contact with students, alumnae, and foundations. In several ways they contributed to the growth and advancement of Washington's programs and perpetuated his philosophy in the recruitment of students, faculty, and curriculum. An early graduate, Mary E. Shaw, had pursued a professional career in New York City and in her will left $38,000 to Tuskegee Institute. Another graduate, William V. Chambliss, was a lifetime contributor to his alma mater. By the time of his death he had bequeathed more than $100,000 to Tuskegee.

Washington was also well known as a national figure because his points of view regarding the role of Blacks in overcoming the effects of slavery were in common with White opinion regarding the role of Black citizens in the nation's progress. He became so well known and respected by foundations and other benefactors that he controlled almost all large grants that went for Black causes. He was also consulted by contributors who sought advice about other African Americans who made requests for financial assistance. Washington used this power to exclude from funding any organization that did not agree with his philosophy.

He suggested that Blacks should prove to Whites that they could earn a place in the nation through their hard work. Washington did not wish to remind Whites about their role in instituting and supporting slavery for fear of antagonizing potential benefactors. In contrast to Washington, W. E. B. Du Bois wanted full recognition of Blacks as having rights and privileges equal to those of Whites. Slavery as he saw it was an evil exploitation of Blacks and served as a restrictive environment preventing the inherent capacities of Blacks to emerge.

Unlike Booker T. Washington, Du Bois wrote and lectured about the impact of slavery upon the achievement, intellect and spirit of Black people in the United States, and he did not hesitate to remind Whites about their role in this process. Du Bois was not against vocational and industrial education; simply, it was his view that persons acquiring this type of education also required courses of study in the aesthetics of life. The worker, he thought, was more that a mere tool of production; the best workers would be those who were exposed to the cultural aspects of life. In this regard, Du Bois proposed the education of "the talented tenth."

Du Bois suggested that at a minimum, 10% of the Black population should be identified and funded for a classical education in the service of other Blacks. The plan would ensure that there would be enough Black university professors and leaders to provide the academic service to the remaining 90% of the Black population. The plan would single out Black scholars and provide them with the best university training to enable them to become the best educators, ministers, lawyers, philosophers, writers, and journalists.

Washington and those who sided with him countered that because of Du Bois's own background, he was proposing an elitist program for Blacks like himself to separate themselves from the masses. Du Bois responded that Washington had more than 30 Blacks on his own staff who had university backgrounds of a classical nature, and this was a living example of the model he was proposing. It appeared that Washington won that argument, especially in terms of public opinion of that time, because he convinced many people that he was concerned about the entire Black population and that Du Bois was concerned with only a few. Du Bois assumed the role of training the "talented tenth" from his position of professor of sociology.

Du Bois was a prolific writer and skilled researcher, having all the attributes necessary to provide academic leadership to his plan. As Du Bois was more well known as an international scholar, he was able to pursue his radical ideas with the assistance of a group of well-educated colleagues. From this position he sent out a request to selected intellectuals and well-known liberals to attend a meeting at Niagara Falls, Ontario, near Buffalo, New York. In 1905 twenty-nine intellectuals were invited to attend the meeting.

They proposed a mission that would bring to the attention of White groups the need for them to participate in the freedom-for-all agenda and to educate Blacks as to their role in opposing limitations on their freedoms as citizens. Primary on the agenda was the possible damage done by Washington's speech delivered at the 1895 Atlanta Exposition to 40,000 people. Among other things, it was concluded that Booker T. Washington's conciliatory policy would hurt the cause of full rights for Black Americans, and this proposed new organization should work to head off such setbacks.

In the group was William Monroe Trotter (1872-1934), a brilliant African American scholar who had become the first Black Phi Beta Kappa at Harvard University. Trotter graduated from Harvard in 1895, and he had known Du Bois as a graduate student during that time. By 1901 Trotter had founded his own newspaper, the Boston *Guardian*, and often used its editorial pages to ridicule Washington's recommendations of accommodation. Washington at that time wielded such power and influence that his followers had infiltrated most radical movements, so he was well aware of Trotter's plans prior to his speech. Washington was scheduled to speak at a July 30, 1903, meeting at the African Methodist Episcopal Church in Boston.

Trotter's plans to respond to Washington from the audience during his speech was known ahead of time by Washington, and he had police at the site. When Trotter yelled questions to Washington during his speech, Washington's entourage had Trotter removed from the church by police and arrested. Washington was not satisfied, he tried to get the *Guardian* co-editor, George Forbes fired from his position in the Boston public Library system, and also sued Trotter for libel.

Washington encouraged publications over which he had some influence, to label the event a "riot," and this drew Du Bois into the fray as a strong supporter of Trotter. This was during the height of Booker T. Washington's influence and it was in the best interest of White America to keep him in power because he believed that a hardworking, dependable, docile Black made ideal citizens. It was unknown to Washington and Du Bois at that time, that earlier in his life, their mentor and role model, Frederick Douglass, had made a similar proposal in a letter to a major benefactor.

While residing in Rochester, New York in the 1850s, Douglass had the opportunity to meet Harriet Beecher Stowe, the author of *Uncle Tom's Cabin*, a story that Douglass thought was powerful and compelling. He was profoundly impressed with Stowe's writing and expressed that she had insightfully described the African American experience for that complex time period. He thought that this artful work was important for the well informed and the public at large. Harriet Beecher Stowe's work had also made an impact on readers in Europe, and she was invited to tour several cities abroad. Before sailing abroad, she invited Frederick Douglass to her home in Andover, Massachusetts. During that visit, she informed Douglass that she anticipated considerable earnings from her European tour and wanted to do something for Blacks who had become free from slavery. She was particularly interested in assisting Blacks who had gained their freedom through their own industriousness and cunning.

When the topic of discussion turned to education, Douglass was quick to suggest that a purely academic course of study would not be suitable for the conditions of Black people of the time. He opposed teaching and learning that had the singular focus of industrial education for Blacks that were common at that time. Douglass went on to suggest a setting very similar to the one that Booker T. Washington had been vilified by the Black scholars for proposing. He suggested to Stowe that African Americans required a knowledge of vocational skills such as woodworking, iron-working and leather trades, along with some rudimentary English education. Douglass justified these recommendations as expedient pathways toward lucrative employment for Blacks. The primary thrust of his theory was the immediate need for employment and income for a group of persons who had become disengaged from plantation dependency. The continuation of this disconnectedness from the common pattern of occupation and income in our country would make African Americans vulnerable to unscrupulous Whites in positions of power and undermine their recently acquired status of freedom.

Douglass conceded that their were situations where free Blacks were employed as servants, field hands and common laborers. But for the most part, he stressed that they were denied lucrative opportunities and were too often compelled to be barbers, waiters, coachmen, and other low wage workers. Douglass suggested that it was important to establish in-stitutions where Black youth could learn trades that provided employment opportunities beyond untrained and unskilled occupations. Stowe was impressed with Douglass' ideas about the needs of free Blacks at that time, and requested that he put his recommendations for her role in writing, and she would share them with her colleagues and other perspective benefactors.

These were Douglass' pragmatic solutions to the problems of a group of people who were closed out of the mainstream of political and social institutions in the United States. He also expressed the view that that even the Black "professionals" of that time were too poorly prepared to be hired by people who could afford such services. He expressed pleasure at the modest increase in the number of Black lawyers that were emerging, but lamented the fact that few were able to attract White clients. He thought that this was the reason for Black reluctance to engage the services of attorneys of their own race. It was also his view that too many Black ministers lacked proper education and were generally incompetent. Childhood experiences with opportunistic religious leaders, especially those who suggested that slavery and human cruelty was *God's will*, made Douglass a severe critic of this group.

Douglass discussed these points of view in a private meeting in the home of Harriet Beecher Stowe, and later in personal correspondence to her. Apparently Douglass' theories regarding the education of free Blacks was not known to Washington or Du Bois, for neither used these views of their mentor to buttress their own arguments in speeches or writings. Washington and Du Bois met with various groups of intellectuals, college presidents, foundation executives and groups of Blacks from various walks of life and had a profound effect upon various individual members of these groups. Philosophical and theoretical agreement among these influential African Americans could have provided the basis for an organized assault upon the inequities of their time. Their lack of opportunity, or their unwillingness to cooperatively amass the resources of the nation behind a common cause found Douglass, Du Bois, Washington and their followers splintering in different directions. Their choices for the manner in which they would, as influential individuals press for educational and occupational rights of Black Americans, were nonetheless effective for their times.

Among those influenced by the philosophy of Du Bois was Alexander Crummell, a Black scholar who founded the American Negro Academy on March 5, 1897. Crummell who had been impressed with Du Bois's intellectual drive, assembled a group of Black scholars and writers at the Lincoln Memorial Church in Washington, D.C. At the time of the meeting Crummell was rector of St. Luke's Protestant Episcopal Church in the District of Columbia and a professor of science in the College of Liberia. Among those in attendance were Du Bois; Paul Lawrence Dunbar, the poet; W. S. Scarborough, who held a LL.D. in gothic and Lithuanian languages and was the author of a textbook on Greek languages; and Frank J. Grimke, a graduate of Princeton Theological Seminary.

The American Negro Academy established among its objectives the defense of Black citizens against physical assaults, the publication of scholarly works, the support of higher education among Black scholars, the promotion of intellectual and esthetic awareness among Blacks, and the encouragement of the study and appreciation of art, literature, and science. During the academy's active years many highly respected scholarly papers were published by academy members on topics like voting rights and unfair institutional affirmative action for Whites in the South. After Crummell's death in 1908, Du Bois was elected president.

Crummell had been a student at the Mulberry Street School, a branch of the African Free School in New York City. Among his classmates were Ira Aldridge, George T. Downing, Henry Highland Garnett, Charles L. Reason, Patrick Reason, and Samuel Ringgold. Garnett and Crummell were invited by Peter Williams, a White minister, to attend a high school he had founded in New York City for the purpose of teaching the classics to young Black scholars. After spending a short time there, they heard about a similar school with better facilities in New Canaan, New Hampshire. By this time their parents knew each other and decided together that this was an opportunity worth pursuing.

At the time the New York City group—including Garnett and Crummel—arrived in New Canaan, approximately 30 young Black scholars had enrolled at the school. After the school had been in operation three months, in New Hampshire a group of Whites in the community decided to destroy the "nigger school." From the rumblings in the nearby town, Garnett and Crummell suspected that an attack was being planned. Garnett organized the students into teams, some to secure a shotgun, others to make ammunition while others would be on guard. At about 11 o'clock one night they heard a group of horses approaching, and made themselves

**ALEXANDER CRUMMELL**

ready. A White attacker on horseback rode rapidly past the house shooting into it. Garnett let off a blast from the double barreled shot gun. The great noise from the shotgun blast woke up the country side, and by morning everyone in the area had learned about the attack on the "nigger school." The students were warned by their teachers and school authorities to leave the state for their safety. Soon after, they left New Hampshire unharmed despite the fact that White residents fired blasts from field pieces at their speeding wagon as they were leaving.

It was later reported that New Canaan residents hitched up 90 oxen and dragged the building into a nearby swamp. Crummell and some of the others enrolled in the Oneida Institute of Oneida, New York, a school opened for "Colored boys" by Beriah Green. After completion of his studies, Crummell applied for admission to the General Theological Seminary of the Episcopal Church, but because of his race he was denied. Later he was accepted in the Diocese of Massachusetts to study for the priesthood. Having completed that work and being ordained, he went for additional study at Queens College in Cambridge, England. He completed studies at Queens College and was sent to Liberia, West Africa, as a missionary, later to become rector and a science professor in Liberia College.

Garnett, Crummell's school mate, had been born a slave in Kent County, Maryland, in 1845. His grandfather was an African chief and warrior captured in battle and sold into slavery. He started his professional career after graduating from the Oneida Institute with Crummell. He became a powerful speaker and was often invited to address abolitionist rallies.

Andrew Carnegie and other industrialists of the time were concerned that the Washington and Du Bois public confrontations and the emergence of such organizations as the American Negro Academy, could seriously undermine the docility of the low-wage Black labor pool. The industrialists and politicians also feared the rise of a more militant African American community. Carnegie had been friends with Washington for some time, but he knew Du Bois primarily through his writings and through newspaper reports of his activities.

In 1900 the National Negro Business League was founded, and this was the type of organization for which White America held out its greatest hope. Then in 1902 John D. Rockefeller funded the General Education Board to provide scholarships for Black students to pursue industrial education and teacher training. Next came a panel discussion at Atlanta University, organized in 1904 by Andrew Carnegie to discuss the "interests of the Negro race."

Washington and Du Bois were the panelists in which Andrew Carnegie had the most interest. As they spoke, their philosophical differences emer-

**HENRY HIGHLAND GARNETT**

ged in every facet of the discussion. Washington had come with several proposals he termed as self-help issues, but he could get little support for his proposals. The group adjourned with a pledge toward "absolute civil, political, and public equality." Carnegie was aware that the Niagara meeting, planned by Du Bois was gaining momentum among Black and White intellectuals, and that Washington's power was starting to wane.

Meanwhile Trotter's intellect and skill as a newspaper editor would create a great alliance between himself and Du Bois during the early stages of the Niagara movement. After the first meeting of the organization in 1905, they began to formulate a Declaration of Principles, to be distributed nationally. The following issues were written by Trotter and put forward in narrative form as a national mission statement for the new organization:

1. Enable full civil rights and suffrage.
2. Abolish all forms of virtual slavery, lynchings, and discrimination.
3. Abolish discriminatory policies of labor unions.
4. Provide free and compulsory education for all citizens.
5. Make available vocational schools and higher education to all citizens.
6. Develop a means to appoint and elect judges who are just.
7. Abolish the convict-lease system prevalent in the South.
8. Build and staff orphanages and residential centers for delinquents.
9. Highlight the elimination of prejudice in Christian churches.
10. Eradicate Jim Crow laws.

Among Du Bois' supporters in the Niagara movement were C. C. Bentley and F. L. McGee, who helped form national committees to attack specific problems and organize a permanent movement that would hold annual meetings. The original group had representation from 13 states and the District of Columbia; the representatives returned to their communities to disseminate the information among their colleagues. Five years later the community groups and their representatives were ready to put together an organization whose mission would be to secure the rights of African American citizens. In 1909 in New York City the same group founded the National Association for the Advancement of Colored People—on the date that Abraham Lincoln would have celebrated his one-hundreth birthday. The original members of the group included some of the most intellectual activists of the day; among them John Dewey, the philosopher; Jane Addams, one of the founders of the settlement house movement that had pioneered kindergartens in the United States; William Dean Howells, novelist, critic and newspaper editor; Lincoln Stephens, and Du Bois.

In 1910, the first issue of *Crisis*, the official publication of the NAACP, was published. With Du Bois as its editor, 1,000 copies were printed with an article written by Du Bois on miscegenation. Du Bois suggested that people should be free to marry anyone they wish. Five years later, another

**W. S. SCARBOROUGH, A. M., LL. D.**

great Black historian, acclaimed as the "Father of Negro History," Carter G. Woodson (1875-1950), founded and edited the *Journal of Negro History.* He was born into a family of 9 children in Buckingham County, Virginia at a time when the state of Virginia provided public education for Whites only. Woodson and an older brother moved to Huntington, West Virginia, where he attended an all-Black high school part time and worked in the coal mines full time. The rest of the family moved to West Virginia a few years later, and Carter was able to attend high school full time, graduating in 1886. He enrolled at Berea College, an integrated school where Black and White students paid their tuition by working at the school. After completing work for a Bachelor's Degree, he returned to Huntington to become principal of Douglass High School from which he had graduated. He left Huntington to further his education, earning his Ph.D. at Harvard University after studying with eminent scholars at the University of Chicago for the master's degree. He became the second African American to earn a doctorate in history from Harvard (Du Bois was the first).

Woodson also followed Du Bois as editor of *Crisis.* In 1915 he and a few intellectual colleagues founded the Association for the Study of Negro Life and History, designed to confront racist literature in books, periodicals, and newspapers. For a period of time in the early 1900s, while Du Bois was preoccupied with NAACP matters, Woodson was the only active research historian in the field. In 1926 Woodson and the association introduced the idea of Negro History Week to coincide with the birthdays of George Washington and Abraham Lincoln. This led to the present-day annual celebration of Black History Month in February.

For many years the NAACP reigned supreme as the primary organization promoting the rights of American Blacks in Congress, in the courts, and in the general population. Their support from the general population, as well as, from Black and White intellectuals, began to show some strain after 1945. Several well-documented articles in Black publications exposed the many racial inequities that existed in the armed forces during World War II. The U.S. Justice Department threatened to charge the critical writers with sedition. The NAACP was called in to mediate the confrontation, and the results virtually censored the Black press. This was not the NAACP that Du Bois or many of his intellectual colleagues had in mind. This action was followed with the founding of the Congress of Racial Equality in 1942 in New York City. This group was dedicated to nonviolent, direct action for the securing of civil rights. Six years later, in 1948, President Harry Truman stunned the military establishment by issuing Executive Order 9981, which eliminated all segregation in the U.S. armed forces. Military leaders warned that Black soldiers were inferior in various ways and that White soldiers would not stand for an integrated military. They were wrong, for the rebellion of Whites in the armed forces against mingling with Blacks in the military never occurred. While the NAACP focused primarily on national human rights, another group formed to address the needs of urban minorities. The National Urban League was founded in 1910 in New York City in response to the "great migration" of African Americans to the cities. By 1915 the number of Blacks moving from rural areas to urban communities would exceed two million.

By 1920 the NAACP had branches all over the nation. Responding to complaints from Black citizens, the NAACP often initiated action in the name of the organization where local Blacks feared White retaliation. In 1939 the organization added the Legal Defense and Education Fund to its operations. This division was assigned to Thurgood Marshall (1908-1992), who received his B. A. degree from Lincoln University in Pennsylvania, earlier known as Ashmun Institute, and graduated at the top of his class from Howard University Law School in 1933. Marshall was to play an essential role on the legal team that argued the 1954 Supreme Court school desegregation case, to be discussed in greater detail later. Later, in 1967, Marshall became the first Black American to sit on the Supreme Court.

The existence of the NAACP, of which Marshall was a member, and which played such a large part in the fight for civil rights for Blacks, can be credited to Du Bois. The present day Tuskegee Institute, with its variety of respected programs and thousands of graduates in many fields all over the world, can for its part, be credited to the vision of Booker T. Washington. Both men made contributions to an understanding of race relations and racial politics for the general public, as well as for the intellectual and business community of the early 1900s, that would call forth the classic dichotomies of Locke and Rousseau. It was inevitable that these two important figures of their time—commenting on the same issues among the most important to an industrializing nation—would engage in confrontation. These confrontations would play out in lectures to large public assemblies, to small and influential groups of industrialists, and intellectual audiences.

Locke and the empiricists, mentioned earlier, had a significant influence on the framers of the nation's Constitution through various principles that reflect individual freedom and liberty. Locke and his followers believed that individual social problems could be solved through logic and reasoning. Prior to this stern philosophy people thought that all knowledge and wisdom was bestowed upon individuals by God or the king. These latter ideas created a concept of fatalism and a permanent caste that would not rebel against feudalism.

Because of his close relationship with the class of planters who came to America from England to exploit cheap labor for tobacco crops—and others with the missionary zeal to Christianize the world—Locke supported Black enslavement and Native American exploitation. He resolved the apparent conflicts between his philosophy and the promotion of slavery by suggesting that Blacks and Native Americans were incapable of properly cultivating lands or establishing civilized governments.

Without a profound knowledge of Locke or Rousseau, Booker T. Washington would make philosophical choices in his prescriptions for Black assimilation into the mainstream of the nation. His view was empirical in that the major thrust of his argument was that Blacks needed *to earn* acceptance from Whites. Inherent in this philosophy was the notion that Whites had a right to their position of power, that Blacks would have to be certified by Whites—who would rate them fairly—should Blacks select their rightful place as designated by Whites.

The purpose of education, according to Locke, is to prepare citizens to be productive in an independent and rational manner. Washington suggested that it was irrational at this time for Blacks to expect acceptance on an equal footing with Whites. It was his view that the *causes* of Black economic and educational deficits were irrelevant at this time. Such things should be set aside, and Black citizens should start *from where they are*, with few expectations beyond what is realistically their present status.

He further suggested that for the good of the nation plantation loyalties to Whites should continue in the new antislavery environment. In his famous speech in Atlanta, Georgia, Booker T.Washington described his philosophy for the general public in what became known as the Atlanta Compromise. Well known as founder and president of Tuskegee Institute in nearby Alabama, he was invited to speak at the special occasion of the opening of the Cotton States and International Exposition.

Washington's address to the exposition marked the first time in history that a Black orator addressed a large, mostly White, audience for any purpose. It was reported by the newspapers of the day that 40,000 people were in attendance, with Black families being allowed to sit in the segregated balcony. As Washington stepped up to the podium, loud applause and cheers came from the balcony, and muted shuffles with some small degree of hand clapping came from the Whites on the main floor. Newspapers and magazines of that time would report that Washington approached the audience with piercing eyes and a commanding manner. The following is an excerpt from Washington's 20 minute speech of September 18, 1895.

To those of my race who depend on bettering their condition in a foreign land, or who underestimate the importance of cultivating friendly relations with the Southern white man, who is your next door neighbor, I would say "Cast down your bucket where you are"— cast it down in making friends in every manly way the people of all races by whom we are surrounded. Cast it down in agriculture, in domestic service, and in the professions. And in this connection it is well to bear in mind that whatever other sins the South may be called to bear, when it comes to business, pure and simple, it is in the south that the Negro is given a man's chance in the commercial world, and in nothing is this exposition more eloquent than in emphasizing this chance. Our greatest danger is, that in the great leap from slavery to freedom we might overlook the fact that the masses of us are to live by the productions of our hands, and fail to keep in mind that we shall prosper in proportion as we learn to dignify and glorify common labor, and put brains and skill into the common occupations of life. . . . As we have proved our loyalty to you in the past, in nursing your children, watching by the sick bed of your mothers and fathers, and often following them with tear-dimmed eye to their graves, so in the future, in our humble way, we will stand by you with a devotion that no foreigner can approach, ready to lay down our lives, if need be, in defense of your interlacing our industrial, commercial, civil, religious life with yours in a way that shall make the interest of both races one. (Ploski & Kaiser, 1971, pp. 133-135)

The response was a resounding reversal of the Black and White reactions in the hall when Washington first approached the podium. As the speech ended, Whites on the main floor applauded a loud and long boisterous approval of Washington's message. Whites began looking around, nodding approval, and congratulating each other on the wise choice of inviting Washington in the first place. The Blacks in the balcony, in contrast, sat stunned. They had entered the hall with self-assurance that this event would mark another step closer to their receiving respect as citizens. Immediately following Washington's speech, they sat muted and betrayed, with their hopes for a different outcome abandoned. And their children were watching.

Many Black intellectuals and Black newspapers condemned the Atlanta Compromise speech; Du Bois thought that it provided some important opportunities for African Americans. "I wrote to the *New York Age* suggesting that here might be a basis of a real settlement between whites and blacks in the South." He went on to suggest that in exchange for equal citizenship, Blacks could agree to support the South with their labor and their vote. "But this offer was frustrated by the fact that between 1895 and 1909 the whole South disfranchised its Negro voters... and passed a series of 'jim-crow' laws which made the Negro citizens a subordinate caste" (Du Bois, 1971 p. 209).

Professor John Hope (1868-1936), of Roger Williams University in Nashville, Tennessee was in the audience along with other Blacks of various scholarly orientations. Like many others he was infuriated that the president of a Black institution of higher education would make such a speech.

His interpretation of the speech was that Washington was promoting an acceptance of inequality as a permanent way of life for African Americans. This was, on the face of it, an unexpected philosophical position for Booker T. Washington to take, given that he had experienced a childhood like the one he described in his autobiography. Booker T. Washington was born a slave on a plantation in Franklin County, Virginia, near a small postal-delivery crossroads named Hale's Ford. He reported in his autobiography:

**PROF. B. T. WASHINGTON**

My life had its beginning in the midst of the most miserable, desolate, and discouraging surroundings. . . . I have not been successful in securing any information that would throw an accurate light upon the history of my family beyond my mother. She, I remember, had a half brother and a half sister. . . . Her addition to the slave family attracted about as much attention as the purchase of a new horse or cow. Of my father I know even less of than my mother. I do not even know his name. I have heard reports to the effect that he was a white man who lived on one of the near-by plantations. (Washington,1989, pp. 1, 2)

Washington's mother was a plantation cook, and her one-room cabin served as living quarters for her, Booker and two other children. Their bed consisted of a bundle of rags called a *pallet,* that rested on a dirt floor.

During one of his speeches as president of Tuskegee, he was asked about his youth. He gave a thoughtful reply to this question in his autobiography.

Until that question was asked it had never occurred to me that there was no period of my life that was devoted to play. From the time that I can remember anything, almost every day of my life has been occupied in some kind of labor; though I think I would now be a more useful man if I had had time for sports. . . . I had no schooling whatever while I was a slave though I remember on several occasions I went as far as the schoolhouse door with one of my young mistresses to carry her books. The picture of several dozen boys and girls in a schoolroom engaged in studying this way would be about the same as getting into paradise. (Washington, 1895 pp. 6, 7)

Washington's descriptions of his childhood bear poignant witness to the type of upbringing that was common plantation life for Black children of that period.

On plantation life in Virginia, and even later, meals were gotten by the children very much as dumb animals got theirs. It was a piece of bread here and a scrap of meat there. It was a cup of milk at one time and some potatoes at another. (Washington, 1985 p. 9)

There is a noticeable absence of bitterness toward Whites in Washington's autobiography. He actually comes close to supporting the period as having positive influences on Black life, especially for artisans. He often stated that well-respected, talented, craftsmen and craftswomen of his generation probably learned their craft on a plantation. During the Civil War his mother married a slave from a nearby plantation, and their owners cooperated in allowing them occasional visits. Washington Ferguson and Booker's mother—Jane Burroughs—had a daughter and named her Amanda. Unknown to Booker at the time, Jane Ferguson gave Booker his White father's surname, Taliaferro. During the Civil War Ferguson left the plantation for a job in the West Virginia salt mines in Malden. It took the Union Army about two years to enforce the proclamation in Malden as well as in most communities,  so it was not until late in 1865 that the Ferguson family was free to travel to Malden to join their father and stepfather.  Booker and his brother, John, in a very short time secured jobs at the mine packing barrels. Sometime later their family  took in a homeless boy named James. The salt mines attracted many Blacks to the area for jobs that for most of them, actually paid salaries.  Booker was determined to attend school and did not see that as a possibility as long as he worked in the mines. He was further inspired when he overheard some fellow workers in the mine discuss a school for Blacks where you were allowed to work off your tuition costs.

As a child his desire for education was so strong that he was on  constant alert about any information regarding opportunities to be taught.  He reported in his autobiography that "from the time I can remember having thoughts about anything, I recall that I had an intense longing to read." Soon after the family was able to live together in West Virginia, Booker pleaded with his mother to get him a book.  He relates that his mother's perseverance enabled her to get a used copy of  Webster's  spelling book at a time when no Black person in his village could read. With his mother's encouragement he taught himself the alphabet phonetically.  "In all my efforts to learn to read my mother shared fully my ambition, and sympathized with me and aided me in every way she could . . . though she was totally ignorant, so far as book knowledge was concerned, she had high ambitions for her children."

During Booker's teen years there came to his village a young Black man who had learned to read in Ohio.  Black residents of the village found out he could read and arranged for him to read the newspaper to them at the end of the day.  This became a major event in the Black neighborhood. Booker related later, "How I used to envy this man! He seemed to me to be the one young man in all the world who ought to be satisfied with his attainments." The coming of this teen inspired the community to engage in a quest for their own school.  The community learned that another young man from Ohio with considerable education had recently arrived.  Each family who wanted to learn contributed toward a salary for him so that he would spend a day with each family.

Children waited in great anticipation for  "teacher's day" in their modest homes. The young teacher was finally able to make arrangements to attend day school during the early morning hours and part of the day if he could work in the mines for at least five hours a day. It was common in those days for schools to accommodate work schedules for chores around the farms and local factories. Word passed quickly throughout the Black communities in 1891 that a school was being built in Kanawha Valley.

By the time the new school was chartered, Booker had already made plans to attend. However,  work in the salt mines had increased his family's income, and his father refused to let him attend the new school for Blacks.

Booker later described this experience as "one of the keenest disappointments that I have ever experienced." Booker and his mother were able to work out a compromise with his father to pay a teacher to provide lessons at night. "These night lessons were so welcome that I think I learned more at night than the other children did during the day."

The small school Washington attended during his early years was expanded along with the increase in Black residents. Approximately 20 years after he entered Hampton Institute in Virginia, in 1891, the West Virginia Collegiate Institute, financed by the state, was opened for Black students in the county.

In addition to providing educational services for African American citizens, the building of schools was used to advance the interests of politicians in much the same way as putting in a new road or securing a post office site for a rural community served political ends. It was also commonly acknowledged among industrialists and state legislators that northern industries would be reluctant to locate in an area where the labor population could not read or write.

By 1915, the year of Booker T. Washington's death, 345 pupils were enrolled in the Tuskegee Institute, staffed by 29 Black teachers. The school offered two levels of courses, elementary and secondary. The elementary level, consisting primarily of studies in English and reading, served as a prerequisite for the secondary level, used for teacher training. The secondary curriculum included science, gardening, and teacher training.

Washington's philosophical approach was influenced by his forced labor as a child, his years at Hampton Institute, and a full confidence in the pragmatic value of manual labor. Washington also promoted a spirit of Black capitalism, in 1900 founding the National Negro Business League. He believed in the market forces of supply and demand, and he thought that Whites would forget racial differences if they could observe African Americans participating in that process.

Washington was pleased with the progress of his students at Tuskegee. He was not, however, pleased with the general progress of race relations in the nation. He had been consulted about the "Negro problem" by two presidents. Over the years he had observed that patience and cooperative behavior on the part of Blacks in support of the White agenda for the nation had done little to change the lives of the majority of Black families in the South.

It was known that during periods of frustration over racial matters in his country, Washington secretly financed African American groups who had a more radical agenda. He was particular disturbed by the White riot in Springfield in August 1908. Two African American males had been jailed in this Illinois town on the suspicion of killing a White man and raping a White woman. As a mob of over 2,000 White residents gathered, a White restaurant owner assisted the police in secretly moving the Black men to a different jail in a nearby town to escape the Springfield lynch mob. The mob was furious to be outsmarted in their attempt to lynch the two Blacks and took their anger out on the restaurant owner. They looted his restaurant, destroyed fixtures, and moved on to attack Black citizens in the town.

White residents attached white cloths to the front of their homes hoping to save themselves from the ravages of the rioters. The rampaging group entered Black neighborhoods and destroyed property, looted homes, and murdered the residents. Newspapers reported that most of the White citizens in the town supported the attacks on Black citizens because they feared that Blacks were beginning to think they were as good as Whites. Also, there appeared to be general agreement among many northern and southern Whites that it was all right to destroy the Black community and drive out its residents for the suspected acts of two Black men. Vigilante "justice" was not a new phenomenon in the nation; it had been an accepted practice in many rural communities without well-organized law enforcement and in those communities with an active Klan chapter.

By 1910, as he approached the age of 60, Booker T. Washington was disappointed that his work had not produced better race relations as he had convinced himself would happen. In the face of increasing Klan activity, lynchings, White race riots, opposition to African Americans' voting, and entrenched racism, he began to fade from prominence. For the last 10 years of his life his philosophy for Black assimilation was frequently condemned by Du Bois, whose articulate and relentless followers would assault Washington's theories in the press and in public forums. In 1900 Du Bois and a group of his intellectual followers helped organize an international conference in London, England. Du Bois delivered his now famous speech at the conference of African and New World Intellectuals, where his often-quoted statement, "The problem of the 20th century, is the problem of the color line," was delivered.

That same year he attended the first Pan-African Conference, where the group drew up a formal protest against Western imperialism and the colonization of African nations. Their mission was to promote self-government for all nations. An organized extension of the Du Bois philosophy would emerge in what became known as the Niagara Movement. From the Niagara group, Du Bois and well-respected White intellectuals, founded the most effective Black organization of its time the NAACP.

William Edward Burghardt Du Bois (1868-1963) was born in Great Barrington, Massachusetts. The family of Du Bois's mother could be traced to the Revolutionary War, and they had farmed in this community of a few Blacks since that time. His father was the son of a seaman from Haiti whose parents were Black and White. They moved to Connecticut early in Du Bois's life, and his father, who had become a barber, deserted the family.

He went to live with his grandfather on the farm in Massachusetts, and by the time he was seven years old his mother moved back to the farm. By 1875 many northern communities had organized some type of educational system for their youth. His opportunities for schooling were consistent and free.

Du Bois was the only Black student in his high school graduating class, and he graduated with the highest grades in the group. In that particular high school it was expected that students with the highest academic records would attend a prestigious New England institution. Instead, this young scholar was sent off to a Black institution in Nashville, Tennessee—Fisk University. When Du Bois entered Fisk, the school had been in operation for a mere 20 years.

Du Bois was startled by the terrible conditions under which Black families lived in the South. What he saw in the South helped to shape the dedication of his career; and one that he would remember the rest of his life.

Fisk University was founded in 1865 by the American Missionary Association and the Western Freedmen's Aid Commission. Early in its development came an emphasis on music and their choir, the Jubilee Singers, became world renowned. In 1871 they made a world tour and raised a considerable amount of money for the school.

By the time that Du Bois arrived as a student, Fisk was controlled by a board of Black and White trustees from the North and the South. Fisk offered college-level and secondary-level education. The college level, the one that Du Bois entered, offered four tracks, classical, education, scientific, and home economics.

By 1915 the institution was experimenting with a new major. The concentration called "social services," included courses in recreation, sociology, statistics, manual training, religion, and domestic science. At the time of William's attendance, there were 45 teachers and a staff comprised of 31 Whites and 14 Blacks. Latin, Greek, and some modern languages were required of all college-level students.

Du Bois graduated from Fisk University in 1888 and attended Harvard University for two years. He earned a bachelor's degree in philosophy but remained an additional two years for studies in history and economics. William's experiences in Boston were mixed with confrontations over racism in the city and at Harvard. His Ph.D. Dissertation at Harvard, completed in 1895, was highly regarded and became the first volume in the publication *Harvard Historical Studies.* At the time of Du Bois's graduate work at Harvard, the board of overseers was seriously considering a quota system to restrict Jews and a residency policy restricting Blacks.

Lawrence A. Lowell, president of Harvard at that time, sided with a small group of White students from the South who objected to Blacks living in the dormitory. This was merely one of the many variations of racial rebuffs that Du Bois encountered in the South and North; and these experiences tended to make him withdrawn and bitter toward the social system. An arrogant and caustic approach to professional matters would emerge as a part of the Du Bois that others saw. An African American scholar with his knowledge and  talents in today's university would not be open to severe criticism; rather, Du Bois's style would be considered a desirable trait. After a period of  advanced studies at Harvard Du Bois taught courses at Wilberforce University in Ohio.  When he left Harvard, he studied sociology at the University of Berlin.  He returned to Harvard as a doctoral student, after spending two years in Germany.  In his autobiography  he wrote, "As a student in Germany, I built great castles in Spain and lived therein.  I dreamed and loved and wondered and sang; then after two long years I dropped suddenly back into "nigger-hating America" (Du Bois, 1971, p. 183).

Du Bois spent a period of contemplation concerning his opportunities that were set in place by both Black and White benefactors.  He thought and wrote about the circumstances of good fortune that continued to occur in his life from childhood. Du Bois "began to realize how much of what I called Will and Ability was sheer Luck!" The prevailing race relations which he had encountered during various experiences were in many ways paradoxical, and lead to a style of interacting with others, where he would condemn a Black as quickly as a White for behaviors or ideas that limited the rights of others. His childhood experiences with adults had a profound and lasting effect upon his adult life, and he recalled, "Suppose my good mother had preferred a steady income from my child labor . . . rather than a dividend from my higher training?"  He remembered his school days as being  the sole African American in the high school, and graduating at the top of his class, and contemplated,  "Suppose Principal Hosmer had . . . no faith in 'darkies', and instead of sending me to college had me taught carpentry (and) I missed a Harvard scholarship?" He was also aware of the significant differences that White foundations had made in the lives of African American scholars like himself, and wrote, " Suppose the Slater Board . . . had distinct ideas as to where the education of Negroes should stop?" (Du Bois, 1971 p. 183).

Du Bois returned home from abroad with very little money and a compelling urge to obtain employment.  He sent letters to several Black institutions and informed friends and colleagues that he was seeking a teaching position.

A Black institution in East Tennessee appeared interested for a time, but finally concluded that Du Bois had too much education for their needs.  He also made application to Fisk University, from which he had graduated, and to Howard University where scholars were familiar with his work, but responses were not encouraging.

His first offer came from Wilberforce University.  Shortly after he accepted the offer from Wilberforce for an annual salary of $800, he received an offer from Lincoln Institute in Missouri for $1,050 to teach mathematics and classics. His integrity would not allow him to reconsider the offer from Lincoln Institute. Later in life he would muse over an offer that he had received from Booker T. Washington to teach mathematics at Tuskegee. After Washington's philosophy about Black education became well known, Du Bois would speculate in conversations among friends about what might have happened had he received the Tuskegee offer first, and thereby inheriting Washington as a colleague and an overseer of his academic work.

Wilberforce was under the leadership of the African Methodist Church, and received aid from the state and the Methodist Board. The religious supporters were interested in spreading the faith, and the state wanted to keep Black students out of their State-run White colleges and universities. Du Bois reported that he almost lost his job over an incident involving him inadvertently walking into a group of students about to have a religious meeting. One of the group leaders said, "Professor Du Bois will lead us in prayer." I simply answered "No he won't" (Du Bois, 1971 p.186).

While at Wilberforce, he met a faculty member who was a graduate of West Point who had been assigned to campus as a military instructor by the Federal government. They were in agreement that the school took too many hours away from academic student's work with their long revivals and frequent religious holidays. Du Bois and a few select colleagues met frequently to discuss their dream of a great future for Wilberforce University. These wistful and reflective conversations with like minded colleagues, together with the courtship of his wife to be, helped to sustain Du Bois in this worshiping encampment immured with a religiosity that was incompatible with scholarship. Du Bois perceived the study of religion as a discipline in philosophy rather than ministerial oratory where followers were exhorted about their daily behavior. Religion of the latter type was, however, the primary mission of the institution and scholars like Du Bois would remain outsiders, in the existential sense of the word.

Du Bois left Wilberforce University under an avalanche of disappointments about salary, his role with students and colleagues and a feeling that he was cut off from the scholarliness of his profession.

In 1896, he accepted a position as assistant instructor in sociology at the University of Pennsylvania. The title of assistant instructor was unusual in that it had never been used before. It was concocted by the head of the sociology department at the university so as not to offend White faculty, many of whom were less competent than Du Bois.

Du Bois conducted what has become one of the great sociological studies on the Black experience. *The Philadelphia Negro* was a journalistic version of the study, and became his second book to be published. After one year at the University of Pennsylvania, he accepted a position as professor at Atlanta University teaching courses, conducting research and developing publications.

When Du Bois agreed to study African Americans in Philadelphia, he thought that the nation's cities were poorly governed, but that Philadelphia was governed in a more inept and corrupt manner than most others. Samuel McCune Lindsay was the chairman of the Department of Sociology at the University of Pennsylvania at the time, and along with members of his faculty identified the "Negro Seventh Ward" as being at the heart of Black problems in their city.

Du Bois accepted his position as researcher with mixed feelings. On the one hand, it would have been common practice for a White professor—and for sure a department head—to expect that a Black scholar would serve as his assistant, and this Lindsay did not do. On the other hand, a White scholar with a Harvard Ph.D., and a reputation for having written extensively, would not be asked to take anything lower than assistant professor.

Knowing the racist nature of most American institutions of higher education, he could speculate on the political battle that Lindsay probably had to wage to get him the meager assistant instructor status. Du Bois' work at the University of Pennsylvania from the beginning surpassed the competence of many of the professors tenured in the department. Despite these circumstances, Du Bois the scholar reported promptly for duty with a complete plan of work, with a proposed work schedule and an outline of methods to be employed.

Du Bois had married while at Wilberforce University, Ohio, and soon found that Wilberforce University paid its faculty when it had money for salaries, and this was infrequent. While one person would have difficulty providing for their basic needs on a modest and uncertain salary, he found it to be a constant source of embarrassment and practically impossible for a husband and unemployed wife to live under these circumstances.

His salary from the University of Pennsylvania, however, was paid on a regular basis, but it was too meager for the Du Bois' to afford much more than a modest apartment of a few rooms in the Black slums of Philadelphia. Despite the difficulties that Du Bois experienced while at the University of Pennsylvania, he thought of this as an opportunity to practice his craft in a manner that was not possible at Wilberforce University. He was convinced that the University of Pennsylvania study would provide him with scholarly gratification.

Among his major concerns was the need for good and reliable information about race in the United States. His work in this domain would make his years of study at Fisk University, his graduate work at Harvard University and even his less than desirable work at Wilberforce University, somewhat authentic and justified. It was his view that academicians and the general public knew little about the problems experienced by African Americans. The cure for this public and professional ignorance, Du Bois thought, could be achieved in part by him generating knowledge through scientific investigation.

Du Bois viewed this scientific endeavor as his personal contribution to the larger mission of correcting the inequities in the nation through a process of enlightenment. His personal sacrifices caused by squalor living conditions for him and his wife, and disesteem by the University of Pennsylvania, he thought, should not detract from this goal. For example, despite his superior scholarship compared to others at the University of Pennsylvania who held the rank of Professor, he made a solemn declaration not to let these aggravations deter him from his goal.

He approached the study of Philadelphia's African American Seventh Ward with great energy, personally interviewing 5,000 persons. He visited libraries in the city, gained access to some private libraries and issued reports to the sociology faculty at the university and requested comments. By the end of the study, he had completed a 200 year history of the Philadelphia Seventh Ward, and mapped and classified the district.

This was the first intimate experience that Du Bois ever had with an African American inner-city community, and he realized that this encounter was important for a variety of reasons beyond the discrete scientific objectives of his investigation. He approached his work with the assumption that just being born in a group did not necessarily mean that one possessed adequate knowledge concerning that group. This was an important self-knowledge experience for Du Bois the scholar and Du Bois the African American in general society. Early in his study, he expressed that he was learning far more from Philadelphia Blacks for his study, than they were learning from him about their community.

The completed report was received by the university as an important study. It was completed in 1898, and published as *The Philadelphia Negro,* in 1899. The work was viewed by scholars as being of the highest quality; and in this context, Du Bois wanted greater recognition of his talents comparable to what would be granted a White academician under similar circumstances. He was disappointed, however, that after his scholarly performance, the University of Pennsylvania failed to offer him even a temporary position.

He was aware that it was not his work, but his race that limited his career, but this did not help to diminish his bitterness. This bitterness was compounded by his knowledge of the many personal stories of Black scholars who had been denied positions at White colleges and universities. Du Bois was also aware that his White classmates from Harvard were having career experiences far different from his own. Even those who graduated with lower academic scores were becoming full professors at prestigious universities at a time when he could not obtain a position as an instructor or lecturer at these same institutions.

His journal publishing and research interests included crime, health, education and economics. After 18 months at the University of Pennsylvania, Du Bois accepted a position at Atlanta University in Georgia. In

1896, he was approached  by President Horace Bumstead of Atlanta University, and asked to come to Atlanta University and head their work in sociology, and direct new conferences that were being planned to study the problems of Black Americans.

Atlanta University was founded in 1867 by the American Missionary Association  as a teacher training institution with a secondary level. By the time that Du Bois  arrived, there were almost 600 students at various levels of study, and the institution was controlled by an independent Board of Trustees.

Atlanta University at that time was one of the most well known professional institutions for Black students in the nation, and had a reputation for graduating highly competent scholars.  The normal school (teacher preparation), was far ahead of most teacher training institutions in the country.

They pioneered the campus school concept, where children attended a grade school in the near proximity of the university were students were assigned to teach as a part of their overall studies.  Children benefited from being exposed to current methods in teaching/learning, and at the same time teachers in training were afforded a convenient  practice site. A similar system was developed at Tuskegee Institute and at the University of Chicago.

The Atlanta University laboratory school offered kindergarten and elementary classes, admitted children of the campus faculty,  as well as from the surrounding   poor neighborhoods. In 1915, there were 33 professionals on the university teaching staff—29 were White and 4 were Black. The secondary school was divided into teacher preparation and college preparatory divisions.  The college preparatory division was of four years duration and included Latin, Greek, English, mathematics and history. At the college level there were 44 students, and they had a choice of two concentrations.  They could pursue classics and philosophy or science and mathematics.

The Atlanta University Conference for 20 years held annual meetings and compiled data on African American issues. Scholars from all over the nation used these reports in their studies of racial issues.  The Free Kindergarten Association of Atlanta was organized by professionals who were associated with the campus kindergarten and elementary education programs.  By 1915 five free kindergarten classrooms were operating on the campus for Atlanta's Black children from poor families.

In these various scholarly positions Du Bois continued to refine a philosophy that emphasized the rights and dignity of all persons.  He did not set himself apart from the rest of humanity.  In this regard he would frequently be at odds with Booker T. Washington and his supporters. Unlike Washington—who was more interested in pragmatic pursuits like education for vocational trades and preparation for life skills—Du Bois had studied the Greek philosophers and was very much in touch with his own philosophy.

Like Rousseau, he could be classified as a romanticist.  Although he agreed with Booker T. Washington  (and John Locke), on the *value*  of education, Du Bois believed deeply that individuals brought a sense of self to the *experience*  of being taught. He had a strong sense of aesthetic values and the creativity of scholarly pursuits.  Booker T. Washington did not feel that the past experiences of Blacks should interfere with their training for the future. As Locke had suggested, the learner comes to the experience as a blank slate to be "written on"  by the teacher.  In that spirit, Washington thought that African Americans should leave behind their past experiences as they enter the classroom; he believed they should become wholly immersed in their training that should be designed to make their careers compatible with their citizenship in the nation.

Washington did not reject all past experiences outright; he simply  felt that experiences that would fit the prescribed program of the classroom were the most acceptable. He often suggested that plantation life had provided many valuable skills for slaves, and many of these talents were helpful in making freedmen productive members of society.

He had lived in the deep South, knew the people well, and witnessed the conditions for African Americans at their worst.  In many parts of the lower South conditions hardly changed after slavery, especially in Alabama, where Tuskegee was located.  In contrast Du Bois  had grown up free in a community that provided opportunities with relatively little discrimination. Washington's experiences were vastly different. He remembered  his childhood as a wretched period in his life, controlled by adults around him, and devoted to waiting to become an adult so that he could direct his own ambitions.

In later life Washington spoke of regretting having no time as a child for play or sports. Du Bois, on the other hand, viewed childhood as a privileged period in a person's life time when youngsters should be allowed to experience things around them with minimal adult interference.  He had grown up on a farm in Massachusetts with a grandfather who assigned chores for the purpose of developing a sense of responsibility in young William—rather than for exploiting labor and thereby creating drudgery, as was Washington's childhood experience on the plantation. For William, these chores were a part of the larger farm experience; for Washington they were a source of bitterness.

Washington's role models were his mother, his siblings, and other slaves. Later in life his stepfather would become a peripheral influence.  His mother was the cook on their plantation, so Booker saw all  the other slaves as they would come and go during meal times.  He was known only by his first name and mentioned frequently that he knew nothing about his father.  He would later learn that his father was a White man from a local plantation who could not, given the social system, openly acknowledge Booker's existence.

Du Bois's family, in contrast, had owned land in Massachusetts since the Revolutionary War and Du Bois could trace his heritage to people who were free. His grandfather was his role model until his mother moved back to the farm and began to participate in raising him. William was encouraged as a young student in a school system that did not segregate pupils based on race. He graduated from high school as the brightest student in his group. He was graced in a way Booker was not. For Booker, learning to read was a passion for which he had to scheme, connive, and work around a depressing job to achieve.

These two different men who would become the intellectual giants of their times were both influenced by Frederick Douglass, a Black pioneer in the antislavery movement. Booker T. Washington probably got the idea that Blacks should, "Cast down your bucket where you are," from Douglass for Douglass had advocated that Blacks should remain in the South as freedmen. Du Bois probably got his ideas about the dignity of all individuals from Douglass' view that all persons should be granted equality.

Frederick Douglass (1817-1895) was the most active Black abolitionist and women's rights activists of his time. In his autobiography he reported that he was born in Talbot County, on the eastern shore of Maryland, "remarkable for nothing that I know of more than for the worn-out, sandy, desert like appearance of its soil, the general dilapidation of its farms and fences, the indigent and spiritless character of its inhabitants, and the appearance of ague and fever" (Douglass, 1892). The first few pages of Booker T. Washington's autobiography would bear a remarkable resemblance to the opening pages of Douglass' work. I do not imply that Washington copied from the work of Douglass, just that their experiences associated with being born in slavery affected them in similar ways. Douglass described his beginnings with further eloquence; "It was in this dull, flat, and unthrifty district or neighborhood . . . among the laziest and muddy streams, surrounded by a white population of the lowest order, indolent and drunken to a proverb, and among slaves who, in point of indolence and ignorance, were fully in accord with their surroundings, that I, without any fault of my own, was born, and spent the first years of my childhood."

Grandparents played a significant role in his early life—as with Du Bois. "My first experiences of life . . . began in the family of my grandmother and grandfather. They were considered old settlers in the neighborhood." As with slaves of that time, Douglass was uncertain about his age. "I never met a slave in that part of the country who could tell me with any certainty how old he was." Such information was seen as non-essential by the slave owners, and in later years when birth dates were necessary for legal transactions, the family member who could write—or a neighbor—would record such information in the family Bible. The family Bible was accepted as legal proof of date of birth and related information.

Time was not a concept that slave owners thought slaves should be concerned about. Slaves were required to work at their assigned tasks as long as sunlight was available. As Douglass reported, "Few at that time knew anything of the months of the year or of the days of the month. They measured the ages of their children by the spring-time, winter-time, harvest-time, planting-time, and the like."

In his autobiography Douglass talked about his father in almost the same manner as did Booker T. Washington. He reported that he knew almost nothing about his father because this sort of information was not seen as necessary for the roles required of slaves. By law, the child was identified through the mother's condition as slave or free. The slave child's father might be a freedman, but this did not matter as to the child's status. A slave child's father was often not only free but White. It was common for such White fathers to sell their own children as one would any other slave. There were exceptions, as when such children were raised under the supervision of Blacks working in the White plantation residence. This preferential treatment would sometimes extend into adulthood to the time when they would be sent off to a Black university like Wilberforce or Howard. Such institutions were founded, in part, for the education of African Americans of White fathers.

Frederick's grandmother was held in high regard by Blacks and Whites, especially during his childhood years. She was responsible for protecting him from many of the drudgeries that slave children generally experienced.

Because of her special status as a slave, she was able, for a period of time, to shield her grandson from the harshest treatment of slave children. He wrote in his autobiographically about the few enjoyable experiences that his grandmother's protectiveness afforded him. He was able to day dream about a better life while sitting on the banks of a little pond near the mill where he could throw his pin-hook fishing line into the water and pretend that he was getting nibbles and really fishing, while casually observing the steady flow of people coming to get their corn ground.

Frederick's childhood, under the partially sheltered environment created by his grandmother was a short one. He was soon to learn the sad fact that the house of his childhood belonged not to his grandmother, but to someone he had never seen. He was also saddened to learn that not only the home and lot, but his grandmother and all the little children around her belonged to the same person who everyone called, "Old Master."

Frederick was also soon to learn that he would be taken away from his grandmother's protectiveness, because old master removed all Black youth from their parents to live with him. As he approached eight years of age, the time came for his grandmother to separate from him as she had done many times before with other children. Later in Douglass's life, app-

**HON. FREDERICK DOUGLASS**

roximately 70 years of age, he still retained the details of his memory of separation from his grandmother and grandfather.

He was transported to the old master's house where he met three other children. He was introduced to these strangers by his grandmother who encouraged him to play with them. They all appeared to be more aware of this process than Frederick, and in their resolve they made the best of the circumstances through their games. Frederick, not being fully aware of the significance of the moment, refused to participate in their play. Frederick's grandmother finally told him that these children who were inviting him to play were his brother and sisters, and that he should join in play with them. He recalled the gentle manner in which his grandmother revealed this startling information, with a tone that implied that he needed to know his kin. His grandmother pointed out Perry as his brother, and Sarah and Alice as his sisters. He did not really understand their relationship to him, because brothers and sisters born of slave women and slave masters were often unknown to each other. They would on occasion discover their brothers and sisters through rumor, or when commerce and trade transactions revealed their relationship.

Eventually, Frederick's grandmother managed to coax him into leaving her side, and for a while he watched his brother and sisters play. He was soon to learn from one of the children that his grandmother had gone, and at that moment of panic and aloneness, he knew that her absence would be permanent. Heartbroken in the midst of this realization, he fell to the ground and cried, refusing the comfort being offered by his newly discovered siblings. Grief and resentment formed his mixed emotions that were created by an act of deception and abandonment by a grandmother who he had learned to love and trust. The deep emotion of this experience would help form his determination and dedication as an adult to commit his energies toward the eradication of the oppression of Black Americans and women.

Frederick might not have been mature enough to understand the complex nature of a system that removed children like himself from their parents to be given away to others, with the apparent complicity of Black parents, but he often pondered the slave condition that made Whites the owners of Blacks. As an adult he recalled a sense of confusion as a child about the institution of slavery that placed Blacks in a subservient role in relation to Whites. These perplexing questions were weighty issues to be left unresolved for a child of Frederick's age. So, like many slave children with his pensiveness, he observed adults among him and tried to make sense of their world through the actions of those with whom he could identify. And Frederick, being a very thoughtful and insightful child, contemplated issues that advanced his understanding of certain matters. He recalled that adults had told him that God was the master of all things good and wonderful, and that God had made all things as he thought they should be. And, that this God had made Black people to be slaves and White people to be their masters. He was also told that God was good and that he knew what was best for everyone and all things. The wretched conditions that resulted from slavery, he thought, were opposed to any ideas of goodness with which he was familiar. Frederick contemplated his present circumstances, and this led to questions about how people come to know that God had designed slavery, and its Black-White context. He also puzzled over the reality that not *all* Black people were slaves, and not *all* White people were masters.

Frederick recalled as an adult that when he was about six years old, his Aunt Esther was romantically involved with a young Black man on a different plantation. Her White master, who also had sexual interests in Esther, had forbidden her to see her Black lover. Whenever she was discovered returning from these visits, she was severely beaten by the White master. From his sleeping rags on the floor, Frederick observed one such incident through spaces between the wall boards. He observed his Aunt Esther tied by her wrists with a rope that was attached to a wood beam. Her shoulders were perfectly bare. Behind her stood the slave master with a cowhide in hand. To young Frederick, the beating of Esther was the most cruel and painful event that he had ever witnessed. He thought that the blows were delivered with the intent of inflicting intense pain and agony beyond reason. Frederick was deeply affected by this childhood observation, and noted that when Esther was let down she could scarcely stand. This experience left young Frederick terrified, stunned and bewildered. It undoubtedly contributed to his tenacious resolve later in life to defy such oppression.

Esther continued to visit her Black lover and would on occasion be caught, followed by a beating. Douglass was deeply disappointed that Black adults failed to come to Esther's aid and that Whites tolerated the practice. He was unclear as to the meaning of this inaction. Was this evidence of Black helplessness, White indifference or another example of God's will? Such beatings did not always result from any flagrant infraction of plantation rules. If an overseer thought that a glance or a gesture from a slave implied impudence or defiance, being tied to a tree and flogged within sight of other slaves would often ensue. Not all victims, however, were passive.

When Frederick was about seven years old, he witnessed a public flogging of a Black mother of five children who was charged with impudence by the overseer. By the time he successfully tied her to the tree, she had fought him off with all of her available strength. Frederick identified with the children, who were about his age, as they pelted the attacker with rocks and other objects. The overseer eventually tied her to the tree, but he was now covered with blood and bruises and fighting off her crying and struggling children.

He then carried out the flogging as brutally as one could imagine. As the blows became progressively harsh, she never ceased denouncing the overseer with gestures and epithets. This struggle took so much out of the overseer that he became ill soon after and died.

Douglass the child witnessed the struggle put forth by a woman who refused to be subdued, and soon became aware that courageous and defiant slaves were whipped less often. He observed that one particular Black man on the plantation was never whipped because he refused to submit, even though it might have meant that he would have been shot.

The childhood of Frederick Douglass was mixed with experiences of very different varieties, and he described these events with vivid recollections. His experiences, though, were often not in common with those of other slaves, but the basic deprivations would not be different. Douglass reported that he seldom received severe treatment from his masters, but the lack of both food and clothing, nonetheless, led to a cruel childhood existence. For Frederick, the lack of clothing often kept him almost nude. The problems for all children of slavery emanated from an absence of common basic needs. Frederick later in life remembered a childhood where pigs in the pen had leaves, and horses had straw, but that Black children had no beds. The slave child's regular diet of corn meal mush was placed in a large tray or trough. This meager offering was placed on the floor of the kitchen or out of doors on the ground, as one would feed animals.

When Douglass was about eight or nine years of age, he was sent as a house servant to a family in Baltimore; and the woman of the house taught him to read after his daily chores were done. This was the only formal academic instruction that he received during his childhood. It is remarkable how this rudimentary instruction proved sufficient for Douglass to develop into an intellectual, a writer and an orator, with enough skill in each domain to project a compelling influence upon his audiences. As he described the experience of being taught as a child, later in his adult life, he reported that he was driven by an inner desire to master this *art*. As was common practice of the time, his mistress read the Bible often and the mystery of her extracting meaning from pages in a book overwhelmed young Frederick's curiosity. He worked hard to please this woman of the house who possessed these magical reading skills, and she in turn treated him with some respect for his stage of maturation. He began to feel grateful for her acknowledgement that he was a human being. Within this accepting environment, he gained the courage to ask her to teach him to read. She agreed that after his chores were complete, she would read with him. In a very short time, he was able to recite the alphabet and recognize simple words and phrases.

Ms. Hugh Auld, called Miss Sopha by Frederick, was pleased and surprised at the pace with which young "Freddy" was learning to read.

Occasionally he thought of himself as a child member of the Auld family, because gradually, his mistress was almost as accepting of him as she was of her real son, Tommy. While Tommy held the place on her lap, Freddy owned a place by her side. He became attached to his mistress; and more than anything else, wanted her to be pleased with him.

As Frederick's reading ability went beyond the mere recognition of the alphabet and uttering short phrases, his mistress appeared to recognize the direct assault that teaching a Black child to read would have on the caste of slavery. She reacted as if discovering for the first time that her act of kindness had transformed a docile slave child into an adult slave of the future with a strictly forbidden talent. Now, whenever he was discovered reading in one of his private places—probably because of orders from her husband—Ms. Auld would become violent and take his reading material from him. But it was too late to completely close off Frederick's relentless pursuit of knowledge.

Doing errands for his mistress in town he met White age mates who eventually shared their homework and assisted him with reading. In gratitude for their acceptance of him as a playmate, he cited Gustavus Dorgan, Joseph Bailey, Charles Farity, and William Cosdry with particular fondness. In return for their roles in advancing his knowledge he converted them into anti-slavery advocates. He also encountered White adults who came to know and trust him. They gave him small sums for chores like errands and boot polishing.

From these modest earnings he bought two books; *Websters Spelling Book* and *The Colombian Orator.* These were highly cherished possessions that he took with him whenever possible. He was particularly moved by a piece in *The Colombian Orator* that depicted an interchange between a slave and his master. The slave's skillful articulation of the untenable nature of slavery was so compelling that the master gave him his freedom.

After the death of her husband, Douglass' mistress sent him into the country as a field hand. By now Douglass was reading with comprehension and thought of himself as capable of teaching others. He started teaching reading to fellow Blacks under the guise of conducting religious meetings. When Whites found out that these sessions involved more than praying and singing, they canceled the meetings. After his "school" was shut down, he left for Baltimore. After disguising himself as a sailor he managed to board a ship bound for New York. Once in this northern city, It was not long before he became affiliated with the abolitionist movement. His activities called for his presence in various cities of the northeast.

He was appointed as an agent of the Massachusetts Anti-Slavery Society and became embroiled in a legal battle to prevent the Rhode Island Legislature from passing a law to restrict Black voting rights. He became a well known lecturer, and was invited to speak to thousands of organizations on the subjects of the rights of Blacks and voting rights for women. In 1890 he was appointed council General to Haiti, but resigned in 1891 when he realized that U.S. business interests were motivated solely by opportunities to exploit Haitian workers.

In 1896, African Americans of Philadelphia founded a teaching hospital and named it the Frederick Douglass Hospital Nurse-training School. By 1916, the nursing program, as a part of the Frederick Douglass Hospital, had 19 nurses in training. The first training school for Black nurses in the United States was in 1891 at the Provident Hospital in Chicago, Ill.

In 1919 in Paris, France, Du Bois organized the first Pan-African Conference with the main agenda an affirmation of the need for self-determination among African nations. This remarkable man was an inspiration for well-known activists, educators, and journalists as well as for ordinary people. He was active during the lifetime of Booker T. Washington and W. E. B. Du Bois. Douglass was a political activist, newspaper editor, scholar, ambassador, and writer and the first Black leader of national prominence in the United States. Washington was aware that Frederick Douglass and Du Bois were more philosophically aligned with each other more than either were with Washington's ideas. In 1906, eleven years after Douglass' death, Booker T. Washington published *Frederick Douglass*, a book that described more of a Douglass that Washington wished had been, rather than the eminent scholar that really was. It was also apparent that Washington's book revealed a lamentable conclusion to the life of a great man with whom he would never again have the opportunity to reconcile his different approach to African American assimilation. Washington died nine years later in 1915.

Not unlike Booker T. Washington, W. E. B. Du Bois was disenchanted with what he perceived was an awfully slow pace toward positive race relations in his country. In his nineties, his response to these disappointments was to join the Communist party. This membership angered residents in his home town, and in response they protested against a plan to erect a memorial as a celebration of his achievements. Both men would nonetheless have permanent monuments of their own making. Du Bois will always be remembered for his founding of the NAACP, and Washington will not be forgotten for his founding of the now highly respected academic institution Tuskegee University.

African American women have always assumed a prominent role during critical periods of the African American experience in our nation. During slavery that role was taken by Sojourner Truth and Harriet Tubman; after that period thousands of Black women served as teachers throughout the South, some in the Freedmen's Bureau. Also thousands of Black women taught their children to read and write at home by using the only book present in practically every home, the Bible. They taught their children to read at the same time they were establishing a legacy for the Black family and the Black church. Black women enacted a major role in establishing the

**IDA B. WELLS**

Black church as a common meeting place for the many organized efforts against racism and racist policies in our nation.

Ida B. Wells-Barnett (1864-1931) was among a small group of African American women who fought against lynching in the south. Born in Holly Springs, Mississippi, she was forced to give up her studies at Rust College to support five younger brothers and sisters after the death of her parents.

Statistics on the lynching of Blacks were collected and reported by Tuskegee Institute. It was reported that by 1950, more than 3,000 blacks had been lynched since 1882. More than 1,200 Blacks were lynched during the ten-year period of 1890-1900. A prominent crusader, Barnett used a newspaper she edited, *Free Speech*, published in Memphis, Tennessee, and an anti-lynching pamphlet, *The Red Record* to publicize the issue. She was also a correspondent and writer for several newspapers including *The Detroit Plain Dealer, The People's Choice, The New York Age, Our Women and Children* magazine, and the *Christian Index.* Her colleagues in the national African American press called her the "Princess of the Press."

Barnett, a school teacher in Memphis, started teaching at the age of fourteen, and directed the work of the Anti-Lynching Bureau of the National African Council. A prolific writer, she distributed many of her pamphlets to keep African American and White attention focused on the horrors of lynching, an act tolerated by the public's apathy and by the criminal justice system of the time.

Her newspaper, *Free Speech,* became such a powerful instrument of change that whites took drastic measures against it. Her articles supporting a local Black grocery business—started a chain of events that led to the death of the Black grocer and his partners, and to the demise of *Free Speech.*

For many years, a White grocery store was the only place in the Memphis Black community where food could be purchased. Three Black men who were respected for their fair-dealing, opened a store in the same community. After the Black merchants became successful, a group of White business men with the aid of a local newspaper—the *Commercial Appeal*—and the White controlled police in Memphis, concocted an elaborate ruse that led to the arrest of the three Black grocers. Within a week, the Black men were removed from the jail by a White mob and lynched. The White mob then went to the store of the murdered grocers, helped themselves to merchandise, and destroyed fixtures.

Ida B. Wells-Barnett, as she was known at that time, was attending a conference in New York along with friends including, Bishop Daniel A. Payne, Fannie Jackson Coppin, and Thomas Fortune, editor of the *New York Age* (a Black newspaper). Wells was met at the train station by Fortune, who immediately informed her of an important story in the local newspapers. Wells reported the incident in her autobiography.

He handed me a copy of the *New York Sun* where he had marked an Associated Press dispatch from Memphis. The article stated that, acting on an editorial of the *Commercial Appeal* of the previous Monday morning, a committee of leading citizens had gone to the office of the *Free Speech* that night, run the business manager, J. L. Fleming, out of town, destroyed the type and furnishings of the office and left a note saying that anyone trying to publish the paper again would be punished with death. (Duster, 1970 pp. 61-62)

Barnett took her anti-lynching campaign to Europe and various parts of the United States through personal appearances and lectures. In 1908 she founded and became the first president of the Negro Fellowship League. Later, her work was primarily in Chicago, where at that time the settlement house movement had emerged as an important neighborhood institution for poor families of all races. She became a community organizer, social worker, and probation officer, all in the spirit of the settlement house movement. Her work was later recognized by the citizens of Chicago, and several memorials in her name survive today.

During this same period, Charlotta Bass became an active opponent of the Ku Klux Klan. She founded and edited the oldest African American newspaper in the West, the *California Eagle*. She used the newspaper's pages to bring attention to racial inequities in the United States. Born in Rhode Island in 1890, Bass attended Columbia University, Brown University, and the University of California. She served as western regional director of the Republican party, campaigning for Wendell Wilkie in the 1940 presidential election. Many Black Americans of that period were becoming disenchanted with the traditional political organizations because of their disinterest in racism in employment and the activities of race hate groups like the Klan. In the early 1950s Charlotta Bass left the Republican party and with a group of Black and White liberals founded the Progressive Party of California. She later became the Progressive party candidate for Congress from the 14 District in Los Angeles County. At the 1952 Progressive Party's Convention in Chicago, she was selected the party's candidate for vice president of the United States, thus becoming the first African American—and woman—to be chosen for the second highest elected position in the nation.

Sadie Alexander was the first African American woman to earn a Ph.D. in the United States. Born in Philadelphia in 1898 Alexander graduated with honors from the University of Pennsylvania in 1918 and became the first African American woman to be admitted to the bar in the state of Pennsylvania. She was very active in the National Urban League and served on the league's board of directors.

Fannie Lou Hamer (1917-1977) was born in Montgomery County, Mississippi. At the age of two, Fannie Lou's parents and their 20 children moved to Sunflower County, Mississippi, to work on the plantation of E. W.

Brandon. By the time Fannie Lou was six years old, she was picking cotton for the profit of the Brandon plantation. For children in Fannie Lou's community there were few opportunities for schooling. When it did exist, classes were held in dilapidated buildings for three or four months out of the year. Despite these depressing circumstances for Mississippi children, Fannie Lou developed a love for reading. As a child she picked up anything, like pieces of old newspapers and scraps of labels from cans of produce and packaging, just to read the words. It was reported that during her limited six years of schooling, she read poetry and was successful at spelling bees.

After the age of 40, Hamer became a role model for many southern Black women who observed her civil rights activities in the 1960s, and she was a challenge to Black men who for many years had not resisted Mississippi racist politics. She was fired from her job when she tried to vote, and she was beaten and jailed when she attempted to register others to vote. In the process she embarrassed Black professionals into taking a stand against the harsh treatment of the South's Black poor, and they in turn pulled resisting Black ministers into the civil rights movement and negotiated for the use of Black churches for rallies. Hamer recruited members for the NAACP, the Southern Christian Leadership Conference and directed many voter registration drives. She was also keenly aware of the necessity of bringing in outside help from northern Whites because of the constant fear under which Mississippi Blacks lived. Hamer knew that a visit to the Delta from a contingent of well-known Whites would yield media coverage in the liberal press and focus attention on the grinding poverty and political oppression in Black Mississippi life.

Her powerful message espousing equality among the races became so pervasive statewide, that U.S. Senator James O. Eastland, who had become an international symbol of the nation's racist policies, decided not to run for reelection because he faced almost certain defeat in the new political climate created through the work of Fannie Lou Hamer. For many years before the turn of the political tide Eastland controlled Sunflower County politics because of entrenched Black de facto slavery on White-owned plantations. Eastland campaigned on racist policies and the Mississippi voters returned him to Congress, and to the chairmanship of the powerful Senate Internal Affairs Committee. Eastland charged that the Communist party was behind the civil rights movement, and for the purpose of intimidation used his congressional committee power to "investigate" educational, labor, and arts organizations. Later for a period of time he managed to prevent funding for Head Start in Mississippi.

Fannie Lou Hamer was among the first of the civil rights leaders to suggest that Black history should be taught in grade schools. She fought for free lunch programs for poor children to ensure that they received proper nutrition. She was aware of the burden of hunger among southern

Black children, aware that poor health and nutrition robbed Black school-children of their motivation to learn. She also campaigned for better salaries and job security for Black teachers, who, at that time were under the control of Whites. Hamer participated in hundreds of demonstrations and marches, confronted the leadership of the Democratic party at their national convention, stood up to the president of the United States, and gained the respect of all civil rights activists of her time and place.

Another important activist was Rosa Parks whose action in December of 1955 brought Martin Luther King Jr., into the civil rights movement of the 1960s. She was born February 4, 1914, and as a child attended the campus school for children where teachers enrolled in Alabama State Normal School for Colored Students, did their practice teaching. At that time, this campus school was the only facility in the county where African American children were able to go beyond sixth grade, so Parks attended school with her mother. Rosa's mother was a teacher attending the college on the same campus to renew her certification. Her father and the men in his family were carpenters who traveled to build houses. Rosa grew up near the campus of Tuskegee Institute.

The State Normal School For Colored Students, was founded in 1873 by an act of the Alabama state legislature as Lincoln Memorial University at Marion, Perry County. The name was changed and it was moved to Montgomery, Alabama, in 1889. Its financial support came from the Slater Fund, the Peabody Fund, and the state of Alabama. The board of trustees were all White and appointed by the governor.

While Rosa was attending the school's kindergarten, her mother was taking secondary-level courses, the school had an enrollment of 714 students; 575 were at the elementary level, and 139 at the secondary level. There were 29 Black teachers and 2 White teachers on the staff. Secondary-level studies included bookkeeping, English, education, science, Latin, history, and practice teaching. At the industrial level courses were offered in blacksmithing, carpentry, wheelwrighting and sewing for the girls. Art drawing was offered to males and females.

Until she was 11 years old Rosa attended a grade school in Mt. Zion, Alabama, where her mother was the only teacher. When Rosa was 11 her mother enrolled her in the Montgomery Industrial School for Girls in Montgomery, Alabama. This school was founded in 1886 by two White women, Alice L. White from Massachusetts and H. Margaret Beard, who served as co-principals. It was designed as an elementary day school for Black girls. White had come to the deep South along with many other White teachers from the North to assist in advancing educational opportunities for Black children. Her school became known as "Miss White's School," and it was not welcomed by the White residents of Montgomery. In the early days of the school's development local Whites burned the school down several times.

The Montgomery school was also known as the school for Colored girls and at the time of Rosa's attendance 325 girls were enrolled under the tutelage of ten White female teachers. The curriculum accommodated students from kindergarten through the eighth grade. The industrial courses included cooking, basketry, hygiene, and sewing, all at the practical and theoretical levels. Literary courses included arithmetic, English, physiology, psychology, and foreign language.

The desire to live in a fair and free society is probably a universal human trait. In the same social context, having to observe others accorded rights and privileges denied to you because of some biological difference between you and the oppressing privileged group increases that desire. The oppressing group will identify an innate difference, perhaps skin color, language, or way of life. These differences are then used to justify oppression, to provide an excuse for unfairness for even the most-well meaning people. The Bible, color differences, lack of intelligence, have all been among the many justifications for keeping African Americans in a lower caste.

When African Americans did not fit the stereotype, they were considered "different" from their own group, or perhaps it was thought, they had been accorded a special privilege by a White. Rosa Parks's grandfather understood these phenomena. He taunted southern Whites and defied their restrictions. Parks was so impressed with her grandfather's wit in knowing how far to push his defiance, without placing his family in harms way, that even in her seventies she could recall with great detail her childhood experiences derived from observing her grandfather interact with local Whites. "I remember sometimes he would call white men by their first names and not say "Mister." He was taking a big risk. My grandfather had a somewhat belligerent attitude toward whites in general." Children are always watching; they want to know how they can make sense of their world. "Any little thing he could do, he did it, it wouldn't be anything of great significance, but it was a small way of expressing his hostility toward whites." (Parks, p. 17).

This maturing, observing child was developing her own personality, struggling for a positive definition of self in an oppressive environment replete with denigrating messages of inferiority for her and the people with whom she identified. We will probably never know precisely how the interaction between her environment and her sense of self created the person who defied oppressive laws by refusing to give up her seat to a person she could not define as superior to herself.

On December 1, 1955, Rosa Parks made history when she boarded a bus and was arrested because she refused to give up her seat to a White passenger when directed to do so by the White bus driver. This was not the first time that such a law was broken by a Black passenger, though the occurrences were rare. The Rosa Parks incident was highly significant because it led to Black citizens' organizing against discrimination through boycotts and set off a steady stream of Black protest in the South. Rosa Parks was the perfect catalyst because of her calm, refined, and elegant manner in the face of being arrested and jailed. The Montgomery bus boycott gave Black Alabama residents their first political victory since Reconstruction, and engaged the attention of Dr. Martin Luther King Jr., who was brought into the movement at the time of the boycott by the young people of Montgomery. And for the next decade, the children were watching.

## REFERENCES

Avery, S. (1989). *Up from Washington: William Pickens and the Negro struggle for equality.* New Jersey: Associated University Presses.

Bond, H. M. (1966). *The education of the Negro in the American social order.* New York: Octagon Books.

Bullock, H. A. (1967). *A history of Negro education in the south: From 1619 to present.* Cambridge, MA: Harvard University Press.

Douglass, F. (1892). *Life and times of Frederick Douglass: Written by himself* (reprint Collier Books, 1962).

Du Bois , W. E. B. (1970). *The souls of black folk.* New York: Simon & Schuster.

————. (1971). *The autobiography of W. E. B. Du Bois.* New York: International Publishers.

Duster, A. M. (1970). *Crusade for justice: The autobiography of Ida B. Wells.* Chicago: University of Chicago Press.

Embree, E. R. (1936). *Julius Rosenwald fund: Review of two decades.* Chicago: The President's Report.

Hawkins, H. (1962). *Booker T. Washington and his critics: The problem of Negro leadership.* Lexington, MA: D. C. Heath and Company.

Jones, T. J. (Ed.). (1916). *Negro education: A study of the private and higher schools for colored people in the United States* (Bulletin No. 38, Vol. 1). Washington, D.C. Department of Interior, Bureau of Education. (reprint Arno Press, 1969).

Mills, K. (1993). *This little light of mine: The life of Fannie Lou Hamer.* New York: Dutton.

Parks, R. (1992). *Rosa Parks: My story.* New York: Dial Books.

Penn, G. I. (1891). *The Afro-American press, and its editors.* Springfield, MA: Willey & Company.

Ploski, H. A. & Kaiser, E. (1971). *Afro USA: A reference work on the black experience.* New York: Bellwether Publishing Company.

Toppin, E. A. (1971). *A biographical history of Blacks and America since 1528.* New York: David McKay Company.

Washington, B. T. (1906). *Frederick Douglass.* Philadelphia: George Jacobs & Company.

————. (1989). *Up from slavery.* New York: Carol Publishing Group.

# V

# The Decades That
# Followed Slavery

*We know positively of case after case where innocent men have died horrible deaths. We know positively of cases that have been made up. We know positively of cases where black men have been lynched for white men's crimes. We know positively of black men murdered for insignificant offenses. All that we ask for is justice— not mercy or palliation—simply justice. Surely that is not too much for loyal citizens of a free country to demand.*

—Ida B. Wells

The 1920s witnessed the end of an era of Black scholars who had been educated in a variety of church-related, church-supported, and Freedmen's schools like the African Free School, where the emphasis was on classical academic education. The new wave of intellectuals included not only a small group of scholars who had attended institutions like Harvard and Princeton but also a much larger group trained as public school teachers, preachers, and vocational artisans in the Booker T. Washington tradition. It was the end of an era of Black scholars who as children had been taught secretly in plantation cabins, in small Black churches, and by the daughters and wives of plantation owners, who in some cases were their half brothers and sisters.

Not until the 1930s did the Black institutions of higher learning replace some of their industrial courses with academic ones and upgrade their offerings from elementary-and secondary-level studies. By the 1940s basic industrial education remained as a focus in Black high schools, but only as vocational education teacher training at the college level. By now public schooling was divided into Black and White either by law or because of residential patterns. In several cities where liberal traditions prevailed, as in New York City, children from the more affluent Black families attended schools with White students. There were also schools where a majority of the children were White and from poor rural and immigrant families.

Children who attended segregated schools in the South told stories of how they got the discarded materials from the White schools in their towns. Their books were those previously owned by children in the local White schools, and the names of White children were still on the inside covers. The Black children also received basketball uniforms that were handed down from the local White schools, and not in their school colors. They looked to their Black teachers to put things right, but their teachers had no power and very little influence. In fact, the teachers' jobs existed at the will of the local politician and/or the White superintendent of schools.

Blacks and southerners were the first to feel the negative effects of the Great Depression of the late 1920s and the early 1930s. They were also more deeply affected, and they took longer to recover. By 1933 the federal government inaugurated a variety of emergency educational programs to improve literacy among poor Blacks and Whites. By this time Black voters had left the ranks of the political party of Abraham Lincoln and shifted their support to Franklin Delano Roosevelt's Democratic party. In their view, FDR had saved the nation from total economic disaster, and he did not leave Black citizens of the plan. In 1935 the Federal Emergency Relief Program and the U. S. Office of Education initiated a variety of educational projects. The various projects that constituted the overall literacy initiatives were administered by the Works Progress Administration (WPA). Among those programs were school building and construction, student aid, adult education and nursery schools.

The school-building program provided loans and grants to communities through the Federal Emergency Administration of Public Works to improve public schooling in Black and White communities. Many of these schools are still in use today and can easily be identified because they bear names like Booker T. Washington, Frederick Douglass, Ida B. Wells, and Phillis Weatley.

Student aid programs were administered through the National Youth Administration (NYA) which enjoyed a reputation for racial fairness in the allocation of funds. In 1936 the NYA set aside a special fund to aid Black students at the college and university level. This was also indirect aid to Black colleges because a majority of the Black students attended Black institutions. Black students in many southern and rural areas were limited in regards to higher-education assistance because they lacked opportunities for secondary education where they lived. Under such circumstances, they would be ineligible for college or university admission. It was suggested by Black professionals assigned as field agents that Black students affected by such community limitations should be financed to attend a high school in the nearest community available. Records did not report any implementation of such a policy.

Adult education was a high priority of the Federal Emergency Relief Program. With support from the Julius Rosenwald Fund, a statistical survey was conducted throughout the South to help determine the extent to which emergency educational activities were being put to use. In those southern states from which data were assessed, it was determined that 26% of their populations were enrolled in adult literacy programs. Black adults represented 38% of the total enrollment, and 31% of the teachers were African American. Some disparity was reported in teacher load. White teachers averaged 29 pupils per class, and Black teachers were reported to have had an average of 40 pupils per class. The average monthly salary for White teachers was $52.80 a month, compared with $42.45 a month for Black teachers. Adult education funds were allocated to states based upon the percentages of adult literacy. It was calculated that the need for adult literacy programs was greater among Black populations than among White, even though there was a general need for greater literacy for all citizens, especially in the South. As a result, many more Blacks than Whites were enrolled in literacy programs throughout the South. Nursery schools for Black children were supported by federal funds in 14 southern states. In 1934 there were 54 emergency nursery schools established for Black children. By May 1937 the number had grown to 160. This progress was due partly to the assignment of a full-time Black administrative assistant to oversee the allocation of resources for programs benefiting Black children. The Rosenwald Fund also assigned a full-time field officer to assure that the allocation of funds in the southern states was done equitably.

The record of the WPA's administration of the program indicated a relatively high degree of effectiveness and fairness, except for teacher salaries in some instances. They were effective in that by 1935 over 200 thousand Black students and over 350 thousand White students were enrolled in emergency education programs. These programs hired more than 5 thousand Black teachers and more than 12 thousand White teachers. A degree of fairness was built into the process because the FDR administration required an assurance that Black children and professionals would be fairly represented in the benefits. As a part of this process, Black professionals were integrated into all levels of the program at the federal level and in the field. A division of "Negro Affairs" was also established in Washington, D.C., to ensure fairness.

Federal programs and an increase in public school opportunities for Black teachers and children called forth a more assertive Black population that started to demand equity in salaries and in employment. Between 1939 and 1947 the NAACP increased its membership from little more that 50 thousand to 450 thousand, with more than 1,000 branches. With a growing industrial preparation for an impending World War II, Black leaders in labor unions began putting pressure on the president to eliminate racial discrimination in the workplace. With the support of Eleanor Roosevelt and a threatened *March on Washington* by the Black labor leader Asa Philip Randolph.  In 1941 FDR issued Executive Order 8802, which made it a federal offense to discriminate in the employment of workers in the defense industries.

Asa Philip Randolph (1889-1979) founded and became president of the first Black labor union to be chartered by a major labor federation in the United States.  Randolph was born in Crescent City, Florida, where his father was a minister of a small congregation of the African Methodist Church.  He graduated from high school by attending the Cookman Institute in Jacksonville, Florida.  This institution would later merge with a school founded by Mary McCloud Bethune in Daytona Beach and become Bethune-Cookman College.

After completion of his studies at Cookman,  Randolph moved to New York City, where he was employed in a variety of  menial jobs such as elevator operator, porter, and waiter.  He attended City College of New York in the evenings after working full time during the day.   By 1917 Randolph had learned enough about capitalism from his studies at City College and his experiences in the workplace to organize a small elevator operators' union.  Together with Chandler Owen, a law student, he founded *The Messenger,* a politically socialist publication.  Owen and Randolph labeled it, "The Only Radical Negro Magazine in America."  Randolph also thought of himself as a pacifist and served a brief time in jail for opposing World War I.  He was fired from several jobs because of  attempts to organize workers.  He thought of himself as a Socialist and resisted all attempts to associate his politics with communism.

The Pullman Company had special railroad cars that rented privileges to passengers who wished to sleep and eat while traveling to and fro by rail.  Black workers served passengers as cooks, porters, and maids.  They were required to work over 300 hours a month for $70,  including tips.  When they complained or attempted to organize, the Pullman Company fired them.  As the pressure built on the Pullman Company, the management set up a company union that made a few cosmetic changes that did not satisfy the few remaining militant workers.

The appalling conditions under which the Pullman car porters worked was well known to Randolph and to many Blacks in the general population.  When approached by several porters, Randolph agreed to assist them in setting up a union of substance.  In August 1925 he began to commit many hours to the new union; and by 1928 more than half  the Pullman car workers, all Black, had joined The Brotherhood of Sleeping Car Porters.  Randolph turned *The Messenger* into the official publication of the  union and  created a new subtitle, *The Official Organ of  the Brotherhood of Sleeping Car Porters.*

Randolph and the leadership of the union tried to secure better working conditions from the  Pullman Company but were unsuccessful. They agreed to strike for better working conditions. Such a large segment of the Black male population was employed by the Pullman Company, that failure would mean an economic loss to the Black community resulting in fewer dollars for neighborhood goods and services and church coffers. People who owned community enterprises were fearful that the Pullman Company was powerful enough to sustain any job action by this small unionized group. Several Black leaders, ministers, and publishers denounced Randolph as an agitator, a Communist and an atheist. The label "outsider" also proved damaging in some quarters because Randolph had never worked as a Pullman porter. Even Thurgood Marshall had as a young adult worked as a railroad porter. For various reasons the parent union, the American Federation of Labor (AFL) ordered The Brotherhood of Sleeping Car Porters not to strike.

By 1935 A. Philip Randolph had signed up such a large number of porters as union members, and a labor law modified in 1934, made the Brotherhood so much more powerful than it had been in the past, that the Pullman Company agreed to accept the union as the collective bargaining agent for the porters. That led to improvements in working conditions, and salaries, and to a pension plan. As the AFL merged with the Congress of Industrial Organizations (CIO), Randolph became its vice-president.

Randolph, and Bayard Rustin, another graduate of City College of New York, were the planners of the March on Washington in 1963 made memorable by Martin Luther King's "I Have a Dream" speech. It was Randolph and Rustin who carefully crafted the cooperative mood of the March on Washington by negotiating various levels of participation for all the Black groups, from moderate to radical. Such diversity could very well have led to unproductive dissension.

The successful negotiation by Pullman workers during the 1930s was the most well known collective action of its time. Many other grievances were being put forth by Black workers from various professions, especially by public school teachers. Professional Blacks known not to take direct action now had A. Philip Randolph as their model. Black teachers filed lawsuits in places where they faced disparities between their salary and the salaries of White teachers. Legal attacks were also launched to equalize the allocation of resources, especially in the South, where traditionally Black schools were given less than White schools on a per pupil basis. Approximately 30 cases would be filed on behalf of Black teachers by 1950. Of those presented, only four cases were lost mostly on salary equalization. But teacher militancy was growing and gradually setting the stage for the civil rights movement.

In 1949 Black parents in Summerton, South Carolina, brought a complaint before their school board regarding overcrowding in the Black high school. After a reasonable waiting period, without evidence of action from the school board, the NAACP joined the parents and filed a lawsuit requesting an end to the town's system of segregated schooling. This approach took the school board by surprise because it was expecting to defend against a "separate and equal" doctrine. The same legal approach was used by the NAACP when it joined with parents in Farmville, Virginia. In May 1951 the NAACP and Farmville Black parents filed a petition of complaint against segregated school facilities. A District of Columbia case involved the NAACP and parents filing similar requests. A case filed in Topeka, Kansas, argued that the assignment of children to separate public school facilities was inherently unequal. In response to a Wilmington, Delaware, parents' petition, the Court agreed that Black children should be allowed to attend an all-White school until their school was brought up to the same standard. In May 1954 all these cases were put to rest by the Supreme Court's decision against the inequality inherent in "the separate but equal doctrine" by rendering a decision that was calmly read by Chief Justice Earl Warren.

## BROWN V. THE BOARD OF EDUCATION

On May 17, 1954, the U.S. Supreme Court convened in its regular manner, and what started off as a ordinary day unexpectedly gave birth to a tremendous civil rights movement that extended into the 1960s. Chief Justice Earl Warren started reading the opinion on a court case that was one of five argued by Thurgood Marshall, mentioned earlier, and a team of NAACP attorneys. Warren reported for the Court, "We conclude that in the field of public education the doctrine of 'separate but equal' has no place. Separate educational facilities are inherently unequal." Thereby the NAACP, founded by W. E. B. Du Bois and his intellectual Black and White colleagues in 1909 on Abraham Lincoln's one-hundreth birthday, became the organization that forever changed the racial makeup of the nation's public schools. At the time of this decision 17 states and the District of Columbia required Black and White children to attend separate schools. The battle for equal educational opportunities in the nation had become the mission of many young Black lawyers educated in the South and the border states, as well as those who had received a classic education in northern White colleges and universities. These young scholars had viewed *Plessy v. Ferguson* as their challenge to reverse in the Supreme Court. In 1896 the Court held that segregation was legal in all areas of life in the United States as long as the separate facilities were *equal*. It was commonly acknowledged that at the time of the decision Black facilities were nowhere near equal to those available to Whites. In acknowledging this disparity, the White-dominated courts offered that in time things *could* be made equal. In actual practice, though, things had gone in the other direction. For example, from 1900 to 1940 practically all the high schools for Black children in the South were located in major cities. During this same period, with the aid of the General Education Board, the South engaged in a vast program to provide secondary schools for its White youth. This was a part of a national movement to make secondary education available to children from working-class families, and not solely to youth from affluent families that could afford private schools.

One of the few high schools for Black youth was in Augusta, Georgia. Ware High School, which stood as a sources of achievement and pride, was located in Richmond County and had developed a reputation for academic excellence. The strong academic studies at Ware was a continuation of a tradition first established in Augusta by Lucy Laney through her creation of the Haines Normal and Industrial School in 1866. This important ground work was discussed more fully in chapter IV.

The community had pressured the county authorities over a period of time, and Ware High School school was established after a bitter battle between Black citizens and the Whites who controlled the public schools.

During the 30 year period after the emancipation proclamation, secondary education was not considered a priority because of the need for basic elementary schooling. In this regard, Lucey Laney in establishing her school, had placed her city of Augusta ahead of most Southern communities.

In July 1897—following national trends—the White school board of Richmond County voted to close Ware High School, citing the need for more elementary Black schools; it proposed to hire four Black teachers to support this new policy.

The Richmond County Black parents had little trouble organizing opposition to the school board's decision, and they petitioned the Court for a reversal. *Cumming v. School Board of Richmond County, Georgia* was carried to the U.S. Supreme Court. The lawyers for the Black parents of Augusta, Georgia, argued that the Court had ruled in the *Plessy* decision that separate was allowed only if facilities were relatively equal. The U.S. Supreme Court rendered its opinion through Chief Justice John Marshall Harlan that the case made for Ware High School did not prove that the White school board's action was based solely on race. The Court failed to consider the fact that *two* White high schools existed in the county, and that White teachers were paid much more than Black teachers for the same teaching duties. This disparity represented a clear violation of *Plessy.*

This Supreme Court decision aggravated an already negative climate among Black law students and hardened their mission to overturn *Plessy.* The *Cumming* ruling was one more example of a racist controlled court system so bigoted that *Plessy* would be used against Blacks whenever possible, and that it would be ignored if its application provided even modest opportunities for Blacks. In this case, the U. S. Supreme Court chose to ignore *Plessy,* thus setting the stage for southern states to proceed with the development of secondary schools for White students, while ignoring the needs of Black students. Whites were aware that eliminating Black student access to secondary schools would substantially reduce their opportunities to qualify for college.

Ware High School was closed in 1897, and a survey conducted 20 years later reported that southern cities were providing public high schools for over 75,00 White children and *none* for Blacks. This policy continued through the late 1930s until FDR initiated wide-scale public works programs that included building schools in many communities in order to create jobs and enable the nation to emerge from the Great Depression. This phenomenon will be discussed more fully in chapter VII.

The struggle to overturn Plessy could be seen as beginning with the personal mission of a not so well known African American named Charles Hamilton Houston (1895-1950). Houston, the major professor of Thurgood Marshall at Howard University Law School, was considered an expert on the U. S. Constitution. Houston served as dean of the Howard University Law School from 1924 to 1935 and there instilled in his young Black scholars the zeal to pursue the overturning of *Plessy* as a part of their overall mission to gain equal rights for Black people. Houston was born and grew up in Washington, D.C. into a family that had been free for many generations. By the time he reached high school age, his parents had acquired a relatively comfortable level of living for African Americans in Washington at that time. Both parents were achievement oriented and pushed him to do well. Houston attended the Garrison Elementary School, and the M Street High School, both known as "Colored" schools. M Street High School enjoyed a national reputation among professionals who knew it as having an academically oriented curriculum and teaching staff.

At the time of Houston's attendance the school administration and faculty were extremely protective of their academically oriented mission and resisted efforts to make the school a vocational/industrial training institution. The curriculum consisted of art, English, French, Greek, German, history, mathematics, science, music, and physical education. Prestigious institutions like Amherst, Bates, Brown, Dartmouth, Oberlin, University of Pennsylvania, and the University of Pittsburgh were awarding its graduates scholarships, based upon teacher recommendations and student achievement.

After high school graduation Charles was offered a scholarship to the University of Pittsburgh. He had his mind set on Amherst College, however, and convinced his parents of his choice. His father was an attorney who specialized in civil cases, and his mother was a hairdresser to women from the White affluent families of Washington. Charles's parents were doing well financially, and they agreed to pay for Amherst, thereby permitting him to turn down the University of Pittsburgh scholarship.

Houston was the only African American student in the class of 1915, and he graduated with honors in English. After graduation, for a brief period, he taught English at M Street High School, now renamed Paul Laurence Dunbar High School. Like many people in the general public, Hamilton thought of teaching as a relatively simple process of imparting information to an eager and receptive young audience. After he learned how difficult it was to teach in grade school, he abandoned the idea in favor of attending law school.

But first came service in World War I. After serving as a 1st Lieutenant in the army during the war, he applied and was accepted by the Harvard University Law School. He excelled as a scholar at Harvard and became the first African American student to serve on the editorial board of the *Harvard Law Review*. He was admitted to the District of Columbia Bar in 1924, and later became the first director of the NAACP Legal Defense Fund; he held this position until his death. His organized team of Black and White lawyers carefully selected cases on a state-by-state basis, successfully gaining admission for Black scholars to attend graduate schools in their own state. Thurgood Marshall, who had been one of Houston's students at Howard Law School, was a member of that team of young legal scholars who approached local courts with cases seeking to assert the basic rights of Blacks. After Houston's death, Thurgood Marshall was recruited as the most reasonable person to replace him. Houston's spirit in pursuit of *Plessy* had been instilled in Marshall by his teacher and mentor through their many years at Howard University and as colleagues in the NAACP.

In December 1952 the NAACP Legal Defense Fund, headed by Thurgood Marshall, was before the Supreme Court representing five cases that had moved slowly through the state courts of Delaware, South Carolina, Kansas, Virginia, and the District of Columbia. The Court scheduled a hearing for a year later, and asked the litigants to submit briefs in the meantime, on *Oliver Brown, et al. v. Board of Education of Topeka, Kansas*.

After Chief Justice Earl Warren rendered the Court's decision in favor of the litigants, thereby dismissing segregation in schools, Thurgood Marshall remarked to his colleagues that the worst was probably yet to come. The Court had also been concerned about implementation, and Marshall knew that Whites would offer great resistance because they had become accustomed to Jim Crow laws as a way of life. Jim Crow was the label given to the many segregation laws established by state legislatures, mostly in the South, to prevent Black citizen's participation in all walks of life. It is a term virtually unknown to school children and their teachers of the 1990s. Marshall's prediction about the difficulties of enforcement with "all deliberate speed' as directed by the Court was true in the North as well as the South.

Educators completely miscalculated the strength of the opposition to desegregated schooling that would come from White communities around the nation. In many areas, segregated mortgage lending patterns, created in part by the Federal Housing Authority's (FHA), discriminatory policies, had already created Black and White residential areas, requiring some children to be transported across sharply drawn geographic lines if desegregation were implemented.

Black professionals and parents in New York City were among the first to attempt to ensure the implementation of the Supreme Court's decision. Professor Kenneth Clarke in New York City, a psychologist who had become well know through his doll studies in the 1950s, and Milton Galamison in Brooklyn, New York, a minister of a large congregation, became active in these early endeavors. Clarke led an organization of Black and White professionals called the Intergroup Committee on New York's Public Schools. The Committee called for a study of lower grades in public schooling, suspecting that teaching and pupil performance in elementary grades doomed Black children to failure in high schools. For his book, *Dark Ghetto;* in 1966, Professor Kenneth Clarke was honored with a prestigious award at the First World Festival of Negro Arts, held in Dakar, West Africa. The book is often used as a reference text in college and university courses. In 1935 Clarke conducted several studies among Black preschool and elementary grade students aimed at determining their sense of self-esteem. Through the use of Black and White dolls he established that Black children rejected Black dolls, and preferred White dolls, even when asked, "Which doll is most like you?" Clarke was asked by the NAACP Legal Defense Fund to conduct the same studies in southern schools to determine the extent to which this Black rejection-White acceptance phenomenon might also be true for children there. The NAACP Legal Defense Fund team was seeking expert evidence, and ultimately expert testimony, as to the damaging effects segregation was having upon Black children in the nation. Social scientists, Black and White, from the most prestigious universities had served as expert witnesses for the NAACP in previous state court cases, but the team thought that an expert who had actually conducted his own studies would be more compelling. After talking to Clarke and observing him conduct some on-site studies of African American children in the South, Marshall was appalled at the self-doubt that welled up in African American schoolchildren as they hesitantly demonstrated mixed feelings about rejecting Black dolls and indicating a preference for White ones. Despite this compelling demonstration, Marshall and members of the team had mixed feelings about the use of Clarke's work in court. Their concerns about the use of the doll studies were tied to the results that reported a Black rejection rate among children in the New York study higher than in a sample of Black children in the South. The NAACP lawyers would later have these results used against them when a segregationist lawyer would point out to the court that the integration policies in New York City had an even more negative effect upon the self-esteem of African American children than did discrimination in the South.

Clarke and Galamison, working in different sections of New York City, each had a respected reputation in the Black community, but they gained little support from traditional organizations. The White-controlled teachers' union in New York City was successful in keeping the traditional civil rights groups like the NAACP out of the fray. The teachers' union by that time was affiliated with older activists like A. Philip Randolph and like Bayard Rustin of the AFL-CIO. The staff of the NAACP Legal Defense Fund did not define the northern busing and housing discrimination within the context of *Brown*. Different divisions within the NAACP were directing their attention to housing and facilities discrimination of a subtle nature in the North and blatant segregation in the South. The slow pace of full desegregation in the North did not get their immediate attention.

Galamison and a group of parents founded the Parents Workshop for Equity. Their investigation turned up a number of predominantly White schools with small enrollments, while an equal number of Black schools were overcrowded. New York City responded by instituting a school building-program that sequestered the Black parents' efforts for a while.

In response, Parents for Equity threatened the city of New York with a massive school boycott. The boycott lacked organization and never occurred, but the fear of future organized action by Black parents was enough to encourage the city to act. The officials responded to the Black parents' complaint about overcrowding by establishing a free transfer program called "Open Enrollment." It was designed to fail. The plan called for selected White grade schools to be identified by school officials as "receiving" schools for parents who wanted to transfer their children to a predominantly White, less-crowded environment. Black parents were given a list of schools available to their children, with no information about the school and only two days to make an appointment to visit the school talk to the principal, and make a decision. It was reported by Black parents who went through the process that receiving principals discouraged Black parents with threats and tales of unsafe conditions for their child being so far away from home. Black children also reported that their White teachers were hostile and that White children were often unfriendly.

In the North White parents organized community groups to oppose busing. Their main argument was that a valuable part of the school day would be sacrificed in traveling to and from school. The cry became, "We do not want our children bused away from their neighborhood schools." It did not take long for researchers to point out that at least half of the schoolchildren in the nation were already being bused. This was being done in many rural communities consolidated into a single school district and in many urban areas children were provided bus passes to attend their school of choice. It was also pointed out that families in affluent suburban neighborhoods chose to have their children bused—or transported in the family car—to a preferred school because of its "good reputation."

With their real concern exposed—that what they really objected to were the minority children at the end of the bus ride—a new phrase was added to the school desegregation vocabulary; *forced   busing.* The rhetoric and political tactics were changed to fit the peculiarities and court rulings in specific state, cities, and neighborhoods. Neighbors would disagree with one another over strategies and condemned other White residents who favored a compliance with the Supreme Court decision.

Few had predicted that such problems would surface with such vigor in northern and southern communities. In many southern communities Christian academies were established for White pupils as a private enterprise.   Because of the political power of Whites in these small southern communities, public school supplies and services were easily transferred to the Christian academies.   When segregated schools became illegal, In one Mississippi county the White school board sold all of the public system's books to the local Christian Academy for a dollar and transferred their children to one of the many Christian academies.   Children from poor Black families and a few children from poor White families were left behind in the old system without books or supplies. A request for an increase in the local school tax to support the public schools was voted down by White parents.

One of the most popular strategies employed by White parents in the North was to comply with desegregation plans as a tradeoff for an agreement with school authorities that  Black and White children would be resegregated inside the school.  In other words, a tracking system would be devised to place White students in "gifted" and "honors" programs, and minority students in other tracks.  Occasionally, one or two Black children would overcome obstacles to higher placement and qualify for one of the top tracks. These students were allowed to be tokens, and White parents seldom objected to the political realities of the need to have at least one Black pupil in each class.

Attitudes toward the rightness of segregation had been put in place by the U.S. housing policies of the 1930s and 1940s.   Mortgage loan guarantees were created in 1934 by the establishment of the Federal Housing Administration (FHA), and the loan guarantees of the Servicemen's Readjustment Act of 1944 (the "G.I." Bill).  These actions created an enormous increase in suburban housing through liberal lending policies at low mortgage rates.  Thousands of White families left the cities, and Black families moved into these integrated communities.  Gradually, attractive opportunities became available for White families to regroup in the suburbs. This *White flight*  left the cities, with their deteriorating tax bases, to Black families.

The FHA, real estate interests and lending institutions agreed on policies of racial segregation.  The FHA manual distributed to mortgage lending institutions informed them that they must investigate the areas surrounding the community where mortgage loans were to be made to "determine whether incompatible racial and social groups are present. It is necessary that properties shall continue to be occupied by the same social and racial classes." It has often been assumed that rhetoric promoting the notion that Blacks' moving into a neighborhood would reduce property values was the work of racist White neighbors when in reality that idea was disseminated by our own Federal government. In information issued to banks, it stated, "A change in social or racial occupancy generally contributes to instability and decline in values." Mortgage lending institutions understood clearly from the government's own documents that mortgages made available to integrated communities would not likely be guaranteed by the FHA or the G.I. Bill.

Despite the legal pressure this policy came under after the Supreme Court ruled against racial housing covenants in the 1948 case of *Shelly v. Kramer,* practically no changes were made in the field. In the 1960s Levitt & Sons built Levittown in several suburban areas. The Levitt homes in Long Island, New York, were built to accommodate 82,000 residents. Not a single African American family was granted a mortgage to be admitted to this development of homes. Levitt & Sons continued to work with the Veterans Administration (VA), and the FHA, in this restrictive manner as did hundreds of other developers. The far-reaching consequences of federal housing and mortgage-lending policies made a profound contribution to segregated residential and schooling patters in the United States.

In Atlanta, Georgia, Black and White political groups were called together for a compromise in the spirit of the 1954 Supreme Court decision. White city leaders offered to support the election of a Black mayoral candidate and the hiring of a Black superintendent of schools in exchange for a Black leadership promise not to press for the desegregation of all area schools. An agreement was reached, but the national office of the NAACP informed the local group they were displeased with such an arrangement. This left Atlanta city schools virtually all Black, and that condition remained in the 1990s.

After some deliberations at the national office, the executive board of the NAACP suspended the Atlanta chapter from the national organization and removed local officers from executive positions. In several communities, local NAACP officials have been known to trade-off on their NAACP affiliation in their aspirations to gain political positions.

For many writers, the *Brown v. the Board of Education* decision marked the beginning of the civil rights movement, because the burden of implementation was left to Black parents and the NAACP. Thurgood Marshall and his team of lawyers from the Legal Defense Fund pressed the Supreme Court for an order to enforce the ruling in the cases that were litigated. Marshall argued that the Court had to make a clear declaration to the states that they should start to desegregate immediately, and that they must file reports with the court assuring compliance by a specified date.

Marshall did not get from the court the response he wanted. Implementation of the desegregation decisions was remanded to the U.S. District Courts so that they could enforce the Supreme Court's decision. They were directed to ensure that school districts as dependents, made a "prompt and reasonable start toward compliance."

Black parents began filing suits in many parts of the South to force their school districts to comply with the law of the land. They received little help from the courts and none from Congress, and the president of their country ignored them. During 1955-56 it appeared to Black parents in the South that the *Brown* decision was an empty victory. Boycotts by Black families of local businesses were started in more than a dozen southern communities, and more court petitions were filed. White merchants retaliated by refusing to sell to politically active parents, and White employers fired Blacks from their jobs or evicted many from their share crop homes. Federal courts would hand down rulings that were ignored by local school boards, and by 1958 there were more Black children in segregated schools than before the *Brown* decision.

In desperation, Black parents petitioned their state and local courts as private citizens to obtain an enforcement of the Supreme Court's decision. Such litigation cost in excess of $10,000 for each case. Several bills were introduced in Congress to authorize the U.S. Justice Department to act on behalf of Black parents to relieve the burden of the cost of private litigation. Such legislation was always defeated. The Congress was in no mood to vote against a constituency that turned out to be more racist than even the Supreme Court had surmised.

Black children, many for the first time, observed their parents in a struggle that promoted the philosophy that White children were not superior to Black children. White resistance to the Supreme Court decision was often violent. In Alabama, where no schools were desegregated three years after the Supreme Court decision, the state legislature made it illegal for the NAACP to conduct business in their state.

In 1956 Fred L. Shuttlesworth, an Alabama minister, helped found the Alabama Christian Movement in Birmingham. One of the group's first acts was an attempt to integrate the local all-White high school. Reverend and Mrs. Shuttlesworth attempted to enter the school to register their children. A White mob attacked the family, beating Mrs. Shuttlesworth with a chain that knocked her to the ground; she was kicked in the face and her husband was stabbed; in addition, their children were terrorized.

Throughout the 1950s Black citizens could not rely on the president or Congress to enforce school desegregation laws except in some high-visibility cases that received national attention. In 1957 the Supreme Court ordered the desegregation of Central Rock High School in Little Rock,

Arkansas. The governor summoned the state's national guard to prevent nine Black students from entering the school. With national media focused on the situation, President Eisenhower ordered federal troops to Little Rock to enforce the Court's order. The Arkansas National Guard was also placed under federal authority.

In New Rochelle, New York, a federal judge ruled in 1961 that the board of education had created and maintained a segregated high school. Judge Irving A. Kaufman ordered the New Rochelle School Board to submit a plan to desegregate Lincoln High School. This was the first court case that ruled against de facto segregation of public schools in the North.

In 1964 Congress passed the Civil Rights Act. With the passage of this act the burden of personal litigation and its expense to enforce the Supreme Court's *Brown* decision would no longer be the responsibility of individual Black parents. Southern school authorities had often claimed that the *Brown* decision was too costly for their states to implement. In 1965 the passage of the Elementary and Secondary School Education Act provided funds for school districts to promote integration in the public schools.

Then in 1966, a federal district court judge ordered the most far-reaching implementation of the *Brown* decision that had ever been witnessed in the deep South. Federal District Court Judge Frank M. Johnson, Jr., directed the Lowndes County School Board to desegregate all grades within two years. It was further ordered that Black teachers should be integrated into the new arrangement, and that a free choice transfer program should be put in place. In that same year, the U.S. Circuit Court of Appeals for the Fourth Circuit ruled that the Virginia School Board of Prince Edward County was in contempt of court for using state funds to assist White parents who wanted to enroll their children in segregated private "academies" to avoid the Supreme Court's desegregation decision. Also the same year a federal district court ordered the Plaquemine Parish in Louisiana to develop a free transfer plan to desegregate grades six through twelve.

In Mississippi, in 1966 a remarkable negotiating process, initiated by Charles Evers and the state branch of the NAACP drew up an agreement with local White school authorities to enroll 13 Black children in previously all White schools in Fayette, Mississippi.

Charles Evers (1923-   ) was born in Decatur, Mississippi. His brother, Medgar Evers, served as a field secretary for the NAACP and was active in civil rights issues. After Medgar was murdered in 1963 for his involvement in civil rights, Charles became politically active and appeared to have had many skills appropriate for the times in Mississippi. He was able to identify White Mississippi moderates and work with them slowly toward inevitable circumstances. A year after his brother was murdered, however, three young civil rights workers—two White and one Black— were murdered in Mississippi.

While Evers was growing up, his family owned a contracting business and operated a funeral home. Evers obtained his college degree in 1950 at Alcorn A&M, a Black college in Lorman, Mississippi. He had majored in teacher education with a concentration in social studies but he decided to administer the family's business interests in Philadelphia, Mississippi, rather than teach. In 1957 he moved to Chicago where he taught for a while and conducted a real estate business. At the time of his brother's murder, he was expanding his business interests in the North.

Soon after his brother's murder Charles returned to Mississippi to take over his brother's post with the NAACP. He very quickly became astute in small-town Mississippi politics, and his political endeavors led to his election as mayor of Fayette, Mississippi, in June 1969. Fayette at that time was a town of 1,700 Black and White residents. It was described as a "shantytown," with most of its Black residents living below the poverty level. The position gave Charles Evers a political base with very little power but great visibility, an asset to his negotiating style thus enabling him to make changes. After winning the election Evers told the citizens of Fayette, "We are not going to allow our power to abuse you or mistreat you like you have mistreated us. We are going to show you what love and working together can do."

Charles Evers was one of the many Blacks elected mayor during the 1960s. Kenneth B.Gibson was elected mayor of Newark, New Jersey; Richard Hatcher became mayor of Gary, Indiana; in Charlotte, North Carolina, Howard Nathaniel became mayor; in Dayton, Ohio, James Howell McGee became mayor; Carol Stokes was elected mayor of Cleveland, Ohio, in 1967, and that same year, Walter E. Washington became district commissioner of Washington, D.C. And the children were watching.

## REFERENCES

Dunn, F. (1993). The educational philosophies of Washington, Du Bois, and Houston: Laying the foundations for Afrocentrism and multi-culturalism. *Journal of Negro Education, 62* (1), 24-34.

Logan, R. W. (1969). *Howard University: The first hundred years.* Boston: Beacon Press.

Sawyer, G. S. (1969). Southern institutes: An inquiry into the origin and prevalence of slavery and the slave trade. New York: Greenwood Publishing. (Original work published 1858).

Vincent, P. F. & Anderson, J. D. (Eds.). (1978). *New perspectives on Black educational history.* Boston: G. K. Hall & Company.

West, E. H. (1972). *The Black American and education.* Columbus, OH: Charles E. Merrill Publishing Company.

Woodward, C. V. (1966). *The strange career of Jim Crow.* New York: Oxford University Press.

# VI

# The Controversies Over African American Intelligence

*There exists no data which should lead a prudent man to accept the hypothesis that I.Q. test scores are in any degree heritable.*
—Leon Kamin, Princeton

Our government spends a great deal of money on various programs for children and families. These programs follow public policy initiatives that originate in the U.S. Congress. Hearings are held, various committees are activated and laws are made to implement programs approved or mandated by congressional action. Another part of the process might involve committee hearings where certain issues are discussed, data are collected, and information is generated. More often than not, funding for programs and projects that make it successfully through the congressional process have also been through *quid pro quo* bargaining in various committees. Following that, a project will still need the *allocation* of funds before a check is issued by the U.S. Treasury. It is also true, that programs that are designed for children are sometimes intended to benefit others. Children can get lost in a maze of Federal rules and guidelines that emerge from the actions of members of Congress who define their mission, in part, to maximize their chances for re-election through the acquisition of resources for their state and district.

For example, the federal government appropriated $2.4 million to local school districts for special educational services to benefit low-achieving students from poor families under Title I of the Elementary and Secondary Education Act of 1974. These allocations were based upon a formula that used poverty data from the most recent census figures. In 1977 Albert H. Quie of Minnesota petitioned Congress to use standardized test scores instead of poverty/census data to determine the allocation of Title I grants. Such a change would end up providing more to some communities and less to others.  The Quie proposal was opposed by civil rights groups because, in their view,  Title I was intended to address the negative effects of poverty on school children, and academic deficiencies that tend to arise from social inequities.  Congressman Quie suggested that not all poor children were academically deficient, and that Title I was an academic program and not a poverty program. The U.S. Office of Education commissioned the Decima Research Company to conduct a study of Title I, and they reported that only about one half of the children in Title I could be considered low achievers based upon the criteria stipulating the need for a certain number of public school children scoring at least one grade behind. Since grants were awarded to schools based upon overall achievement average, and not to individual students, there was also a likelihood that some needy students were overlooked because their school did not qualify.  This is probably one of the least convoluted of the various approaches to funding educational programs. For example, Head Start funds have been diverted to bolster the images of members of Congress back in their home districts by allocating "research grants" to their favorite university when the administration has valued their support as critical.

In the 1950s Congress was holding hearings that would have far-reaching funding policies for educational and social policies related to educational opportunities for Black children. Several sessions held by congressional committees heard testimony from White academicians that Black children had intractable learning deficits and that desegregation would place them in unfair competition with the more bright White children, with whom they would vie for the classroom teacher's time.  The argument went on to suggest that White children, who are academically superior to Black children, would be waiting for the classroom teacher's attention, which would necessarily be directed to slow-learning Black children. Theories of intellectual deficits among Black children are often used to influence educational, social, and economic policy.  There were those who suggested that the expenditures of public funds to remove academic deficits of poor and Black children would yield few benefits because Black children were genetically fixed at a lower I.Q. level than their White age-mates.

The effects on Black families from  the national resistance to the Supreme Court's desegregation decision, the continuous battles Black parents waged to get equity in education, the dilapidated buildings and underpaid Black teachers in their neighborhood schools, and the pilfering of school supplies to assist White "academies" over a period of years, should be factored into the Black-White disparities in school performance in the 1960s and 1970s.

The battle for federal funds for disadvantaged children and their schools was waged at the congressional level.  Research studies were being introduced to show that vocational and trade school training, and not academic education should be the goal for Black grade school children. Presenters of these findings offered solutions that would fund research to study the most effective ways to match the industrial training of Black pupils with the needs of private enterprise. Such a policy would divert funds from programs that were designed to offset the effects of poverty on the young, to individuals and institutions who conduct research. Programs like Head Start, the argument went, would yield very few benefits for the public funds expended because such programs were aimed at intellectual growth, the very domain in which Blacks were "genetically" inferior. The Booker T. Washington-W. E. B. Du Bois philosophical confrontations were being revisited in the 1970s!

Organizations and individuals whose purpose it is to influence public policy, school curriculum, and access to education frequently cite the I.Q. score differential between Blacks and Whites. The most recent missive launched in this direction was a popularized version of the Black-White I.Q. theme titled, *The Bell Curve: Intelligence and Class Structure in American Life,* by Richard J. Herrnstein and Charles Murray. Herrnstein was a Professor of Psychology at Harvard University, and Murray had been one of his graduate students. This book was brought to public attention with remarkable coordination of print and TV media. During a one week period it was reviewed in *The New York Times Book Book Review* and the *New Republic*, and author Murray was given a lengthy personality-biographical treatment in the *New York Times Magazine*. This was followed by interviews with Mr. Murray on various media outlets during the following weeks where he discussed his book in detail.

One of the several active groups that is involved in funding enterprises related to Black-White I.Q. score differences, but with an emphasis upon work that suggests Black genetic deficiencies, is The Pioneer Fund, incorporated in 1937 and based in New York at that time, for the expressed purpose of "research for racial betterment." The fund has been known to provide grants to researchers and scholars whose approached to work has been anti-school integration and anti-busing. A report on the fund in 1977 indicated that for the past 20 years it had supported the research of scientists who believed in the genetic inferiority of Blacks.

It was also reported in 1977 that Dr. Ralph Scott, a professor of education at the University of Northern Iowa, used a part of his grant for seminars on antibusing and anti school integration in Boston, Massachusetts, and Louisville, Kentucky, and financed a graduate student to conduct seminars on antibusing in Mississippi. Pioneer was also reported in 1977 to have funded Dr. Frank C. Mcgurk, Dr. Audrey Shuey, and Dr. Travis Osborne, of the University of Georgia. The Pioneer Fund appeared to be interested in two broad fields related to human growth and development; (1) research in the field of what they define as improving the population through the control of mate choices, and (2) *dysgenics*, the study of the means to reduce dysfunctional human characteristics in a population. Herrnstein and Murray, among other things, would qualify for the dysgenics aspect of the Pioneer Fund's mission, in that, they expressed concern over what they observed as U.S. women with low I.Q. scores reproducing at a much higher rate than U.S. women with higher I.Q. scores.

In 1977, Pioneer grants had been accepted by administrators and faculty at the University of Northern Iowa, the University of Southern Mississippi, the University of California at Berkeley, the University of Georgia, and the Montana College of Mineral Science and Technology.

There never appeared to be a scarcity of White academicians who actively identified measured I.Q. differences as an index of Black inferiority. Three men, however, appeared to have volunteered to be more proactive than others in delivering this message to learned audiences, public media, and to anyone else who appeared interested. This group included Arthur Jensen, an educational psychologist at the University of California, who had received substantial funding from the Pioneer Fund; professor William Shockley, a professor of Engineering Science at Stanford University who received the Nobel prize for his share in the invention of the transistor, and was also a recipient of grants from the Pioneer Fund; Richard Herrnstein, the co-author of *The Bell Curve,* also received support from the Pioneer Fund.

In one of his earlier books, *I. Q. in the Meritocracy,* Herrnstein stated that " . . . as the . . . complexity of human society grow, there will be . . . a low capacity residue that may be unable to master the common occupations, cannot compete for success and achievement, and are likely to be born to parents who have similarly failed . . . " While these points of view seem common among Pioneer Fund recipients, it is also true that there were many White scholars who were embarrassed and enraged by the "science" of some of their colleagues and used their own work to refute the often-reported conclusions of Jensen, Shockley, Herrnstein and others.

It is rather extraordinary that given all the worthy causes in society, and atrocities related to the ravages of racism, anti-semitism and colonization, a prestigious foundation and a group of learned scholars would devote their energy and resources to projects intended to discredit the intellectual capacity of African American people, who constitute only 12% of the U.S. population.

The greatest controversy over Black and White differences in I.Q. scores occurred when the editors of the *Harvard Educational Review,* in the late 1960s invited professor Jensen, to write an article describing his work on Black and White I.Q. The article, "How Much Can We Boost I.Q." revealed the nature of its content in its title. Jensen was reintroducing the nature-nurture argument to the academic community. Several questions were debated: To what extent is intellectual capacity fixed by virtue of inherited genetic characteristics from one's parents? Can what we measure as intelligence be changed through experiences? Jensen concluded that probably only 15-20% of a person's intellectual potential could be modified through enriched experiences. This would leave approximately 80-85% of one's I. Q. score to heritability.

His article in the *Harvard Educational Review* concluded that Blacks are genetically inferior to Whites in areas of abstract performance and creative thinking tasks. This, he suggested, partly accounted for a persistent 15% lower performance of Black students compared with White students on standardized I.Q. tests. Jensen said that for the most part these differences could not be modified by experience.

The same theory, with few variations, would be supported by Shockley, who for several years was an invited speaker on many college campuses, and by Richard Herrnstein of Harvard. Jensen cited reports from other studies that supported his findings. As will be discussed later, the twin studies conducted by a respected research psychologist, who Jensen cited to support his heritability argument, were fraudulent. Jensen's contentions started a debate that was furthered by others who responded in journals, books, and other periodicals to such an extent that Jensen's point of view was referred to as "Jensenism."

There was a tremendous number of request for reprints of Jensen's article, which raised such a furor, that editors of the publication refused to send out copies without including a selection of rebuttals to Jensen's thesis. It is also fair to say that too many critics depended upon a quick read of the reports of Jensen's article, and not upon the article itself as a primary source of information. Most of the criticism that was directed at Jensen's work was probably deserved, but some of it missed the criteria for appropriate and acceptable scholarly discourse.

In 1977 the American Association for the Advancement of Science elected Jensen to the status of fellow, much to the disappointment of many members. Jensen's name was on a list of scientists recommended to the full membership for this recognition, and the entire list was approved. A later vote to remove Jensen's name was defeated. The most vocal critics of retaining Jensen's name on the list was William Wallace, director of Health Career Programs at Harvard University, and anthropologist Margaret Mead. Dr. Williams resigned from the organization when it refused to strike Jensen's name from the list. Margaret Mead did not, commenting that she needed to work within the organization.

Probably the most compelling evidence capable of proving the heritability of intellectual functioning, as opposed to the acquisition of such skill through experiences, would be to test sets of identical twins raised in completely different environments; then, at various intervals in their lives, to administer a respected valid and reliable standardized test.

As a part of the initial process one would need to locate an adequate number of sets of identical twins (a reliable sample size) and assign them to be reared in different homes—preferably an equal number of affluent homes and impoverished homes. Such an intrusive assignment of infants for the sake of experimentation could not, of course, and should not be be conducted in today's scholarly environment.

Another possible approach to subject selection could be to locate sets of identical twins raised apart because such an arrangement was deemed best for the children at the time of their separation. Certainly an adoption decision could have been made by parents for various reasons. Separated identical twins under study must be raised apart assuring different environmental experiences. If one child was adopted by a sister of the child's mother, and the other twin by a different sister living in the same town, this would not qualify as being raised in *different* environments. Identical twins would have to have been raised in environments that would provide different experiences in order to qualify as subjects for a twin study investigating the power of inherited characteristics. This points up one major problem of establishing a reliable experiment to measure the strength of heritable human characteristics.

Jensen and his followers were fortunate enough to have this problem solved for them by one of the most respected researchers in British psychological circles. His name was Cyril Burt. His work was so respected that he was knighted by the Queen of England and referred to affectionately in scholarly circles as the "father of British Psychology." Sir Cyril Burt was a long time advocate of theories supporting the genetic inferiority of Blacks. In his long term studies on the subject, he reported a substantially large number of identical twins, raised in different environments. Burt's twin studies were so respected that they were often cited by Jensen, Shockley and Herrnstein. In Jensen's article for the Harvard Educational Review, Burt's work was identified as a major factor in the article's conclusion.

In 1967 Leon Kamin, a professor at Princeton University, was asked by his students to investigate the barrage of racial inferiority literature appearing in reported studies and public media. Since Burt had reported the largest sample of identical twins, Burt's work was included in the Kamin investigation. Professor Kamin examined documents from as far back as the turn of the century and discovered tremendous misuses of scientific "evidence" for political purposes and as a means to control minorities of various types. He described his work in an important book titled *The Science and Politics of I.Q.*

Kamin criticized the validity of Burt's twin studies and concluded that Burt's data which had been published in scientific journals, were unreliable. Kamin was severely criticized in research circles and even labeled a Communist because it was reported that as an undergraduate at Harvard he had attended several meetings with students who had been identified as such. His detractors did not explain what Kamin's political orientation as an undergraduate—many years earlier—had to do with his criticism of Burt's defective research. When Kamin pointed out discrepancies in Burt's reporting that were too glaring even for Burt's supporters to reject, the errors were attributed to "carelessness." For the remainder of 1977 and almost all of 1978 Kamin was under attack for his criticism of the "father of British psychology", a man who had earned more accolades than any other psychologist in the world.

During the latter period of the controversy, Sir Cyril Burt died. It was only fitting then, that someone should write a story about this great man's contributions to the scientific community. During the process of collecting information on Burt, Oliver Gillie, a British investigator turned up some startling facts about Burt. Burt's papers were found, but the two persons he had listed as collaborators or assistants were not found, nor were they thought to have ever existed. It was also believed that he wrote most of the articles that appeared in journals he edited, despite the fact that they were attributed to others. A substantial number of studies were published by Burt in the *British Journal of Statistical Psychology*—one with a co-author named Howard—that were consistently cited by Jensen, Shockley, and Herrnstein. The co-author "Howard" could not be located, and a careful review of Burt's reported statistics after his death found falsifications. A study reported under the name of J. Conway on, *Class Differences in General Intelligence: II* was also suspect because investigators could not confirm that Conway was not actually a pseudonym used by Burt. In one of Herrnstein's major works, *I. Q. In The Meritocracy*, he referenced the work of Burt a dozen times.

In response to the article, *I.Q.* by Herrnstein in *The Atlantic Monthly* in 1971, many students demonstrated against the Harvard professor. Faculty protested in various forms including letters to the Harvard campus newspaper because of what they thought was more racist propaganda than scholarly research. Professor Richard A. Musgrave of Harvard was among those who were dismayed by the Herrnstein article, but who did not condone the student demonstrations that disrupted Herrnstein's classes. He did, however provide his scholarly perspective on the *Atlantic Monthly* article in a letter to the *Crimson,* (the campus newspaper), with a copy to Herrnstein:

Speaking as a social scientist . . . the evidence mentioned in the article seems to me to be extremely skimpy. . . . I do not see the empirical data cited to support such a conclusion with a degree of probability acceptable in a sophomore paper on statistics... ( *I.Q. In The Meritocracy*, p. 54)

Professor Herrnstein's reply by letter stated that:

Dear Professor Musgrave: Lest you confuse the skimpiness on the evidence in my article (for heritability of I. Q.) with skimpiness of evidence on the subject in general, I hasten to refer you to the following sampling:

1) Burt, C. The genetic determination of differences in intelligence: A study of monozygotic twins reared together and apart. British Journal of Psychology, 1966, 57, 137-153. (*I.Q. In The Meritocracy,* p 55)

Professor Herrnstein listed a total of ten references, with the fraudulent work of Burt listed first as in the above response to Professor Musgrave. Of the other nine references listed in Herrnstein's reply, some based their conclusions on Burt's work as a primary source while others made reference to Burt as a secondary source. This exchange took place between Musgrave and Herrnstein in December of 1971, before Leon Kamin was to publish his suspicions about Burt's studies.There were others who examined the work of Burt and drew similar conclusions. In 1978, D.D. Dorfman of the University of Iowa reported that all of Burt's data were fabricated, and that there were no real subjects involved in Burt's reported studies of identical twins raised apart. Professor Dorfman also reported that Burt arbitrarily placed numbers on a table in a manner to indicate high correlations between twins he reported raised apart. After the publication of his articles citing Burt's work, Arthur Jensen reported that he had also been suspicious of data used in Burt's studies. The Dorfman findings were corroborated by others, but this did not deter Jensen, Shockley, or Herrnstein from pursuing their deficit theories. The academic community remains angry with the messenger who exposed Burt, and continue to ignore the critical role of Professor Leon Kamin in exposing Burt's fraudulent work.

A short time later, group-administered I.Q. tests came under attack from parents and advocacy groups. This led several states by 1978 to bar the use of I.Q. tests, including New York, the District of Columbia, Massachusetts and California. The Society for the Psychological Study of Social Issues issued a press release informing the public that no direct evidence existed to support the notion that innate differences exist between different racial groups. They added that it would be virtually impossible to determine if such differences did exist until social conditions among groups were equalized.

Despite what we learned in the 1970s about Burt's discredited work, some scholars in the 1990s are attempting to restore his creditability. J. Phillippe Rushton, the author of *Race, Evolution, and Behavior* (1995), mentions the work of Burt without reference to what we now know about his falsifications. To his credit, Rushton acknowledged that he received financial support to write his book from the Pioneer Fund.

The measurement of intelligence in young children is more of an art than a science. Given the present state of the art we would be on safer ground to test the instrument instead of the child. Alan Kaufman, professor at the University of Alabama cautions that:

Any intelligence test for . . . assessment requires the examiner to go beyond the simple IQ's and try to make sense out of **why** the child scored the way he or she did. And proper use of IQ tests with the gifted or the potentially gifted children demands that they be used in conjunction with other tests and criteria. (Kaufman, p. 158)

In 1977 the lawyers for six African American children filed a suit against the Department of Education in California charging that its clients were placed in special classes for the "educable mentally retarded" based upon their I.Q. test scores which were below 75 for each child. After being tested on a "culture fair" test, the children achieved scores between 17 and 38 points higher.

In 1974 a federal judge in California issued a temporary ban on the use of I.Q. tests to track children in public schools. A survey revealed that African American children constituted 27% of all children in remedial classes, but they were only 9% of California's schoolchildren. The court agreed that this disparity was unreasonable.

There seems to be conflict between tests that lend themselves to quantification and standardization for various subgroups in different skill areas and tests that measure qualitative differences or some meaningful content. Even the test method of data collection, as opposed, for example, to the sampling of behavior episodes, is increasingly viewed as untrustworthy. When such tests are administered in groups, the reliability and validity tends to further decrease.

Important differences exist between the way children behave in natural settings, in their neighborhood playground, for instance, and the way they behave in school settings and a testing room. There are differences in responses to questions asked by adults who are familiar to the child in the teaching-learning environment and those asked by strange examiners. There are significant differences in motivation to do well for children who are anxious, fearful, bored, or positive about the testing situation. Moreover, children may have abilities available to them in some situations but not in others; and we know little about conditions in which *capacity matches performance.*

There is a need to distinguish in testing between *learning ability*, as measured by qualitative progressions from sensorimotor through formal operation and thought, and quantitative measures of the *amount of information* that learners acquire through the use of abilities available to them. Also, we often ignore the fact that the indices of behaviors or characteristics tests purport to measure are not the same as the behaviors or attributes themselves. Nor is the proficiency, which increases with the practice in taking tests, the equivalent of competence in whatever the test is designed to measure.

The usefulness of intelligence testing has become debatable. Even the general public is now aware that the I.Q. question has become a racial, social policy and political issue. It is true, however, that different *abilities and skills* of children in schools should call forth different expectations of how and what they learn. Distinctive methods of teaching should be applied where appropriate. There are an infinite number of group differences in I.Q. scores to be found if one really thought it important to seek out such differences. It is believed, for example, that there are probably stable differences between the children from farm families and those of families residing in an urban housing project; and between Jewish children influenced by whether their parents came from Poland, France or Germany. There may well be differences between the children of college professors and carpenters, or policemen and social workers. Until research can begin to pinpoint the nature of these differences so that specific characteristics of intellectual functioning and how they affect academic growth can be described, their implications for teaching and learning are not very helpful.

Andrew Hacker, in reviewing the work of Herrnstein and Murray (*The Bell Curve*), reminded us that over the past fifty years, White scholars have agreed not to make genetic distinctions between White U.S. residents. African Americans, however, have been deemed a visible and accessible target; and, according to Hacker, it is "better for white sensibilities, to focus on presumed black deficiencies. But this is neither surprising or new." In the face of such racialist agreements among "scholars," not to report White I.Q.s by ethnic origin, Hacker goes on to cite differences in intellectual performance between White U.S. citizens who have achieved a college degree, and had a history of at least three generations in our country.

Due to our agreement not to sort out white I.Q.s by national origin, I will have to use census information on the number of people who have entered and completed college. . . Irish 21.3 percent; Italian 21.9 percent; German 22.1 percent; Polish 23.4 percent; Swedish 27.5 percent; English 28.6 percent; and Russian 51 percent. True it takes ambition, discipline and family encouragement to get to and through college. Still a certain kind of mental capacity is minimally necessary. (Hacker, 1994, pp.13-14)

## THE NATURE VS. NURTURE DISCUSSION

What constitutes a person's intelligence and how that intelligence is acquired are issues central to the nature-nurture debate. Some would argue that *nature* (i.e.,genes), determines a person's intellectual capacity; for example, that smart parents usually produce smart children. The argument goes on to suggest that children whose parents are not smart will not inherit characteristics that will enable them to do well on intellectual tasks; the gene pool from which these children emerge cannot provide smart genes. Then there are those who believe that genes are important, but that persons who are relatively healthy can be intellectually *nurtured* through experience and can overcome whatever deficits they might bring to the learning environment. It is also true, they believe, that gene action requires an interaction with environmental influences. Yet those on both sides of the argument agree that there is a place for nature and nurture in the construction of intelligence. The nature proponents, however, believe that genes overwhelmingly dictate what we call intellectual functioning, and those who support nature in the equation believe that environment is a more critical factor.

Herrnstein and Murray, in *The Bell Curve*, emphasized the public policy implications of their work, and suggested that it does not matter to them whether a mother has low scores because of nature or nurture. Their concern is that her offsprings will follow her pathway into poverty and become an expense to more intellectually competent taxpaying citizens. This mean spirited approach, and the use of data derived from various racialist sources, compelled the editor of *The New Republic* edition that devoted more than half of the issue to reviews by selected scholars, to defend the motives of Herrnstein and Murray and stated that, "Neither is a racist. . . . neither author is weirder or darker than any other writers to be found on our pages." Richard Nisbett, professor of psychology at the University of Michigan, was among the scholars who reviewed *The Bell Curve* in that issue and expressed a somewhat different view.

Such coolness about evidence that contradicts their position together with uncritical warmth shown toward supporting evidence is found throughout the painful sections of the book dealing with race and the modifiability of I.Q. This is not dispassionate scholarship. It is advocacy of views that are not well supported by the evidence, that do not represent the consensus of scholars and that are likely to do substantial harm to individuals and to the social fabric. (Nisbett, 1994, p. 15)

To support their White positive/Black negative I.Q. thesis, Murray and Herrnstein did not conduct studies themselves, but cited the work of others. Lynn, Owen, and D. H. Crawford-Nutt were referenced by Murray and Herrnstein as major sources of support. In 1995, as a part of a book review of *The Normal Curve* in *Scientific American*, Leon Kamin examined these sources and other supporting evidence cited by the authors. Kamin reported that selected sources of support were misrepresented, distorted, and in some cases the referenced studies were poorly conducted.

Owen's studies were cited as a source of support by Murray and Herrnstein, but as Kamin pointed out, Owen did not assign I.Q. scores to subjects and the developer of the test that Owen employed "insisted that results on the . . . tests cannot be converted into " I.Q." Kamin described the manner in which referencing the work of others, as was done by Murray and Herrnstein, can create a trail of misrepresentations.

A. L. Pons did test 1,011 Zambian Copper miners . . . his data were summarized in tabular form in a paper by  D. H. Crawford-Nutt. Lynn took  the Pons data from Crawford-Nutt's paper and converted the number of correct responses into a bogus average " IQ" of 75. Lynn chose to ignore the substance of Crawford-Nutt's paper, which reported that 228 black high school students in Soweto scored an average of 45 correct responses . . . *higher*  than the mean of 44 achieved by the same-age white sample. (Kamin, 1995, p. 100)

Kamin expressed a critical view of a major source selected by Murray and Herrnstein.

Lynn's distortions and misrepresentations of the data constitute a truly venomous racism, combined with scandalous disregard for scientific objectivity. Lynn is widely known among academics to be an associate editor of the racist journal *Mankind Quarterly* and a major recipient of financial support from the nativist, eugenically oriented Pioneer fund. It is a matter of shame and disgrace that two eminent social scientists, fully aware of the sensitivity of the issue they address, take Lynn as their scientific tutor and uncritically accept his surveys of research. (Kamin, 1995, p. 100)

At the turn of the century, psychologists who supported the nature hypothesis seemed to be winning the argument because the idea of a fixed intelligence from birth, was the conventional scholarly wisdom of the time. We now know that an I.Q. score is often not a fixed entity and can be subject to substantial variation over a person's lifetime.

We also know that both nature and nurture  make significant contributions to what we call intelligence.  The important question to ponder is not *how much*  each domain might contribute to the whole of intelligence but the nature of their relationship and *how* that enables intellectual functioning to emerge in individuals.  In his book, *Intelligence and Experience*,  J. McViker Hunt, and many other studies support the theory that intelligence is not an innately fixed entity, but an intellectual functioning modified by experience. In *What is Intelligence?*  by R. J. Sternberg and D. K. Detterman, S. Scarr (1986) suggested a much larger role for experience in the growth of individual intelligence.  "Human intelligence, as measured by traditional tests and by more contemporary information processing tasks, is about 50% heritable; the remaining variance is largely due to individual experience" (Scarr, 1986, p.19).

The migration of Black families from the South to the North provides additional insight into how experience and environmental factors affect the I.Q. scores of African American children.  Studies have indicated that Black children who migrated from the South showed a steady improvement in I.Q. test scores relative to their length of residence in the North.  In 1935, Otto Klineberg administered intelligence tests to southern born Black children living in New York City; and he made a comparison of groups with different lengths of residence in the City. The scores of the southern-born children increased steadily with increased length of residence. In addition, the scores of those with several years of residency began to approximate the scores of children born in New York City.

A similar study in Philadelphia supported the notion that changed environmental factors alone could account for a significant increase in scores on I.Q. tests. A 1951 study by E. S. Lee found a continuous trend upward in I.Q. scores of southern-born Black children, related to their length of residence in Philadelphia. It was also shown that at point of entry, children who had migrated from Southern schools tested significantly lower than Philadelphia children; but after several years in attendance they showed no significant difference in scores.

Another study reported that teacher attitudes about a child's possible success could substantially improve or depress the child's I.Q. score. In 1968 R. Rosenthal and L. Jacobson set out to make a group of teachers believe that certain children who were not doing well at the time were actually "late bloomers" and would do well academically. The teachers communicated their new expectations to their students, and the pupils' performance and I.Q. scores increased significantly.

Several other studies have highlighted the significance of the environment (nurture), in the growth of intelligence. A 1971 study on ninth-grade pupils by Peggy Sanday, professor of anthropology reported that their I.Q. scores seemed to be more a reflection of the student's educational environment rather than racial aptitude. Professor Sanday also reported from her studies, that . . . "Environment and genetics are important but middle-class social interaction also results in higher I.Q. scores for whites as well as blacks."

In 1976 Sandra Scarr and Richard A. Weinberg of the University of Minnesota reported on a study that investigated I.Q.'s of Black children raised in middle-class White homes. The study involved 176 children who had been adopted. In the total group, 130 were Black and 46 were not. White children who were generally adopted earlier in their lives had an average I.Q. score of 111, compared to an average I.Q. of 106 for the Black children. The researchers suggested that the younger children are when adopted and the better they are cared for in the early years, the higher their I.Q. scores will be later in childhood. They also expressed the belief that environmental factors have a strong influence on intelligence, and that Black-White differences are " . . . neither inevitable nor unchangeable."

## WHAT IS MEASURED BY I.Q. TESTS?

The idea of an intelligence test to determine school performance can be traced to T. Simon and A. Binet, who in the early 1900s were contracted by the Paris minister of public instruction to devise a test to identify children suspected of being mentally retarded, so that they could be properly placed for special attention.

These early diagnostic measures were based upon assessing various *factors* related to reasoning skills, and it was assumed that these selected intellectual abilities (factors), contributed to a single general intelligence. There has been no single element in defining the measuring of intelligence that has survived over time with greater persistence than the theory that intelligence can be determined by this single factor—labeled the *g* factor.

The concept of general intelligence as it relates to school performance was introduced in the United States by a Stanford University professor, Lewis M. Terman in 1916. Professor Terman used the Binet and Simon instrument as a basis for developing the well known Stanford-Binet test of intelligence. This instrument has undergone various modifications since its introduction and is currently the most widely administered test of intelligence. As with the Binet and Simon instrument, the Stanford-Binet test of intelligence purports to determine general intelligence from selected factors deemed to be essentials of intellectual performance. The revised Stanford-Binet—first published in 1916—still provides a single score that purports to reflect general intelligence.

The Wechsler Intelligence Scale for Children-Revised (WISC-R), is the next most commonly used instrument. Both WICS-R and the Stanford-Binet are designed to be administered individually, with the Stanford-Binet emphasizing verbal responses more than the WISC-R. The WISC-R is designed for children 6 to 16, and consists of 12 subtests (2 are optional). Half of the items are verbal, and half do not require verbal responses.

Ronald Taylor and Stephen Richards studied the intellectual differences of Black, Hispanic, and White children using the WISC-R. Their results were reported to show that Black children performed better on verbal tasks, White children scored higher on tasks that required abstract thinking and knowledge of facts, and Hispanic children performed better on visual-spatial tasks. Taylor and Richards cautioned that these results might be indicators of "educational needs," rather than intellectual deficits for either group. Further, they suggested that attention should be given to teaching patterns to accommodate areas of weak performance. These results could also be a proxy for differentiations in *cognitive style,* to be treated later in this text.

In the 1990s, the state of the art in measuring intelligence among school children for various purposes, like screening for the placement of children in classes for the gifted, has led to the selection of the Wechsler Intelligence Scale for Children-III (WISC-III), as well as the Wechsler Preschool and Primary Scale of Intelligence - Revised (WPPSI-R). Both tests demonstrate an improvement in acknowledging the subtleties of race and gender. The preschool version has more than 40% new items, and the new items in the WISC-III total more than 30%. Many experts in the field remain critical of instruments designed to measure intellectual functioning in children. In order to compensate for an inherent flaw in the most recent version of the WPPSI-R, the test developers added bonus points for speed. In response to this strategy, one reviewer suggested that:

Giving bonus points for speed to preschool children seems silly from a developmental and common-sense perspective. Sure, brighter children will tend to solve problems more quickly than less intelligent children, and that relationship will hold even at the preschool level. But young children sometimes respond slowly for a variety of reasons that have more to do with maturation or personality. For example, a young child might respond deliberately because of immaturity of experience in test taking, underdeveloped motor coordination, insecurity, or a reflective cognitive style. (Kaufman, 1992, p. 158)

The widespread use of these traditional instruments occurs at a time when information-processing theorists and others are suggesting alternative approaches, and in the process creating a receptive scientific environment for imaginative and inventive constructs. Guilford, for example, described intelligence as encompassing *five operations* (divergent production, convergent production, cognition, memory, and evaluation). The same model included *six products* (units, classes, relations, systems, implications and transformation). It also included *four content areas* (figurative, semantics, behavioral, and symbolic). These three domains would generate 120 cells. Some cells match abilities typically measured by standardized intelligence tests, whereas others represent a multidimensional structure of intelligence. For example, *memory* for *symbolic relations* would subsume operations and a form of content. Guilford conceptualized these measurable abilities as *factors* that contributed to individual general intelligence. In his book, *Frames of Mind,* Howard Gardner (1983) created a great deal of interest when he proposed that individuals have at least seven different intelligences. Gardner's "intelligences" appeared to be more related to *cognitive styles* than intelligence; however, the notion that individuals possess more than a single intelligence stimulated a great deal of thought among psychologists who took their discussions beyond the dominant theory of one factor from which all intellectual functioning is derived.

Spearman, (1904) constructed intelligence tests in such a way as to insure the concept of a single factor, *g*. In such a design, Spearman started with the idea of a *principal component*, using a single axis, with other abilities projected at right angles and rotated for the highest potential. By selecting a principal component concept and projecting each vector (subordinate factors) onto the axis, Spearman could always yield a single factor—but he conceded that there might be a specific factor unique to a particular test. An excellent discussion of this procedure can be found in Stephen J. Gould's *The Mismeasure of Man* (1981).

L. L. Thurstone was among the first to suggest that the human organism was far too complex for intellectual activity to be determined solely by a single human factor. In 1938, he developed what he labeled *primary mental abilities* and introduced to the intelligence-testing community multivariate analyses to operationalize his theory. Thurstone's test batteries were developed for three age levels, with approximately six tests designed to measure a separate ability. Thurstone's theory suggested that intelligence cannot be determined by measuring a single ability, rather, multiple factors like verbal ability, deductive reasoning, spatial ability, and perceptual speed are essential to a unified theory of intelligence. Thurstone rejected the principal component approach to factor analysis, and he proposed a rotated factor axis that in essence eliminated *g* in the process. Despite Thurstone's new approach to the reexamination of a seasoned theory, it remained the view of Spearman and his followers that Thurstone's "set of abilities" contained an underlying element common to all measures of ability that could be defined within the framework of *g*. There is some dispute as to the original inventory of factor analysis. Burt claimed this distinction, but most writers give the credit to Spearman. The work of these early theorists still dominates a great deal of today's scholarly thought on the subject of intellectual performance and I.Q. testing.

Despite the persistence of *g* theorists, the practice of intelligence testing began to incorporate Thurstone's multifactoral analyses. Following Thurstone's publication of a test battery of primary mental abilities, others started to develop multivariate instruments to measure separate abilities.

Gesell (1949) for example, developed an age scale to measure infant development. The Gesell developmental schedules defined four areas of behavior but did not claim these were measures of intelligence. The areas included adaptive behavior (subject's reactions to objects), motor behavior (subject's control of body), language behavior (vocalizations and speech), bodily expression, and personal-social behavior (interpersonal relations). Many of Gesell's followers, however, used the Gesell model to develop instruments to assess these behaviors and labeled their instruments "measures of intelligence."

At several intervals in the history of various approaches to assessing intelligence, single-factor theorists have had to defend against occasional assaults. It has been suggested—as mentioned earlier— that persons have at least seven different intelligences. The expanded view of what constitutes intelligence has called attention to another construct called *cognitive style*. Whereas teachers are encouraged to recognize intelligent behavior that might not be tapped by traditional intelligence tests, they must also recognize variations in how learners approach their schoolwork. It has also been known for some time that personality and temperament are important variables in the teacher-learner relationship. And as more attention is being given to the learner, educators will become open to the fact that children bring to the learning environment a great deal that needs to be considered in educational planning. Environments where the *control of children's experiences*, as in Locke's *tabula rasa*, have given way to more *freedom of experience,* as in Rousseau's *Emile*, cognitive style has emerged as a means of recognizing and appreciating individual differences.

## COGNITIVE STYLE THEORY

*Cognitive style* has also been referred to as *psychological differentiation.* A complete review of cognitive style research is presented by Samuel Messick (1976) and his collaborators in *Individuality in Learning.*

Cognitive style has emerged as a construct that refers to the particularized modes individuals employ in perceiving, remembering, organizing, and evaluating information. These individual characteristics are not described as information content or intelligence; however, there can be dynamic interactions among them. The effects of cognitive styles are also inherent in all human activities related to emotional, psychological, and social environments.

Each individual has preferred ways of organizing all that is perceived and remembered. Consistent individual differences in these ways of organizing and processing information and experience have come to be called *cognitive styles.* These styles represent consistencies in the manner or form of cognition distinctly different from the content or the level of skill displayed in the cognitive performance. They are conceptualized as stable attitudes, preferences, or habitual strategies determining a person's typical modes of perceiving, remembering, thinking, and problem solving. As such, the influence of *cognitive style* extends to almost all human activities that implicate cognition, including social and interpersonal functioning. Studies of cognitive style categories have been expanded by I. B. Myers and K. C. Briggs to include constructs of personality theory. In literature and practice this concept has been referred to as the Myers-Briggs Type Indicator (MBTI).

In the early 1900s, Katherine C. Briggs began a systematic observation of personality types in human interactions. Her primary focus was individual behavior related to experience and information processing. At the same time, she devoted a great deal of time to reading biographies. With her discovery of the work of Carl C. Jung, she began to realize that his descriptions of psychological types were highly compatible with her own interests that included personality typologies. After a thorough study of Jung's personality theory, during formal and informal encounters, Briggs and her daughter—Isabel Briggs Myers—began observations of personality types.

In the early 1940s, Briggs and Meyers started developing self-report questions that would lead to assessments of individual personality types. By 1975 the MBTI had gone through a series of field tests and modifications, and was in widespread use by professionals in a variety of fields. Designed to identify individual preferences in regard to perception and judgment, the MBTI is a self-report test for students grades 9-16 and adults. The basic form of the MBTI includes four dichotomies that allow for the scoring of preferences along a bipolar plane: extroversion-introversion, sensing-intuition, thinking-feeling and judgment-perception.

By now, most human services professionals are aware of the extroversion-introversion construct because over the years it has become the most widely discussed aspect of Jung's theory of personality types. Jung perceived of introversion and extroversion as basic human attitudes, with introverted persons demonstrating a tendency toward detachment, thoughtfulness, a desire for clarity and understanding of ideas, and a preference for proven concepts. Extroverted personalities, in contrast, are outgoing, sociable, sometimes impulsive, and they use the surrounding environment for stimulation.

The other dichotomies are, thinking-feeling, sensing-intuition and judgment-perception. Thinking types approach experiences in a logical analytical fashion with strong objectivity. Feeling types are more subjective and tend to approach experiences with a sensitivity toward the feelings of others accompanied by the desire to be accepted. Sensing types attend to problem solving matters with objectivity, preferring procedures that have been tested and certified. Intuitive types, on the other hand, explore new ways of solving problems and receive inspiration from successful experiences. Judging types prefer decisiveness in a planned orderly structure. Perceiving types prefer to postpone final decisions and grant themselves ample time to ponder the issues and consequences. Type theory suggests a dynamic interaction between these four types, therefore, sixteen different cross-categories are possible. For example, an Introvert could be sensing, feeling and judging.

The MBTI represents an important area of cognitive styles assessment because of its potential usefulness for classroom teachers, career counselors, workers with the gifted, and therapists in the public domain. Although the work of Myers and Briggs is not usually considered when cognitive styles are discussed in literature, their work, nonetheless, makes an important contribution to the study of this construct. Traditional cognitive styles have been identified and placed in these categories:

### Field Independent

Approaches object relations in an analytical fashion with the ability to discern objects as discrete from their context. A tendency toward impersonal preferences in social encounters.

### Field Dependent

Approaches object relations in a global manner with less competence in analytical functions. Demonstrates a preference for social interactions and displays superior social skills.

### Reflectivity

Ability to formulate alternative hypotheses and consider various alternatives to problems that contain uncertainties.

### Impulsivity

A tendency to offer a quick response to the solution of problems that contain response uncertainties despite the fact that their response might be incorrect.

### Conceptualizing

Three developmental modes of utilizing selected relationships in concept formations. Younger children have a tendency to use relational attributes (relational conceptualizing), with older children displaying a preference for descriptive details (analytical-descriptive conceptualization), and in adulthood a preference is expressed in the class membership (category) of stimuli (categorical-inferential conceptualization).

### Leveling

A tendency toward egalitarian structuring in memory assimilation by not differentiating between objects and events but, rather, by incorporating similar events into related experiences.

### Sharpening

Demonstrates the capacity for memory detail that can isolate events without confusing similar events or objects with each other, and will occasionally perceive of differences between events (even minor ones) of the past and present in an exaggerated form.

### Breadth of Categorization

Individuals can demonstrate preferences along a bipolar plane in terms of tolerances for different types of error. Individuals of narrow categorization are conservative about errors of inclusion. Individuals with tendencies toward broad categorization are more tolerant of including deviances.

### Sensory   Modality

Individuals demonstrate a consistent pattern in the manner in which they experience the environment. Studies have identified three categories of information-processing preferences in this style.   Kinesthetic types (physical and motoric thinking), auditory (verbal thinking), and visual (spatial and figural thinking).

### Social   Interactive/Motoric

Individual tendencies toward a preference for a socially interactive environment, where Sensorimotor constructs enhance action-oriented modes of information processing.

### Cognitive   Complexity

Individual tendency to interpret experiences utilizing a variety of distinct concepts and alternative perspectives, with the ability to finely articulate the power and magnitude of each stimuli.

### Cognitive   Simplicity

Individuals with a tendency toward undifferentiated categorization of stimuli, not particularly skilled at processing dissonant information, and occasionally demonstrating a lack of interpersonal maturity.

## COGNITIVE STYLE AND BLACK CHILDREN

There are indications that Black children as a group tend to prefer learning environments that encourage social interaction among pupils and teachers. During neonatal growth periods, and the Sensorimotor stage as identified in the theory of Piaget, it appears that Black infants are more advanced in motor performance than their White peers. In this regard, the work of neonatal and child development specialists have highlighted some important findings relevant to socialization and child-rearing practices in Black families. In 1946 Benjamin Pasamanick of the Clinic of Child Development, School of Medicine, Yale University, conducted a study in New Haven, Connecticut, on 53 Black infants, who were compared to three different groups of White babies from foster homes (57), institutions (22), and from two-parent households of well educated parents (20).   Pasamanick reported that female babies—Black and White—were more accelerated in development than males.  The institutionalized White group was negatively affected by their impoverished environment. Babies living in poor housing conditions did not do as well as those in better housing. On "fine motor, adaptive, language, and personal social behavior Black babies did as well as white ones. In other areas investigated, Black infants showed a definite acceleration in gross motor behavior."

Pasamanick used well chosen words and descriptors to avoid identifying differences between groups as "racial." This was a period of great debate in the literature, in university seminars, and in conferences of learned organizations regarding "Negro" and White intelligence comparisons. Numerous studies were published from southern environments comparing Black children whose families were living in poverty, with White children growing up under completely different, affluent circumstances. These poorly balanced studies reached such an absurd level that one of the most respected scholars in the North suggested that . . . "It is safe to say that as the environment of the Negro approximates . . . more closely that of the White . . . inferiority tends to disappear." He went on to suggested that "the real test of Negro-white equality . . . can be met only by a study in a region in which Negroes suffer no discrimination whatsoever and enjoy exactly the same educational and economic opportunities . . . as the environment of the Negro approximates more and more closely that of the white . . . inferiority tends to disappear" (Klineberg, 1935).

In 1953 Judith R. Williams and Roland B. Scott of the Howard University School of Medicine and Pediatric Services at Freedmen's Hospital reported on a study of over 100 Black infants to determine if the advanced motor development of Black infants reported in Pasamanick's study, which had become known as The New Haven Study—was innately racial. Their study involved infants from three different income groups. They reported that babies raised by low-income parents showed superior motor development, when compared to babies from higher income families. They concluded that differences in motor development were linked to childrearing practices and the way the infants were handled by their parents. For Williams and Scott this ruled out any genetic explanation for the behavioral differences.

In 1965, a larger study was conducted by Nancy Bayley of the institute for human Development, University of California. Her investigation involved over 1400 babies from 1 to 15 months in age. She reported that all babies scored equally on mental measurement, but Black babies scored higher on motor scales when compared with White and Puerto Rican infants.

Mary Salter Ainsworth, in *Infancy in Uganda* (1967) described in great detail the childrearing practices of parents in an African community. Families were observed raising their children from birth, and careful records were maintained to chronicle and interpret these observations. The study focused upon infant development in the context of family and village. Observations were made in Buganda, a province in Uganda on the African continent. Data were derived from conversations and questioning, as well as through the use of other techniques in various settings between 1954 and 1955. Among the many important differences between African children raised in this African community and those raised in European-oriented environments were in the experiences provided infants by parents and significant others. Using a scale developed by Arnold Gesell to describe normal levels of development for European infants, Ainsworth reported that African infants reached their Sensorimotor milestones earlier than European infants. The Sensorimotor milestones included sitting with support, sitting alone, crawling, creeping, standing with support, standing alone, walking, and trotting. Ainsworth sought confirmation from Marcelle Geber (1957), a researcher who had previous experiences with testing infants. "Geber examined 252 infants and young children. Her findings not only substantiate but greatly elaborate our own."

News regarding advanced Sensorimotor development among African infants appeared during the time that the U.S. congress was hearing testimony from leading psychologists regarding Black inferiority as an argument against school integration. Ainsworth was aware of the volatile nature of her report and chose not to become embroiled in the political implications of her findings. But it did not end there because research in the United States wanted to investigate the extent to which this phenomenon might be true for African American children. Several studies had been conducted in the United States, but they were confined to scholarly journals away from the general public.

Classroom teachers introduce the curriculum, set the rules for learning experiences, and conduct academic activities. These activities are designed to enable learners to maximize their knowledge acquisition. *Cognitive style* researchers have reported that learners bring a variety of personality and information-processing differences to the classroom, and this information can be useful to teachers. It has been common practice, however, for grade school teachers not to value racial and cultural differences when they are not compatible with the mainstream culture. This is reinforced when the teachers' own childhood and education training has followed a sociocultural pattern similar to the one embraced by the school system where they are employed. For example, some Black teachers are among the severest critics of Black English, and they join many White teachers in lamenting that this neighborhood practice stands in the way of children learning "good" English.

Socially active African Americans are more likely than White males to be suspended for being too active. At one extreme, some of the more active students are medicated with Ritalin or similar substances, and many other socially active students are among those in trouble for expanding the expectations of the system. In 1975 the Washington Research Project reported that African American boys are four times as likely to be suspended from school as their White peers for similar infractions of the rules.

The teacher's knowledge of cognitive style theory provides a theoretical basis  for modifying the classroom environment  for the purpose of expanding the number of ways that children can *process each learning experience*.  Variations in the way that children process information in school settings have been reported by several researchers. A study by A. Dershowitz in 1971 suggested that fathers in the Orthodox Jewish families seldom participate in the daily child rearing practices of their sons. Mothers in these families take the more dominant role. Dershowitz compared a group of Jewish Orthodox boys with a comparable group of White Protestant boys. As he had hypothesized, the Jewish boys were characterized as more *field  dependent*.

In 1974 Manuel Ramirez III of the University of California at Riverside, and Douglas R. Price-Williams, of the University of California at Los Angeles, conducted a study of *cognitive styles*  that included Mexican Americans, African Americans, and Anglo Americans in Houston,Texas. They reported that children from families that emphasize respect for authority with a strong religious affiliation and group identity more often than not tend to be *field dependent.*  Those families that support the child's freedom to question authority and have ties to  friendship groups outside of the family tend to be *field  independent.*

Differentiations in cognitive styles call for teachers to use varied ways to help students learn.  From time to time schools do experiment with teaching/learning designs in creative and innovative teaching methods. Too often this creativity and innovation is exhausted in the pedagogical process, where the teacher's expectations for the student's displays of learning tend to repeat old comfortable methods. In other words,  materials might be presented in a manner that acknowledges various styles of processing information, but too often classroom practice will ultimately demand traditional pupil performances like recitations, paper-and-pencil tasks, or similar displays of classroom etiquette upon which to base pupil achievement—and  provide proof that learning has taken place. Many schooling patterns promote quietness and docility which on occasion are opposed to the behavioral characteristics of many African American students from moderate—to low— income families. This makes it difficult for them to comply with the demands made upon them by the system.

For these children to set their own behavior norms should not surprise us.  Their behavior can be viewed as disruptive when the planned environment for learning lacks the elements that accommodate their Sensorimotor style.

## COGNITIVE STYLE AND THE BLACK ATHLETE

Athletics in general and sports in particular are performing arts. This art form, like ballet, gymnastics, football, basketball, soccer or modern dance, requires information processing at the highest levels of performance, with accompanying Sensorimotor control of the body's muscle functions. The ball carrier, defensive and offensive players, the dancer, the gymnast, all must integrate a tremendous amount of information and body involvement into cognitive processing behavior to produce a superior display of performance.

Information processing and intellectual requirements for performance in gymnastics and sports are not fundamentally different from cognitive endeavors that do not necessarily call forth competitive physical interactions, responses and performances. An essential element that is common to all intellectual functioning is problem solving through the processing of information. Performance associated with problem solving skills are useful indices of intellectual capacity.

In classroom settings, problems are often presented in a well structured format with the necessary information provided or close at hand. Problems to be solved in athletics and sports, however, are ill structured with myriad variations of individual encounters unfolding within the field of play and during planning sessions. A careful observation of a brief episode in a basketball game, football game or tennis match, for example, would reveal a performer processing a tremendous amount of information. The successful athlete must have the cognitive capacity to differentiate between players, isolate spectator noise, execute memorized play action, and assess when the set play must be abandoned or modified and a more suitable plan of action must be inserted in pursuit of a "goal," while simultaneously calling upon the organism for extreme outputs of physical and mental response. To reach world-class performance standards and retain that level, one must have the intellectual capacity to process this type of information in an extremely brief time.

The high levels of mental and physical abilities employed during gross motor activity (athletic performance), however, might not be available to the same individual in the static environment of the quiet classroom. It is in this context that educators need to be aware of the sensory active *cognitive style* that tends to influence the information processing of many African Americans. The gross motor advancement discovered among populations of African American babies in all likelihood remains a part of their lifestyle as they mature in various environments. It should not surprise us to find that Black athletes dominate certain sports and are represented in championship play far in advance of their representation in the general population.

There are many voices that cry foul when athletes do not receive high paying contracts, or graduate from the university where they have performed in exchange for tuition. These voices ignore the fact that at the higher levels of achievement, there is very little room at the top. Team sports that generate the millions of dollars as entertainment have limited rosters. Thousands of children with interests and skills in athletics are screened at many steps along the way through grade school. They will not tread the pathway to professionalism. Universities create the final pool from which most highly paid athletes are selected. To enter the world-class category, one must play for a college or university for that is where athletes want to be—and that is where professional scouts are watching. To be seen, tested, and exposed to the top draft selection process, one must attend a post-secondary institution of higher learning. In the field of dance—another entertaining art form—one must have been in a post secondary institution like the Dance Theater of Harlem or the School of American Ballet or a similarly highly visible school to be considered for professional work. In the arts, as in athletics, attending does not guarantee a lucrative career upon graduation. Being accepted to study at that level is an important step. However, upon exit from a school of art or a four-year university program, a highly proficient graduate might spend some time without employment in his or her field. Why, then, should we consider competitive circumstances unfair to college athletes who do not graduate or receive a high-paying contract?

Professional athletes have often been the children of the immigrants, the poor and Blacks. It has never been popular to suggest that members of any of these groups are intellectually endowed. The public tends to resent the possibility that professional players might earn more than the owners of the teams for which they play. Prior to the 1960s educators generally assumed that one could be proficient in academics or athletics, but not in both. We should not ignore evidence to the contrary. Many athletes on scholarships have balanced studies in law, psychology, teaching, business and medicine, with a demanding practice schedule. University and professional athletes are now serving successful careers in the U.S. Congress, in the academic world as university professors and athletic directors, and in various positions of prestige in the private sector and in the U.S. government.

Historically, group differences have been used by the majority population, or the most affluent, to justify special privileges they grant to themselves and their children. Group differences are defined as deficits in the minority, or less affluent group. For example, in the Southern states after the Civil War Black citizens paid taxes that supported schools for Whites only. Whites justified this practice by convincing themselves that Blacks were incapable of intellectual pursuits and should be confined to menial tasks mostly designed to serve the needs of Whites who could afford to buy Blacks or pay for their services. Justification was also found in interpretations of Biblical passages.

Currently in public schools with population reaching 40% African American, Latino, or any other minority of color, a common practice is to install a policy of "ability grouping," which in effect means resegregation within the school building.  Screening procedures are implemented to assure that minority or poor children qualify only for those classes (tracks) that place them with each other. This tracking could be based on achievement tests or I.Q. scores, language differences, or whatever supports the objective, which could be an appeasement of the majority group or the prevention of White flight. Such objectives are irrelevant to those who advocate for what is best for children in school. When special tracking is designed for the "disadvantaged," too often such programs create a learning environment  in which these children are not exposed to the full basic curriculum necessary to meet the needs of *all*  children. Thus, programs ostensibly designed to improve the lives of all children are too often intended to benefit only a few.

# REFERENCES

Ainsworth, M.D.S. (1967). *Infancy in Uganda: Infant care and the growth of love.* Baltimore, MD: Johns Hopkins University Press.

Barnes, M.L., & Sternberg, R.J. (1989). Social intelligence and decoding of non-verbal cues. *Intelligence, 13* (3), 263-287.

Bayley, N. (1965). Comparison of mental and motor test scores for ages 1-15 months by sex, gender, birth order, geographic location and education of parents. *Child Development, 36,* 379-411.

Bieri, J. (1961). Complexity-Simplicity as a personality variable in cognitive performance behavior. In D.W. Fiske and S.R. Maddi (Eds.), *Functions of varied experience.* Homewood, Illinois: Dorsey Press.

Binet, A., & Simon, T. (1916).*The Development of Intelligence in children.* Baltimore: Williams & Wilkins.

Birch, H.G., & Lefford, A. (1967). A visual differentiation, intersensory integration, and voluntary motor control.*Monographs of the Society for Research in Child Development, 32* (2), serial # 110.

Bissell, J. White, S., & Zivin, G. (1971). Sensory modalities in children's learning. In, G.S. Lesser (Ed.), *Psychology and Educational Practice.* Glenview, Ill: Scott, Foresman.

Bloomberg, M. (1967). An inquiry into the relationship between field independence-dependence and creativity. *The Journal of Psychology, 67,* 127-140.

Boykin, W.E.(1978). Psychological/behavioral verve  in academic/task performance: Pretheoretical considerations. *Journal of Negro Education, 47,* 343-354.

Bracken, Bruce A. (1987). Performance of black and white children on the Bracken Basic Concept Scale. *Psychology In The Schools, 24* (1), 22-27.

Brandt, R. (1988). On assessment in the arts: A conversation with Howard Gardner. *Educational Leadership, 45*  (4), 30-34.

Broverman, D.M. (1964). Generality and behavioral correlates of cognitive styles. *Journal of Consulting Psychology, 28,* 487-500.

Broverman, D.M. and Lazarus, R.S. (1958). Individual differences in task performance under conditions and cognitive interference. *Journal of Personality, 26,* 94-105.

Brown, H. J. (1985). Cognitive style and learner strategy interaction in the performance of primary and related maze tasks. *Research Quarterly for Exercise and Sport, 56* (1), 10-14.

Bruner, J.S., & Tajfel, H. (1961). Cognitive risk and environmental change. *Journal of Abnormal and Social Psychology, 62,* 231-241.

Buescher, T. M. (1985). Seeking the roots of talent: An interview with Howard Gardner. *Journal For The Education of the Gifted, 8* (3), 179-186.

Burkhalter, B. B., & Schaer, B. B. (1985). The effect of cognitive style cognitive learning in a non traditional educational setting. *Educational Research Quarterly 9* (4), 12-18.

Burt, C. (1940). *Factors of the mind.* London: University of London Press.

———. (1958). The inheritance of mental ability. *American Psychologist, 13,* 1-15.

———. (1959). Class differences in general intelligence, III. *British Journal of Statistical Psychology, 12,* 15-33.

———. (1961). Intelligence and social mobility. *British Journal of Statistical Psychology, 14,* 3-24.

———. (1966). The genetic determination of differences in intelligence: A study of monozygotic twins reared together and apart. *British Journal of Psychology, 57,* 137-153.

Burt, C., & Howard, M. (1956). The multifactoral theory of inheritance and its application to intelligence. *British Journal of Statistical Psychology, 9,* 95-131.

———. (1957). Heredity and intelligence: A reply to criticisms. *British Journal of Statistical Psychology, 10,* 33-63.

Cattell, R. B. (1963). Theory of fluid and crystallized intelligence: A critical experiment. *Journal of Educational Psychology, 54,* 1-22.

Charlesworth, W. (1976). Human intelligence as adaptation: An ethnological approach. In L. Resnick (Ed.), *The nature of intelligence.* Hillside, N.J: Lawrence Erlbaum.

Coates, S. (1975). Field independence and intellectual functioning in preschool children. *Perceptual and Motor Skills, 41,* 251-254.

Coates, S., Lord, M., & Jakabories, E. (1975). Field dependence-independence, social-nonsocial play, and sex differences in preschool children. *Perceptual and Motor Skills, 140,* 195-202.

Conway, J. (1959). Class differences in general intelligence: II. *British Journal of Statistical Psychology, 12,* 5-14.

Copeland, B. D. (1983). The relationship of cognitive style to academic achievement of university art appreciation students. *College Student Journal, 17* (2), 157-162.

Curti, M.W., Marshal, F.B. & Steggerda, M. (1935). The Gesell schedules applied to 1, 2, and 3 year old Negro children of British West Indies. *Journal of Comparative Neurology, 20,* 125.

Dershowitz, Z. (1971). Jewish subcultural patterns and psychological differentiation. *International Journal of Psychology, 6* (3), 223-231.

———. (1977). Jewish culture and psychological differentiation. *Journal of Genetic Psychology, 130,* 137-144.

Dyk, R.B. & Witkin, H.A. (1965). Family experiences related to the development of differentiation in children. *Child Development, 36,* 21-55.

Einstein, E. (1979). Classroom dynamos. *Human Behavior, 8,* 58-59.

Elias, M. (1979, September 23). No chance for Huck Finn? *San Francisco*

*Chronicle,* p. 17.

Elkind, D. (1971). Two approaches to intelligence: Piaget and psychometric. In D.R. Green, M. P. Ford, & G. B. Flamer (Eds.). *Measurement and Piaget.* New York: McGraw-Hill.

Elkind, D., Koegler, R. R. & Go, E. (1963). Field independence and concept formation. *Perception and Motor Skills, 17,* 383-386.

Federico, P.A. & Landis, D.B. (1984). Cognitive styles, abilities, and aptitudes: Are they dependent or independent? *Contemporary Educational Psychology, 9* (2), 146-61.

Fiske, E. (1977 February 9). Schools in Syracuse cater to active learning styles. *The New York Times,* p. 41.

————. (1977, March 27). An issue that wont go away. *The New York Times,* section 6, p. 58,

————. (1977, October 3). Congress to study change in criteria on Title I funding. *The New York Times,* p. 23.

Fitts, P. M. (1954). The information capacity of the human motor system in controlling the amplitude of movement. *Journal of Experimental Psychology, 47,* 381-391.

Fitts, P.M., & Peterson, J. R. (1964). Information capacity of discrete motor responses. *Journal of Experimental Psychology, 65,* 103-112.

Ford, E. M. &Tisak, M. S. (1983). A further search for social intelligence. *Journal of Educational Psychology, 75,* 197-206.

Frank, B. M. (1986). Cognitive style and teacher education: Field dependence and areas of specialization among teacher education majors. *Journal of Educational Research, 80,* 19-22.

Frederiksen, N. (1984). The place of social intelligence in a taxonomy of cognitive abilities. *Intelligence, 8* (4), 315-337.

Gardner, H. (1983). *Frames of Mind.* New York: Basic Books.

————. (1984). Assessing intelligences: A comment on "Testing intelligence without I.Q. tests." *Phi Delta Kappan, 65* (10), 698-700.

————. (1987). The theory of multiple intelligence. *Annals of Dyslexia, 37,* 19-35.

————. (1988). Creativity: An interdisciplinary perspective. *Creativity Research Journal, 1,* 8-26.

Gardner, H. & Hatch, T. (1989). Multiple intelligences go to school: Educational implications of the theory of multiple intelligences. *Educational Researcher, 18* (8), 4-10.

Geber, M., & Dean, R. F. A. (1957). The state of development of newborn African children. *Lancet, 1,* 1216-1219.

Gesell, A. (1949). *Gesell developmental schedules.* New York: Psychological Corporation.

Getzels, J. W., & Jackson, P. W. (1962). *Creativity and intelligence.* New York: Wiley.

Goldstein, F. G. (1986). Temperament and cognitive style in school-age children. *Merrill-Palmer Quarterly, 32* (3), 263-273.

Goodenough, D. R. & Karp, S. A. (1961). Field independence and intellectual functioning. *Journal of Abnormal and Social Psychology, 63,* 241-246.

Gould, S. J. (1981).*The mismeasure of man.* New York: W. W. Norton.

Hacker, A. (1994, October 31). White on white.*The New Republic,* 13-14.

Halsey, A. H. (Ed.). (1977). *Heredity & environment*. New York: Free Press.

Havighurst, R. (1952). Developmental tasks and education. New York: Longmans, Green & Company.

Hebb, D. O. (1947). The effects of early experience on problem solving at maturity. *American Psychologist, 2,* 306-307.

———. (1949). Organization of behavior. New York: Wiley.

Hechinger, F. M. (1979, January 30). Further proof that I.Q. data were fraudulent. *The New York Times,* p. C4.

Herrnstein, R. J. (1973). *I. Q. in the meritocracy.* Boston: Little, Brown.

Herrnstein, R. J., & Murray, C. (1994). *The Bell Curve: Intelligence and class structure in American life.* New York: Free Press.

Houts, P. I. (1977, May 1). I.Q. test once again disturb educators. *The New York Times Magazine,* p. 21.

Itzkoff, S. W. (1994).*The decline of intelligence in America.* Westport, CT: Praeger.

Jencks, C. (1979). *Who gets ahead.* New York: Basic Books.

Jensen, A. R. (1969). How much can we boost I.Q.? *Harvard Educational Review, 3,* 1-123.

———. (1969). Reducing the heredity-environment uncertainty. *Harvard Educational Review, 39,* 449-483.

———. (1970). I.Q.'s of identical twins reared apart. *Behavior Genetics, 1,* 133-146.

Kamin, L. J. (1974). *The science and politics of I.Q.* Potomac, MD: Lawrence Erlbaum Associates.

———. (1995, February). Behind the curve. *Scientific American.*

Kaufman, A.S. (1992, March). Evaluation of the WISC-III and WIPPSI-R for gifted children. *Roeper Review,* 156-160.

Klineberg, O. (1935). *Race differences.* New York: Harper.

Lee, E. S. (1951). Negro intelligence and selective migration: A Philadelphia test of the Klineberg hypothesis. *American Sociological Review, 16,* 2.

Lichtenstein, G. (1977, December 11). Fund backs controversial study of racial betterment.*The New York Times,* p. 76.

McCelland, D.C. (1973). Testing for competence rather than for "Intelligence." *American Psychologist, 28,* 1-14.

Messick, S. (1972). Beyond structure: In search of functional modalities of psychological process. *Psychometrika, 37,* 357-375.

———. (1973). Multivariate models of cognition and personality: The need for both process and structure in psychological theory and measurement. In J.R. Royce (Ed.), *Multivariate analysis and psychological theory.* New York: Academic Press.

———. (1976). *Individuality in Learning.* San Francisco, CA: Jossey-Bass.

Messick, S., & Damarin, F. (1964). Cognitive styles and memory for faces. *Journal of Abnormal and Social Psychology, 69,* 313-318.

Messick, S. & Kogan, N. (1965). Category width and quantitative aptitude. *Perceptual and Motor Skills , 20,* 493-497.

Miller, A. (1987). Cognitive styles: An integrated model. *Educational Psychology: An International Journal of Experimental Educational Psychology, 7* (4), 251-268.

Monsaas, J.A. and Engelhard, G. (1990). Home environment competitiveness of highly accomplished individuals in four talent fields. *Developmental Psychology, (26) 2,* 246-268.

Morgan, H. (1976). Neonatal precocity and the Black experience. *The Negro Educational Review, 27 (2),* 129-134.

———. (1980). How schools fail black children. *Social Policy, 10,* 49-54.

———. (1990). Assessment of students' behavioral interactions during on-task classroom activities. *Perceptual and Motor Skills, 70,* 563-569.

Myers, I. B., & McCaulley, M. H. (1985). *Manual: A guide to the development and use of the Myers-Briggs Type Indicator.* Palo Alto, California: Consulting Psychologist Press.

Niaz, M. (1989). The role of cognitive style and its influence on proportional reasoning. *Journal of Research in Science Teaching, (25) 3,* 221-235.

Nisbett, R. (1994, October 31). Blue genes. *The New Republic.*

Ohnmacht, F W., & McMorris, R. F. (1971). Creativity as a function of field independence and dogmatism. *Journal of Psychology, 79,* 165-168.

Pasamanick, B. B. (1946). A comparative study of the behavior development of Negro infants. *Journal of Genetic Psychology, 69,* 3-44.

Plank, D. N., & Turner, M. (1987). Changing patterns in Black school politics: Atlanta, 1872-1973. *American Journal of Education, 95,* 584-608.

Posner, M. I. (1966). Components of a skilled performance. *Science, 152,* 1712-1718.

Ramirez, M. & Castaneda, A. (1974). *Cultural democracy, bicognitive development, and education.* New York, NY: Academic Press.

Ramirez, M. & Price-Williams, D. R. (1974). Cognitive styles of children of three ethnic groups in the United States. *Journal of Cross-Cultural Psychology, 5* ( 2), 212- 219.

Rensberger, B. (1978, November 8). Data on race role in I.Q. called false. *The New York Times,* p. 9.

Rosenthal, R. & Jacobson, L. (1968). *Pygmalion in the classroom.* New York: Holt Rinehart & Winston.

Ruble, D. N., & Nahamura, C. Y. (1972). Task orientation versus social orientation in young children and their attention to relevant social cues. *Child Development, 43,* 471-480.

Rushton, J. P. (1995). *Race, evolution, and behavior.* New Brunswick, NJ: Transaction Publishers.

Santostefano, S. G. (1964). A developmental study of the cognitive control leveling-sharpening. *Merrill-Palmer Quarterly, 10,* 343-360.

Scarr, S. (1986). Intelligence: Revisited. In R. J. Sternberg & D. K. Detterman (Eds.), *What is intelligence?* Norwood, NJ: Ablex Publishing Corp.

———. (1981). Testing for children. *American Psychologist, 36,* 1159-1166.

Scarr, S., & Weinberg, R. A. (1976). IQ test performance on Black children adopted by White families. American Psychologist, *31* (10), pp. 726-739.

Scarr-Salapatek, S. (1973). Race, social class and I.Q. In E. Flaxman (Ed.), *Educating the Disadvantaged* (Part II). New York: AMS Press.

Schmeck, H. M. (1971, April). Science group balks at study of race. *The New York Times,* p. 24.

Schmidt, C. P. , & Sinor, J. (1986). An investigation of the relationships among music audiation, musical creativity, and cognitive style. *Research In Music Ed-*

*ucation, 34* (3), 160-172.

Schmidt, G. P. (1984). The relationship among aspects of cognitive style and language bound/language optional perception to musicians' performance in aural discrimination tasks. *Journal of Research In Music Education, 32* (3), 159-168.

Signell, K.A. (1966). Cognitive complexity in person perception and nation perception: A developmental approach. *Journal of Personality, 34,* 517-537.

Singer, R.N. (1968). *Motor learning and human performance.* New York: Macmillan Publishing Company.

Skeels, H. (1938). A study of environmental stimulation: An orphanage preschool project. The University of Iowa.

Skeels, H. & Dye, H. (1939). A study of the effects of differential stimulation on mentally retarded children. *Proceedings of the American Association on Mental Deficiency, 44,* 114-136.

Slack, W. V. ( 1977, November 19). Firmly against taking S.A.T.'s. *The New York Times,* p, 21.

Spearman, C. (1904). General intelligence objectively determined and measured. *American Journal of Psychology, 15,* 201-293.

Spotts, J.V. & Mackler, B. (1967). Relationships of field-independent and field dependent cognitive styles to creative test performance. *Perceptual and Motor Skills, 24,* 239-268.

Staff. (1977, February 25). Election of psychologist as science fellow called enforcement of racism. *The New York Times,* p. 11.

———. (1977, March 27). The value of head start. *The New York Times,* p. 7, Section IV.

———. (1976, April 18). An I Q. study of Black children in white homes. *The New York Times,* p. 7.

Sternberg, R. (1985). *Beyond IQ: A trarchic theory of intelligence.* New York: Cambridge University Press.

Sternberg, R. J., & Detterman, D. K. (Eds.). (1986). *What is intelligence?* Norwood, NJ: Ablex Publishing Corp.

Taylor, C. W. (1964). *Creativity: Progress and potential.* New York: McGraw-Hill.

Taylor, R. L. & Richards, S. B. (1991). Patterns of intellectual differences of Black, Hispanic, and White children. *Psychology in the Schools, 28,* 5-9.

———. (1991). An analysis of the general and specific intellectual factors on the WISC-R for Hispanic and White children. *Diagnostique, 17,* 49-56.

Terman, L. M., & Merrill, M. A. (1937). *Measuring Intelligence.* Boston: Houghton Mifflin.

———. (1973). *Stanford-Binet Intellectual Scale: Manual for third revision form L- M.* Boston: Houghton-Mifflin.

Thorndike, E. L. (1930). *Educational Psychology.* New York: Lenicke & Buechner.

Thorndike, E. (1936). Factor analyses of social and abstract intelligence. *Journal of Education Psychology, (27),* 231-233.

Thurstone, L.L. (1938). *Primary mental abilities.* Chicago: University of Chicago Press.

Thurstone, L.L. and Thurstone, T. G. (1946). *Tests of primary mental abilities for ages five and six.* Chicago: Science Research Associates.

Vernon, P.E. (1972). The distinctiveness of field independence. *Journal of Personality, 40,* 366-391.

———. (1973). Multivariate approaches to the study of cognitive styles. In

J. R. Royce (Ed.), *Multivariate analysis and psychological theory.* New York: Academic Press.

Wachtel, P. L. (1968). Style and capacity in analytic functioning. *Journal of Personality, 36,* 202-212.

Wallace, S. G., & Gregory, R.A. (1985). Cognitive styles: The unaccommodated variable in training design decisions. *Performance and Instruction, 24* (4), 22-23.

Wallach, M. A., Kogan, N., & Burt, R. B. (1967). Group risk taking and field dependence-independence of group members. *Sociometry, 30,* 323-338.

Washington Research Project. (1975). *Children out of school in America.* Cambridge, MA: The Children's Defense Fund.

Wechsler, D. (1989). *Manual for the Wechsler preschool and primary scale of intelligence—revised (WPPSI-R).*

———. (1991). *Manual for the Wechsler Intelligence Scale for Children—Third Ed. (WISC-III).* San Antonio, TX.: The Psychological Corporations.

Werner, H. (1957). The concept of development from a comparative and organismic point of view. In D. B. Harris (Ed.), *The concept of development: An issue in the study of human behavior.* Minneapolis: University of Minnesota Press.

Wertheimer, M. (1945). *Productive thinking.* New York: Harper.

Wilkerson, D. A. (1939). *Special problems of Negro education.* ( Negro Universities Press, Reprinted 1970). United States Government Printing Office, Staff Study #12. Washington, D. C.

Williams, J. R., & Scott, R. B. (1953). Growth and development of Negro infants: Motor development and its relationship to child rearing practices in two groups of Negro infants. *Child Development,* (24), 103-121.

Witkin, H.A. (1949). The nature and importance of individual differences in perception. *Journal of Personality,* (18), 145-170.

Witkin, H. A., Dyk, R. B., Faterson, H. F., Goodenough, D. R., & Karp, S.A. (1962). *Psychological differentiation.* New York: Wiley.

Zigler, E. (1970, May). The environmental mystique: Training the intellect versus developing the child. *Childhood Education,* 402-412.

Zigler, E.& Tricket, P.K. (1978). I.Q. social competence and evaluation of early childhood intervention programs. *American Psychologist,* 789-798.

# VII

# Head Start: The Great Divide

*For the boys and girls who grew . . . to be man and woman, who laugh and dance and play and marry their playmates and bear children and then die of consumption and anemia and lynching.*
                                                    —Margaret Walker

The U.S. government has established an income index to be used by federally funded agencies as a guide for accessing the financial status of families. This is done to determine a family's eligibility for social programs like Head Start. Such programs are called means tested because eligibility is based upon individual or family financial means. This index changes with the annual cost of living, and in 1989 a family of four earning less than $12,675 annually was considered below the poverty line and therefore eligible for a variety of federally supported programs.

Head Start was designed to provide preschool experiences for children ages three to five. Head Start was initiated on February 12, 1965, as a summer program in preparation for large scale plans to provide full year preschool activities involving health, social services and academic activities for children from poor families. Letters were sent to community leaders throughout the nation to call attention to the project, and the response led to thousands of communities registering an interest. The ultimate goal of Head Start was to make an important difference in the lives of poor families—primarily through services to their children. Poor parents want a better life for their children, but they often feel trapped in their condition. They want a better life for themselves too, but their problems are too many and too immense and their resources are too few to change their condition. They have too few skills, not enough political savvy or influence, and not enough knowledge. Too often they are alone with their problems; if unaided they cannot cope with their family responsibilities or the demands of institutions which are designed to advance their interests. Without well designed strategies of intervention by their government, there is a likelihood that their children will repeat this pattern when they become adults with their own families.

Announcing the availability of helpful programs in traditional local media can be effective as a means of informing poor families of opportunities for their children. Those of the so called near poor are often the first to select-in when programs like Head Start are announced. At its highest funded level, even Head Start could reach only 45% of children who are eligible. The very poor are often isolated from other neighborhood adults who could make them a part of the nontraditional network of information. Their children are often shut out of such programs because they have too little information, or apply too late.

The levels of poverty change over time because of a variety of complex factors related to employment and income. Many poor families who have a fully employed adult in their midst remain in poverty because of the relationship between legal minimum wage and family size. Despite popular perception, Black families and White families represent an almost equal percentage of those families living in poverty—Blacks 39%, Whites 38%—with the *greater* number being White. These figures were reported by the U.S. House Ways and Means Committee of the Health and Human Services Department, for 1991. The committee also reported that of the families living in poverty, 17% were Hispanics and 3% were Asians. In this statistical distribution, more than 70% were children.

Head Start was brought to communities through a federal mandate in 1965, but the social and economic environment that enabled such a program to be created has a long history dating back 60-70 years. The decade of the 1930s brought with it the Great Depression, a catastrophic event that actually started in the late 1920s. Southern and rural communities were affected first, but the downhill economic spiral would gain little Federal attention until 1929.

This was a period that witnessed serious economic setbacks in our nation. It included business failures, high unemployment, and the closing of financial institutions for a period of time. Low wages were traditional in many parts of our economy already, so savings were modest, and even much of that was lost when unregulated banking institutions collapsed. Workers in agriculture, manufacturing, and private corporations worked long, hard hours for few benefits and modest wages, compared to worker rights and salaries today.

Citizens were confused and frustrated because their way of life was falling apart around them. President Herbert Hoover and industrial employers like Henry Ford insisted through their speeches and writings, that patience and hard work would bring things back to normal. Both opposed public assistance for needy families. In their view, such aid would undercut individual initiative and play into the hands of those who did not want to work. It took a new president, Franklin Delano Roosevelt, and ten years to bring the country out of economic depression.

Many believed that our economic system—capitalism—had failed and that major changes were essential. To this group of citizens, the change recommended by Communist party leaders appeared to be an attractive alternative. Among their expressed goals was a greater role for the worker, stronger unions and collective bargaining, and a public consciousness about the fundamental ills in our socioeconomic system. Their newspaper, *The Daily Worker*, reached its highest level of distribution in the 1930s and early 1940s. There were other publications that also promoted a worker's rights point of view; these were not directly affiliated with the Communist party.

The party's major message stressed that everything in the United States that could be bought or sold was controlled by a few wealthy men whose self-interests were harmful to workers because among their primary interest was to make labor as inexpensive as possible. The party insisted on a role for the worker in decisions regarding wages, benefits, and work rules.

The Great Depression caused a collapse of many industries; while those that survived controlled operations. The Communist party organized workers to demonstrate at various work sights, and in the process it increased membership considerably. Neighborhood groups offered mutual assistance to the families hardest hit, and large demonstrations were planned in major cities as the party grew.

The party's mission to improve the conditions of workers appealed to a large segment of the population, especially among hourly workers and professionals like teachers, college and university professors and social workers. The party was directly and indirectly responsible for increasing unionism and bringing about many changes in the lives of workers. The party rejected the racist views prevalent during that period, and many Whites were angered by the presence of several Blacks in the top ranks of the leadership.

A few party members, among them Eugene Dennis the President, held the view that Communist Party USA should design its own mission unique to the workers in our country. Others believed that direction should come from the party headquarters in the Soviet Union. It was their view that workers' rights was an international issue and that workers of the world should unite in a common cause. Eugene Dennis argued that the world view could be retained in a model that allowed for national direction in various locations like the United States. The Dennis perspective never prevailed.

Eugene Dennis was indicted during the anti-Communist frenzy following the Great Depression. Dennis and several other leaders would be charged with attempting to overthrow the U.S. government.  Black and White U.S. party leaders would be found guilty and were jailed for various periods of time, even though their unlawful acts never involved violence, weapons, or the threat of violence on their part.

The party's membership dwindled in the 1950s in part because the imprisonment of major party leaders had a chilling effect upon  its members.The final demise of the party as a major force in U.S. politics came when Stalin's role  in human rights atrocities against those who opposed him—which he had continually denied—was proven to be true.

The presidential election of 1934 would inaugurate a Democrat, Franklin Delano Roosevelt, who over time would improve the social conditions of poor families.  Fundamental changes in our economy through the banking system government regulations and federal programs were enacted to create employment and reduce poverty among families.

The year of 1935 witnessed the greatest surge of social legislation that this country had ever experienced.  Major legislation would include a family welfare system, Aid to Families With Dependent Children (AFDC); the Works Progress Administration (WPA); a system of full employment backed up with federal projects; Social Security (FICA); and various job related-programs that put hourly workers, artists, and professionals on salary.  These socialistic programs were integrated into our system of capitalism, and many still remain.

The Congress of the United States, at the urging and direction of the president, operated under the principal that when families in our country are unable to care for the basic needs of their children and themselves, they have a *right*  to expect  their government to come to their aid.  This concept of federal assistance to the poor as a right was new to the United States and would change to a *privilege* when the economy rebounded in the 1940s and the unemployed were Blacks and poor Whites.

After the economic status of middle-and upper-income Whites improved—primarily through economic expansion in preparation of World War II—those who were left at the bottom were primarily Blacks with skills but too few opportunities resulting from discriminatory occupational exclusion because of race.  Exceptions would be found in large cities on the East and West coasts where workers were organized, in part because of the work of the Communist party.

After World War II, federal programs like FHA would enable many middle-class Whites, and a few Blacks to become homeowners.  Once again, though, the common pattern of discrimination would result in the federal government's placement of regulatory guidelines in the FHA legislation that would restrict home ownership by Black families.  In general, the great demand for domestic goods after World War II created manufacturing jobs for the majority of Blacks and Whites.  Families who remained poor—primarily  the under-employed and single parents with children—were often thought to be responsible for their own condition. They were not viewed as a social responsibility as were the poor of the 1920s and 1930s from European backgrounds. The preponderance of persons needing welfare assistance were children, and Whites outnumbered Blacks. In terms of percentages, Black children, however, are almost three times more likely to be poor than White children, according to 1992 data.

More often than not, children in the United States are viewed as a family responsibility and not a social responsibility. Further, the perception of federal aid to citizens as a right replaced it with the view that federal aid, when given to the poor and powerless, is a privilege. From this change in attitude a number of "workfare" programs and reductions in benefits to children in poor families is being legislated state by state. These restrictive legislative actions often take place under an almost bizarre set of circumstances. As suggested by Stephanie Coontz (1992), the politicians who are the most aggressive about promoting "welfare reform" legislation that curtails benefits to poor children received massive government aid in the 1950s and are children of European parents who benefited from the welfare programs of the 1930s and 1940s!

According to legend, after WWII a new, family-oriented generation settled down, saved their pennies, worked hard, and found well paying jobs that allowed them to purchase homes in the suburbs. In fact, however, the 1950s suburban family was far more dependent on government assistance than any so-called underclass family of today. Federal GI Benefits available to 40% of the male population between the ages of twenty and twenty-four, permitted a whole generation of men to expand their education and improve their job prospects . . . Government spending was also largely responsible for the new highways, sewer systems, utility services and traffic-control programs that opened up suburbia. (Coontz, 1992, p. 13)

The lingering effects of poverty that restricted the ability of some families to provide for the basic need of their children would become the major focus of the Democratic president of the 1960s, Lyndon B. Johnson. The improved economic conditions of the 1950s and 1960s that brought secure jobs and home ownership for many citizens did not affect all families. Too many families who were poor in the 1940s were still poor; and their children, who had grown up under poverty were now attempting to raise their own children in a similar environment. This condition was labeled *the cycle of poverty* because for generations too many of the same families and their children seemed unable to change their economic status. Those families who were able to improve their economic status through their own persistence and government social programs moved away from distressed neighborhoods to a better life. In many communities, federal housing programs provided a way out. Such housing was intended as a short—or long—term solution for low income families. Thousands of families used such housing as a period to accumulate enough resources to afford home ownership in a traditional neighborhood. Over the years such housing tended to become a permanent residence for those who, for a variety of reasons, were unable to advance their own economic status.

Gradually, these permanent residents—sharing the same debilitating financial condition—created a neighborhood within a neighborhood to become known as *the projects*. The projects in urban areas would become large high-rise populations of families eligible for practically every social program available to the poor. It seemed unwise to arrange a system that concentrated large populations of economically disadvantaged people in a "city" of their own. These massive building programs were welcomed by financially strapped cities. For a period of time it meant construction jobs, and social service providers saw an advantage to having clients more visible and accessible in one part of the city, rather than scattered over a wide geographic area. In the final analysis, for many cities housing development for the poor solved fewer problems than it created.

Many poor families residing in rural areas moved into cities for the modest advantages of social services, better housing, and employment. They would often become the new residents in the projects, and frequently they were no better off than before. Deficiencies in health and education for poor children were being reported by human services providers in urban and rural communities. By the late 1950s the needs of the poor became too much for communities to sustain, and municipal governments looked to the federal government for help as they had done in the 1930s.

In response to urban and rural municipalities, Lyndon B. Johnson would borrow from the rhetoric of the Great *Depression* and change it to the *Great Society,* in which he envisioned a role for the federal government in improving the lives of poor families.

President Johnson launched the War on Poverty to attack this debilitating condition of poor families on several fronts. Head Start would focus on the children of the poor. It was theorized that poor children needed early intervention programs to assure their starting academic journey through the grades with a good foundation. Studies had shown that for a variety of complex reasons, school success seemed to correlate positively with family income. Children from low-income families tend to do less well academically than children from upper-income families, and children from non poverty families were more likely to arrive at school well fed and healthy. Children from poor families come to school for the first time with fewer academically related cultural experiences and less time in an organized nursery school or day care center.

In response to these often-heard reports, Head Start provided funds to community agencies and school systems to organize centers that would provide health, social services, and academic programs for children from poor families. The largest program for children ever created by the federal government, It became a part of the 1964 Economic Opportunity Act, along with several other programs under the umbrella of Community Action Programs like VISTA (a domestic Peace Corps) and Job Corps. By the summer of 1966 there were over 600,000 children in almost 3,000 childcare centers throughout the nation.

Program planners in the nation's capital encouraged community agencies to submit proposals, while they were enlisting the help of professionals, to find ways to articulate guidelines that would address the medical, dental, nutritional, and academic needs of poor children who would be attending neighborhood-based Head Start classrooms. Even though school learning was accepted as a major goal by the planners, the government's newly appointed executive, Sargent Shriver, would emphasize mental and physical health in the initial stages.

Robert Cook, a physician, was selected chairman of the planning committee. Julius Richmond, dean of the Medical School at New York State Medical College at Syracuse, would later become the national director. Among the other professionals to be brought in later was Mamie Clark, an expert in mental health; and Keith Osborne, Polly Greenberg, James Hymes, and Bettye Caldwell, experts in the field of early childhood education. Attempts were made to create a balance between academic needs and health needs with the ultimate goal that Head Start would be a catalyst for social reform.

Head Start introduced many innovations. It was the first educational program to emphasize a significant role for parents. Its guidelines mandated a consulting role for parents in program policy, teacher and site selection, and funding at the local level. Parents were also included in the budget process, and their elected president signed the proposals prior to site funding. This was a radical departure from the role of parents in the traditional parents-teacher relationships common to PTAs.

Head Start also introduced men as teachers in preschool classrooms and parents as aides to teachers, social workers, and health providers. In many programs this provided incentive for those parents with the time and inclination to complete their own professional education through funding provided by an affiliated program that became known as New Careers.

Head Start seemed to provide new energy for the thousands of advocates for poor families and their children. There was renewed interest in early education for all children at traditional institutions like Bank Street College, and at the many universities where campus laboratory schools in conjunction with teacher training had been inoperation since the 1920s and 1930s, and in public school systems around the nation where kindergartens had been in existence for the same length of time. The fact that our federal government was about to launch an early childhood initiative aimed at children of the poor served to sharpen the attention of parents and professionals at all levels of childcare. Affluent families were not excluded because 15% of the enrollment could be children from families with higher incomes. Head Start also created a political fervor among childcare professionals to make an important difference in the lives of poor families. The timing coincided with the civil rights movement, and Head Start appeared to be a natural connection between grass roots community organizers and their government. There were, however, many skeptics among civil rights groups who feared that this was a government tactic to divert attention from more pressing issues regarding voting rights and empowerment of oppressed southern Blacks.

The professionals from universities and public school systems in the Northeast and far West learned quickly not to expect all families to have the kind of access to childcare services available to northern communities. It was not until the mid-1980s that Georgia would require all communities to provide kindergartens in public schools. Before then, in 1965, the governor of Mississippi had refused to approve the opening of Head Start programs.

Poor parents and community professionals, with the assistance of the Washington office, founded the Child Development Group of Mississippi (CDGM), and received Head Start funds of $1.4 million granted through a college because Mississippi Governor Paul Johnson had threatened to veto the flow of federal funds to community groups for the program. Many poor Mississippi parents viewed Head Start as a benefit for their children, but equally important it provided employment for them and hundreds of other poorly paid Black workers in the state.

The program was open to all poor children and 15% of the non-poor, but White parents rarely enrolled their children. By 1966 CDGM had received $5.6 million in federal grants to provide Head Start services for children. The politicians in the state were stunned by the amount of money flowing to Black residents and eventually gained control of the major portion of the funds. There was also conflict between the voter registration and civil rights advocates on one side and the participants and administrators of anti-poverty programs, like Head Start, on the other. Both groups defined themselves within the "movement" and attempted to resolve their conflicts at the grassroots level. For some rural communities the first programs were set up in homes because the local churches were afraid of being bombed or burned down. In the early stages of the program when local politicians managed to have the funds halted, Black parents continued their work without pay. In rural Mississippi one community reported that poor White parents enrolled their children in several Head Start classes in defiance of threats from more affluent Whites. In the years to come, Head Start parents would make more demands for better quality schools as they learned their rights through their Head Start experience, where parents were required to participate at all levels.

By 1967 funds were provided for research aimed at investigating the positive effects of Head Start. There were many health and nutritional benefits, as well as increased community interest in early education, there also emerged a greater willingness among poor parents to support the work of their local grade schools. However, studies of that time regarding the *academic* gains of the children reported mixed results. Despite the short duration of the program prior to the studies and the flawed nature of several of these studies, the belief that childhood benefits gained from the Head Start experience might not last past the third grade in regular schools was taken seriously by the executives in Washington.

The national director and staff of Head Start expanded the scope of the original model by adding Follow Through. This gave community parents and program directors the opportunity to select an academic, or child development, model for classrooms that would follow Head Start graduates through kindergarten to grade three. The Head Start program that involved parents in actual program planning and created a role for them in the learning and social and medical needs of their children would now be expanded in Follow Through to include local public schools.

The "academic models" for Follow Through programs in the grade schools would be provided by current theorists and practitioners whose work was guided by philosophers and theorists described earlier. Prior to the inauguration of Head Start, teachers and administrators in schools throughout the nation created teaching-learning environments in their schools and classrooms that reflected the theories and practices that they were taught during their own professional training.

Prior to Follow Through, Head Start programs were staffed by professionals from a variety of different teacher training institutions. Some institutions of higher learning grouped grades one through six in a professional program called Elementary Education. There were other colleges and universities that provided a primary grades concentration of study in kindergarten through grade three. This was seldom done by colleges and universities located in states that did not have mandatory kindergarten programs in public schools.

Where kindergarten had existed for some time as a part of public schooling—as in most major cities—the college or university teaching major that concentrated on the education of young children—enrolled teacher trainees in a program of early childhood education. These majors usually studied children from birth to age nine (third grade). Program concentration for early education in colleges and universities through the 1920s to 1950s was often a part of a division of child and family studies, home economics and/or child development departments. These program concentrations were, more often than not, restricted to studies of children from birth through preschool.

College and university campuses where early childhood education was a concentration of birth to third grade, and those programs that were housed in home economics/child development studies, usually had a campus nursery school or similar setting for their students to engage in practice and child study. Early education programs of these types were more concerned about *how* children learn. The aforementioned elementary education program (k-6), was more concerned with *what* children should be taught.

Within the context of these various teacher-training approaches, sometimes overlapping, sometimes completely different, there were also various theoretical and philosophical perspectives on child development and learning. Teachers recruited during the first days of Head Start could come from any one of these various training experiences. Their few differences over pedagogy were overshadowed by the rich diversity to which poor children were exposed.

With the inauguration of project Follow Through, came a rearrangement among programs that would decrease the diversity within programs, but it would provide community groups with an opportunity to select the "model" that in their view best suited the needs of their children. This was seen as an extension of parent involvement, and at the same time it provided opportunities for researchers to assist in identifying the most effective approaches to advancing the academic interests of children from poor families.

The selection process started with national Head Start planners organizing a demonstration of the various teaching-learning approaches to parent and staff groups. Representatives from various colleges and universities and academic professionals were invited to a demonstration conference in Kansas City. Each model was presented by professionals from the institution or university identified with that particular approach to teaching and learning. The following are descriptions of the major models presented to the various communities and selected by them for their Follow Through programs.

The *Bereiter-Engelmann Model,* renamed the DISTAR program, was designed by two psychologists, Carl Bereiter and Siegfried Engelmann. The program was designed to present carefully prepared lessons in language arts, mathematics, and reading. Teaching is done in small, disciplined, and orderly groups with the language of the teacher and the expected responses from the children predetermined. Children are praised—and given a reward—when their performance fits the program's expectations. It is based upon the philosophy of John Locke and the theory of B. F. Skinner. In the early phases of the model, when pupils respond with desired behaviors, they are given a small piece of candy or handshake by the teacher (positive reinforcement). If their behavior is disturbing to the group, they are ignored or placed in isolation away from their peers (negative reinforcement).

At least one study of the effects of the intensive methods of this type of direct instruction found that as children grew older, they were more likely to be involved in delinquent behavior than their age-mates in programs using different models.

The *Bank Street Model* is named for the college that designed the program. Bank Street College in New York City takes its name from its original location. Lucy Sprague Mitchell and Harriet Johnson established the Bureau of Educational Experiments in New York City. To provide an environment for research and child development education, they founded Bank Street College of Education as a graduate school with its own experimental day school. It became one of the most well known early childhood centers in the field. The Bank Street program is based on freedom of experience. Learners are encouraged to initiate their own classroom interactions with materials, the teacher, or other children. Play is seen as children's work, and the use of building blocks and other manipulatives is a part of that work. At other sites in New York City, Bank Street College has conducted programs for children from poor families using the freedom of experience approach. Their work can be identified with the philosophies of Rousseau and Dewey and the theories of Jean Piaget. The Bank Street Model views Piaget's stages as essential to an understanding of children's logical thinking and their level of readiness to make sense of their environment in thoughtful ways.

The *Tucson Early Education Model* was designed by Marie Hughes of the University of Arizona, Tucson. It is built upon the idea that classroom teachers can enable children to develop positive attitudes toward learning. Small-group interaction is encouraged, and the teacher is often engaged in a one-on-one interaction with children. Classrooms are grouped in cross age-patterns to optimize heterogeneous groups for interaction. Materials are in great supply and visible to children, who are encouraged to advance their intellectual skills through group work and projects. The Tucson model is based upon the philosophy of Rousseau and the theories of John Dewey and Jean Piaget. This model accepts the stage theories of Piaget as a means of understanding how to respond to the learner's needs in the classroom's socially interactive process.

Professor Don Bushnell of the University of Kansas proposed a model of teaching and learning for young children called the *Behavior Analysis Approach.* Programmed materials are utilized in a planned, individual instruction mode. It is a skills approach to teaching that employs parents as teachers. Parents are taught techniques that use behavior modification through positive reinforcement techniques. This approach is rooted in the philosophy of John Locke and the theories of B. F. Skinner and John B. Watson.

David Weikart in Ypsilanti, Michigan, proposed an approach in which learning objectives are stated in terms of the planned behavioral goals. Essential to the *Ypsilanti Program* is self-concept and language comprehension. The approach has three dimensions: a curriculum that is cognitively based; a classroom teacher who is intimately involved in the planning, strives to interact with children and participates actively in their learning;  and a cooperative effort between the teacher and a parent in the home to encourage support for the work of the program.  The child's competence at each level is assessed to enable the teacher to guide the child's learning in a sequential manner. Philosophically the program is Rousseau oriented, and it follows the theory of Jean Piaget.

The *Far West Laboratory Educational Research and Development Model* was directed by Glen Nimnich. The model has been referred to as an autotelic approach. The learner's language development, sensory and perceptual acuity, concept formation, abstract thinking, and problem-solving skills are viewed as fundamental to knowledge acquisition. Classrooms and other learning environments are designed to promote a positive self-image through autotelic learning activities that are self-rewarding and detached from teacher reinforcements. The overall environment is designed to be responsive to the learner's cognitive style.  The teacher's role is that of guide to help children solve problems and arrive at their own solutions.  This approach is based on the philosophy of John Dewey and the theory of Jean Piaget.

The *Educational Development Center of Boston, Massachusetts*, utilized a Piaget approach that motivates teachers and parents to define their own needs in terms of what they want children to learn;  through staff development training, professionals will advise as to how these goals can be achieved.  In the Educational Development Center Model, classrooms are fashioned to the needs of the learners and the talents and working styles of the teachers. The classroom activities emerge from staff development and parent-teacher approaches that continue to assess the needs of children, parents, and professionals.  Each classroom is expected to undergo change from time to time as the needs of learners change with their growth and development.  A teacher with considerable experience with children serves as an on-site advisor to the staff.

The *Parent  Education Model*  was similar to a variety of programs that over time have involved parents directly in the education of their infants and toddlers.  At the University of Florida at Gainesville, Professor Ira Gordon had been experimenting with the growth and development of infants and toddlers from economically disadvantaged families.  The Parent Education Model emphasized family life as the core of its intervention strategies. Parents were recruited from the economically disadvantaged community and trained to become parent educators.  It was theorized that parents from the low-income community would have a better chance than an outside professional of being accepted in the home of their neighbors. The minimum requirement for this new role of parent educator was completion of high school. Parent educators were trained by Gordon's professional staff to use materials readily available in the home where they were working, and to develop a comfortable trusting relationship with the mother and child.  The theories of Piaget provide the framework for Gordon's assumptions about how children learn.  The learning tasks used by the parent educators were designed to be age appropriate according to Piaget's stages of early child development.

A study of a Head Start program in Nassau County New York, reported in 1977 that  twice-a-week home visits to teach poor parents how to teach their children raised the I.Q.s of their children 10-15 points upon school entry.  They also had fewer behavior problems and scored higher than a control group.

## THE FUTURE OF HEAD START

After the first ten years of Head Start the government made the decision through funding patterns to support *quantity* more than *quality*. During the 1980s Head Start centers would be required to serve more children with fewer resources.  This trend continued during the 1980s to the extent that the funding per child continued to decline.  The quality of any program for children rests upon the training received by the professionals who work face to face with children and upon the training of those who supervise these practitioners.  In 1965 the classroom practitioners were college-and university-trained teachers who by choice worked in Head Start centers rather than in regular schools.

Head Start centers and classrooms presented professionals with a new and dynamic challenge to use their skills in a way not available to them in traditional public school settings.  The recruitment of males as teachers in early education, the use of poor parents as teacher and social service aides, and close cooperative encounters with medical and nutritional providers in a comprehensive approach to the education of poor children was an attractive career choice for well trained teachers.  By 1980 most of the well-trained professionals no longer worked directly with Head Start children.  The few who remained were used as trainers and/or supervisors for the classroom aides.  Poor parents, who were the teacher aides of the 1960s and the 1970s became the classroom teachers by 1980.

In 1990 the average Head Start teacher's salary was less than $10,000 a year, and the director's salary was less than what beginning teachers in local public schools were earning.  Teachers in Head Start are currently  required to have the equivalent of high school completion, with some college cited as desirable but not mandatory.  A college—or university—trained person is usually assigned to coordinate training and curriculum for a group of several centers in a designated geographic area.

Why has a program for poor families with such a distinguished record faced so many threats of demise?  The reasons are philosophical and political.  In capitalist  societies such as ours, children are viewed as a *family* responsibility and not a *social* responsibility. Public policy in various informal ways require most families to purchase their childcare needs in the private enterprise marketplace. The disparity in family income that enables some families to purchase high-quality services, whereas others can afford only poor services, or none at all, is an acceptable condition of capitalism. A family's quality of life is tied to their income. To change the status of poor children who need the early intervention of preschool services would require local legislative action to require tax-supported public schools to extend the age for school entry downward to accommodate children three years of age or younger. Persons who can afford to pay for childcare, however, and receive a tax allowance for the purchase of such services are not likely to support a plan that would extend the school day to include younger children, thereby increasing the taxes they successfully avoided in the first place.

It is also true that the financial commitment to Head Start tends to mirror the policies of the political party of the president. Under the Republican administrations, Head Start is viewed as a privilege for a group of parents who should be required to pay for childcare that is purchased from private, for-profit providers. Their policy preference was to close-out the existing Head Start program. During Democratic presidencies, Head Start is accepted as one of several programs that enabled poor families to have a better life. The congressional process that sets policy for social programs often results in compromises between the two political camps. For Head Start, it has been a continuous political struggle to avoid complete dismantling.

For some time now, Head Start has existed as a compromise, with fewer resources and more children. In our society too often it is acceptable to assist poor families as long as the assistance is modest—and below the quality of services available to those able to pay.

## REFERENCES

Biber, B. (1970). Goals and methods in a preschool program for disadvantaged children. *Children, 16.*

Coontz, S. (1992, October). A nation of welfare families. *Harper's Magazine,* pp. 13 -16.

Judd, D. R. (1991). Segregation forever. *The Nation. 253* (20), pp.740-744.

Lee, V. E., Brooks-Gunn, J., & Schnur, E. (1988). Does head start work? A 1-Year follow-up comparison of disadvantaged children attending head start, no preschool, and other preschool programs. *Developmental Psychology, 24* (2), 210-222.

Shapiro, E. & Biber, B. (1972). The education of young children: A developmental interaction approach. *Teachers College Record, 74,* 59-60.

Shorr, L. B. (1988). *Within our reach: Breaking the cycle of disadvantage.* New York: Doubleday.

Staff. (1977, March). The value of Head Start. *The New York Times.* section 4 (E),

p. 7.

Ziegler, E., & Valentine, J. (Eds.). (1979). *Project Head Start: A legacy of the war on poverty.* New York: Macmillan.

# VIII

# Exemplary Programs, Methods and Materials

*I was convinced that I was prejudiced in a manner over so many years that some of that prejudice undoubtabley would always be within me.*

—Jonathan Kozol

In many parts of our nation schooling is divided into separate areas or groupings based on children's age, maturation, and readiness to learn. For example, some communities have an early childhood area of concentration for children from preschool (mostly kindergarten) through the third or fourth grade. The middle school concentrates on children from fourth or fifth grade through the seventh or eighth grade. High school, then, usually encompasses grades seven or eight through grade 12. William T. Harris, the superintendent of schools for St. Louis in 1872, started the first public school kindergarten in the United States and later became the U.S. Commissioner of education in 1878. He introduced a year-by-year progression of grades 1 through 12 as a basic requirement for public school completion. This arrangement was similar to that envisioned for state-supported education of the elite in Plato's *Republic.* Harris was well read; he was therefore aware of the work of early philosophers and theorists, and the ideas of the early thinkers were apparent in his approach to the profession of teaching and learning. Active in the kindergarten movement in the United States, he was aware of the impact that early education could have on the academic performance of learners in the later grades; from his ideas about the need for kindergartens, he suggested that, "Froebel has provided a system of discipline and instruction which is wonderfully adapted to this stage of the child's growth, when he needs that gentleness of the nurture and the natural order of the school in due admixture." He was also clear on racial matters related to education frequently speaking out in support of Du Bois's view that Blacks should be afforded academic opportunities equal to those granted Whites.

The growth of the settlement house movement that was started by Jane Addams, Jacob Riis, and others coincided with an awareness among human services professionals that poor immigrant families were swelling the ranks of the urban poor and their children were at great risk. Programs for poor families often meant providing services such as childcare, recreation and games, free milk, and free meal programs for their children. The kindergarten movement was on its upswing at about the same time as settlement houses in cities were looking after the needs of poor families in their neighborhoods. In some cities, settlement houses were actually called *neighborhood houses.*

The National Education Association was also giving a great deal of attention to kindergartens through speeches and the dissemination of materials to its members. As this attention expanded, the organization established kindergarten as its own division. This new attention on Froebel and the kindergarten grew into a lock-step use of the gifts that Froebel had envisioned as manipulatives to support the natural growth of children in a nurturing environment. In trying to establish their own identity separate from grade schools, kindergarten teachers began to use Froebel's gifts for direct instruction of children in the performance based mode. This took the kindergarten method away from the philosophy of Rousseau and Comenius, toward that of John Locke.

The earlier developers of the kindergarten movement in the United States were alarmed at what the Froebel system had become in their own country. In their effort to recapture the essence of the child's garden, a reshaping of thought surrounding child development was emerging.

Along with changes toward the urbanization of the United States in the early 1900s came Charles Darwin's *Origin of the Species,* that diverted scholarly attention away from the spiritual-religious nature of society to an examination of our connectedness with the animal world. Psychologists, many of whom were inspired by the animal experimentation of the Russian scientist, Ivan Pavlov, began experimenting with animal learning in the belief that it had direct implications for human learning. This approach to study involved mice, pigeons, dogs, and monkeys—some bred especially for research purposes. This behaviorist school of psychology would dominate the field of thought in this profession until the 1960s.

Meanwhile kindergarten and early childhood education was holding on to its Froebelian roots, despite the fact that in some examples of the practice Froebel was hardly noticeable. The early education pattern would gradually shift from the nurturing environment traditional in U.S. kindergartens to a more scientific observational mode wherein data were collected from the observations of children in the teaching-learning environment. G. Stanley

Hall, John Dewey, and Edward L. Thorndike were the most notable thinkers involved in the study of child development and were also among those proposing changes in the study of children during this early period. Arnold Gesell invented the one-way observational mirror for the purpose of data collection, and led the way for the growth of child study centers in universities in United States.

It was G.Stanley Hall who introduced the study of childhood experiences through children's social interaction with dolls. He concluded that doll play among children had a profound effect upon early childhood learning, and he made contributions along with Gesell by giving early childhood professionals a discipline of their own. In the mid-1930s Kenneth Clarke, the Black psychologist, used dolls to study race preference among Black and White children.

John Dewey provided the basic philosophy for practitioners, and Gesell pioneered the University Laboratory School with his work at the Yale University Clinic of Child Development. Other scientific observations were conducted to study child development by the the Free Kindergarten Association of Atlanta University which was started by a small group of African American mothers in 1913. The mothers were associated with Du Bois's Atlanta University Conference for the Study of Negro Problems.

Also studying child development were the Iowa University Child Welfare Station, opened in 1917; the Child Welfare Institute of Columbia University's Teachers started in 1925; and the University of California's laboratory school for child study, started in 1927.

By this time the Peninsula School had been operating for several years in California as a school for children of all races. Founded on the principles of John Dewey, it provided education from early years through the middle grades. As the children from Peninsula School entered the local high schools they were usually deemed exceptional and Peninsula School still provides educational services for children through the 1990s. Later, a school on the East Coast, in New York City, was also founded on the principles of John Dewey and others, emerging under the influences of the psychoanalytic movement based on Freud's ideas about psychosexual development. Bank Street College focused solely on early childhood education through its graduate school for teachers and its laboratory school for children. Lawrence Frank, a New York economist, had been conducting studies relative to the social welfare systems in the city and state. Lucy Sprague Mitchell and Harriet Johnson founded the New York City Bureau of Educational Experiments, and they interested Frank in the scientific study of child development. Together they founded the New York City Bureau of Educational Experiments, which prepared the foundation for Bank Street College.

By now Bank Street College for children and the Peninsula School were among several schools that focused more on *how* children learn rather than *what* children should be taught. Following Froebel's ideas, play was viewed as the child's work, and aesthetic experiences loomed large in these programs. They focused on enabling learners to make sense of their world by providing materials, experiences, and supportive adults in an environment of trust and cooperation. Since these programs rely not on direct instruction and activities like memorizing the times table but, rather, on encouraging children to construct their own learning, teachers without special training have found these principles difficult to translate into practice.

Teachers educated at colleges and universities that provided teacher training in early childhood education, as opposed to elementary education, have a far better likelihood of success in the teaching of children below the fourth grade, and this is critical for Black children. As a group, all children appear to learn at the same rate from the beginning of school in kindergarten through the third grade. When measurable differences do occur between groups of Black and White children, it is after they exit the experiences of early childhood. This disparity can be pinpointed with such accuracy that it is sometimes called the *third-grade syndrome.* It is the long tradition of early childhood education that is linked to the philosophy and theory of Rousseau, Dewey, Piaget, and Freud that seems to provide the essence of what African American children need to become competent learners in their own right. This successful encounter with learning in the early grades is due in part to the collaboration between the school and the parents. Early childhood teachers *strive* to remain in touch with parents beyond the point of enrollment; however, it is after the third and fourth grade that teachers and parents begin to lose interest in each other. This is unfortunate under any circumstances; it is more troubling when the teacher is White and the child's family is Black. The family-teacher relationship is *required* at all levels in Head Start programs.

It has become common place to report that African American children tend to lose the gains they achieved in Head Start and then blame the children or Head Start. There is something lacking in the receiving school's performance when it is unable to build upon the academic gains that pupils possess at the time enrollment.

Recently efforts to capture benefits of social interaction in the classroom, as is apparent in early childhood education, middle school and some high school teachers have been experimenting with cooperative education. The fundamental tenets of cooperative education stress group interaction around a common interest. The class is divided into heterogeneous work groups. Their assignments are serious academic projects that require various lines of examination. The teacher determines beforehand the level of skill required to complete the assigned study or project. For example, a project might require students to understand the concepts associated with metaphor or to possess intermediate computer skills. Usually, to allow students to become familiar with the process of cooperative learning, a task is assigned that can be completed in a single class session. The assignment could be for the group to read a brief passage from *Moby Dick,* the novel, and make sure that everyone understands the concept *metaphor.* First, the group assures themselves that each member understands the task. The group then decides how they will proceed with the assignment. The procedures agreed upon by the group might be to have each person read a short passage quietly in a given time frame, say five to ten minutes, and each reader is given the opportunity to present her or his interpretation for group discussion. Finally, the group will compare ideas and obtain a consensus on the final outcome (answer). Cooperative learning encourages students to complete tasks with as little teacher assistance as possible, to negotiate their own conflict resolution, to assure that all members are participants, to become knowledgeable about the academic content, and to complete the task.

It has been reported that cooperative learning enables children to better comprehend content that might otherwise be difficult for them, to appreciate cultural and gender differences, to improve their intellectual skills of enquiry and to develop social skills. Cooperative learning is now being tried at all levels of schooling, and the reports of teachers are encouraging.

## TEACHING ABOUT AFRICAN AMERICANS

It has become a tradition in our nation's schools to set aside the month of February as a time when African Americans who contributed to the growth of our country can be talked about in school classrooms. Civil rights leaders and selected Black activists—primarily Martin Luther King, Harriet Tubman, and Thurgood Marshall— are brought to the attention of students in various ways. Seldom are they integrated, as they should be, into the vast American landscape of all the important people and events considered an integral part of social studies taught throughout the year. The contributions of Black historical figures and the changes and events they have created in American life are set aside during the regular school year, to be studied only during the month of February.

The history of our nation's capitol should include the architectural contributions of Benjamin Banneker. The story of American theater or the study of Shakespeare's work should include one of the foremost interpreters of theater art—Ira Aldridge. The teaching of various periods of significance, such as the Industrial Revolution, should integrate inventors and scientists like Jan Matzeliger, inventor of the machine that revolutionized the shoe-manufacturing industry and made Lynn, Massachusetts, the shoe capitol of the world. Elijah McCoy invented devices that advanced railroad technology in the United States and acquired over 50 patents.  Garret Morgan was another inventor; he made substantial contributions to public safety by inventing a device that became the gas mask for military and civilian rescue work.  He also developed and patented a device that became our present day traffic light.  The toggle harpoon was the invention of Lewis Temple in the early 1800s; its introduction into the fishing industry doubled the catch for the New England fishing industry.

There need not be a fragmentation of  African Americans in academic studies. Neither do such studies have to be limited to an occasional biography in the month of February.  School curriculums are often presented to students in the form of "units" to be studied. This often provides an across-the-curriculum approach that integrates social studies, geography, reading, mathematics, and other areas of study. Such an approach  provides an excellent opportunity to integrate subject matter with African American, Hispanic, and Native American issues and individuals.  A unit on health and nutrition, for example, could include foods common to various cultures and subcultures.  A creative classroom teacher could expand the content and manner in which children create their own knowledge about such matters. Minority children in the classroom can be encouraged to interview adult members of their families, and their work can be integrated into the unit in the same manner as material from traditional sources is used.  The history of Native American and Hispanic early customs of food gathering, healing the sick, and housing could be integrated into such a unit.  White children should  be encouraged to become knowledgeable about customs and contributions of all Americans, whether minority or not.

In this same unit on health  the teacher could bring attention to Daniel Hale Williams, an African American surgeon, who was a pioneer in open heart surgery.  He graduated from the Chicago Medical College in 1883, but because he was Black, he was not allowed to practice medicine in the local city hospitals. He changed this practice by founding  the Provident Hospital as a medical facility and assured those needing medical care that the hospital would be open to all people.

Scholars, practitioners,  and the general public are reminded constantly of a remarkable contribution made by Dr. Charles Drew to the field of medicine. Drew,  an African American, helped develop the idea and the scientific process that led to our present-day "blood bank" administered by the American Red Cross. He was chief surgeon at Freedmen's Hospital in Washington, D.C. in the 1940s. Drew was a graduate of Amherst College and received that institution's most prestigious award for having brought the highest honor to his alma mater.

Students would be fascinated by the life history of one of the most famous African American scientists of our time; George Washington Carver. He was sold as a field hand after his mother, a slave, was sold away  from the plantation where they lived and worked. When Carver was thirteen, his owner traded him for a race horse, and Carver became a worker in the fields. Here he became intrigued with plant life and their growth. He worked hard and managed to finish high school by attending at night. Denied admission by many colleges, he was finally admitted to Simpson College in Iowa. After graduation he was hired as a janitor at what is now Iowa State University, but his ultimate goal was more elaborate than merely cleaning buildings. While working as a janitor he took courses and finally earned a degree in agricultural science in 1894. He earned his master's degree from Iowa State University and was invited to join the faculty. Carver's many scientific discoveries for uses of the peanut and soybean is said to have saved southern agriculture from disaster, because of their total dependency on cotton. Carver ended his career as a professor and researcher at Tuskegee Institute. He is buried alongside Booker T. Washington.

In 1992 a five-volume series of books published for middle—and senior high school readers described in great detail the contributions of various scientists from early philosophers to the 1990s. It is remarkable that neither Drew, Carver, nor any other Black scientists were mentioned in this series. The absence of information about African Americans from regular sources reinforces the need for educators to be more active in making literature that is inclusive, more visible and accessible.

When teachers attempt to put all African American history into one month, they encounter several difficulties. Some teachers approach the implementation of Black History Month though a study of the periods in history they deem appropriate to the subject matter. For example, they concentrate on the "Civil Rights Era" or "Slavery." Another approach is to ignore the time frame of events. Here, with a display of pictures and/or written assignments teachers merely introduce biographical sketches of famous persons and attempt to integrate their deeds into the content and activities for the month.

In many schools classrooms are desegregated, and Black and White children are cooperating in these studies. It is within this context that another problem tends to surface. Some White children begin to wonder why all this Black-oriented material is being emphasized every year at about the same time, and African American students are sometimes embarrassed because their White classmates are learning that their great-grandparents were slaves. White pupils are also learning that their own great grand-parents could have owned slaves, suggesting a heritage of being "master" and therefore somehow superior. Were teachers able to tell the whole story, African American children would perhaps be more comfortable about the subject of slavery. This means that as children learn that Blacks were enslaved and forced into servitude, White children need to be informed that their great-grandparents were the perpetrators of such evil, and that schools, churches and the criminal justice system abetted an unconscionable system of degradation. They should be informed that Whites were responsible for buying and selling Black people as slaves, for Klan beatings, lynchings, and other harmful things to the ancestors of Black children. When teachers suggest that the slavery period was merely a terrible time in the history of our nation, leaving out the details of perpetrator and victim, the message they convey is that slavery just happened—and possibly that slaves were responsible for their own condition.

African American children can have a negative reaction to the topic of slavery drifting off into self-doubt or uncertainty as they comprehend the ramifications of slavery. In the absence of teaching about the roles and responsibilities of both Blacks and Whites during slavery—leaving essential parts unsaid—the victims can be blamed for the events.

It is therefore the role of educators to go beyond the popular biographies that appear on commercial calendars and promotional literature during the month of February and advance the knowledge and interests of all children to give them a historical perspective of African Americans. Immediately following the civil rights movement, primarily during the 1970s, there was a flurry of activities to integrate Black history into school materials. The first efforts were more cosmetic than substantive in that a percentage of the pictures of White children in textbooks then in use were colored brown, but the features of the children remained White.

From 1920 to 1921 W. E. B. Du Bois published *The Brownies Book* for young readers. Designed especially for Black children, this unusual periodical portrayed African American as attractive, intelligent, and important. Unattractive caricature of Blacks in advertisements, newspapers, magazines, and on picture post cards, were displayed by White artists of this period. Popular literature followed this pattern with stories of exaggerated and degrading Black stupidity and buffoonery. In *The Brownies Book,* Du Bois's careful attention to art work depicted Blacks as having attractive physical features and variations in skin tones. Articles, poetry, and stories, informed children about Black activists such as Sojourner Truth and Frederick Douglass. Du Bois's ambition to foster "refined Colored youngsters" was attempted through the magazine's emphasis on racial equality, self-esteem, racial solidarity, and political awareness.

Educators must maintain a critical consciousness about their methods and materials because the most appropriate ones are seldom the most easily available. A search through the professional literature for up-to-date curriculum ideas on a consistent basis is essential. All college and university campus libraries, and many public ones, have on-line access to the Educational Resources Information Center (ERIC) founded through funding from the U.S. Office of Education to provide access to a retrieval system of current research findings in education. ERIC has 16 clearing houses and a central office. The clearing houses are assigned an area of study such as information concerning the gifted, counseling, early childhood and the handicapped. Each clearing house prepares newsletters, catalogs, and indexed documents from researchers and learned societies, as well as proceedings from professional conferences.

*Resources in Education (RIE)* is a monthly and semiannual report published since 1969. More than 1,000 documents in RIE are abstracted which is furnished to libraries for use by professionals and the general public. Materials submitted to *RIE,* include presentations at professional meetings, federally funded research reports, literature from school district projects, and speeches given at professional meetings. The research findings of these documents are not reported in full but summarized. Most materials in *RIE* are also in the ERIC document microfiche collection available at universities, in state departments of education, and in many public schools.

The *Educational Index* (EI) references periodicals, monographs, and yearbooks. The *EI* indexes more than 300 educationally related journals for ten months of the year. It has been providing this service since 1929.

An example of what can be accessed through the ERIC system is the following information on Rosa Parks and the Montgomery bus boycott that many historians cite as the beginning of the 1960s civil rights movement. Herbert Kohl, in the *Journal of Education's* January 1, 1991 issue described an appropriate method of integrating the actual history of events into a curriculum that depicts an important period in U.S. history. Kohl provides information of the little known details that led lead to the boycott. Among other things, children will learn that other residents of Birmingham, Alabama, had defied the city's segregation ordinance.

Children's books are also an important source for curriculum ideas. *Nettie's Trip South* by Ann Turner, and illustrated by Ronald Himler, is an excellent children's book for home or the classroom for it would increase White children's awareness of the slavery period. White youngsters would learn how some children like themselves dealt with their knowledge of slavery and about the role of adults like their parents. Ann Turner uses the contents of her great-grandmother's diary to weave an intimate story of a young White girl's visit to the Old South from Albany, New York. She writes to a friend back home, "Addie, I can't get this out of my thoughts: If we slipped into a black skin like a tight coat, everything would change." The charcoal and pencil drawings enhance the depth of feeling that the words evoke. "There was a fat man in a tight white suit. There was a black woman on the platform. Someone called out a price and she was gone . . . like a sack of flower pushed across a store counter. And two children our age clasped hands but were bought by different men, and the man in the white hat had to tear them apart."

Other important books are available that provide an understandable and accurate view of slavery through biographical stories. *Freedom Train: The Harriet Tubman Story*, by D. Sterling, was written in the 1950s but remains potentially enjoyable and informative reading for any child above the third grade, especially the section that describes Tubman's childhood. It is a good read-to book for any child above preschool. *The Drinking Gourd,* by F. N. Monjo is a story about Tommy, a young White boy who comes upon a runaway slave family (mother and father, with a son about his age) in his family's barn. This is an informative book for beginning and intermediate readers, but it can be read to children in any grade. Illustrations by Fred Brenner help to make this an excellent book about the underground railroad.

Twelve Years a Slave: Excerpts from the Narrative of Solomon Northrup edited by Alice Lucas, is available in print and on audiotape. It is the story of a free African American living in New York who was kidnapped and sold into slavery in Louisiana. He regained his freedom in 1853, after 12 years of bondage. African American actor-singer Wendell Brooks sings work songs and spirituals of the period to add depth to the audio version. This is excellent primary source material for the study of slavery for all grades and even some college courses.

Award-winning authors Patricia McKissack and Floyd McKissack introduced the Great African American Series which includes biographies written for young readers in the elementary grades. The series includes Marian Anderson, the great singer; Louis Armstrong the great jazz trumpeter; Mary McLeod Bethune, the great teacher and presidential advisor; Ralph Bunche, the great peacemaker in the Middle East; George Washington Carver; the great scientist who discovered numerous uses for the peanut; Frederick Douglass, abolitionist and activist for women's rights; Martin Luther King, Jr., civil rights leader and man of peace; Mary Church Terrell, leader for equality; Ida B. Wells-Barnett, an activist against violence; and Carter G. Woodson, Black history scholar.

Frederick Douglass wrote a biographical account of his escape from slavery published as, *Escape from Slavery: The Boyhood of Frederick Douglass in His Own Words.* In a more recent publication, editor Michael McCurdy has attempted to make the Douglass story more accessible to young readers. McCurdy has skillfully selected eloquent and compelling passages from Douglass's original work written in 1845. McCurdy "kept Douglass' own words, spelling, and distinctive punctuation . . . and rearranged (them) for the sake of clarity." Each chapter is preceded with excellent commentary; however, Douglass's references to the cruelty of the most religious slave owners made in the original text, were missing from McCurdy's edited version. It is this latter point that led some reviewers to suggest that Douglass's original writing is superior because it blends history with social commentary. Reviewers also suggested that McCurdy's version could be considered redeemable if it encouraged young readers to seek out the original.

Paintings by the Black artist, Jacob Lawrence which date back to the 1940s, are used to illustrate *John Brown: One Man against Slavery*, by Gwen Everett. This book relates the story of the famous abolitionist who organized a group of Blacks and Whites to attack the U.S. government's arsenal at Harper's Ferry, Virginia. Some historians have suggested that this event along with other issues and incidences, precipitated the Civil War. A skillful teacher can use this story to introduce thought-provoking discussions among young children concerning groups and individuals who have used violent protests in just causes. Jacob Lawrence's work can be seen on public view from time to time in various galleries on college and university campuses and in public museums, as it occasionally tours the United States. Art exhibitions are usually mentioned in local newspapers in the art and entertainment sections, often with a feature story of artists and their work.

*From Africa to the Arctic: Five Explorers*, written by Esther and Donald Mumford and illustrated by Nancy Lee, is a book about early Black explorers of North America, including Estebanico, a Black Morrocan who explored the American Southwest seeking gold; Jim Beckwourth, who discovered the Western River Pass that bears his name; Stephen Bishop, explorer and scout who led exploration parties to the Mammoth Cave system in Kentucky; York, the slave who served as interpreter and provider for Meriwether Lewis and his master William Clark; and Matthew Henson, who along with Robert Peary explored the North Pole in 1909. This book provides informative and interesting material for advanced readers.

Another biographical approach to African American History can be found in *George Washington Carver, Plant Doctor*, was written by Mirna Benitez and illustrated by Meryl Henderson. This book is easily read and understood by beginning and intermediate readers. Carver is depicted as a scientist and concerned citizen who enabled many people to benefit from his work with the peanut plant.

*Runaway To Freedom*, by Barbara Smucher, is a story of the underground railroad. *Great Women in the Struggle*, edited by Toyomi Igus, provides single-page biographical sketches from the slavery period to our current time. Included are Black women artists, activists, poets, writers, entertainers, athletes, and educators.

*I Have a Dream: The Life and Works of Martin Luther King, Jr.*, written by Jim Haskins, is a photographical chronology that covers King's life from childhood to his murder. Vivid photographs of Blacks and Whites who were involved in the civil rights movement in the 1960s is told in words and pictures. *Martin Luther King Jr., Day* covers King's life and discusses our nation's purpose for creating a legal holiday on his birthday. The book has some interesting drawings and photographs, and beginning and intermediate readers would find this book interesting and would learn a lot from the text.

*Points of Rebellion,* by William O. Douglas, associate justice of the Supreme Court, is for intermediate readers. In the text Douglas identifies protest against pollution, poverty, segregation, and other social problems as justifiable activity for citizens.

*Aesop's Fables* contains 223 Aesop tales is illustrated by Arthur Rackham, well known for his illustrations in original publications that have become classics, including *The Arthur Rackham Fairy Book, Wind in the Willows,* and *Peter Pan in Kensington Gardens.* There is also *Aesop's Fables* by A. T. White, which has 40 selected fables from the Aesop repertoire and is illustrated by Helen Siegel. Another version,*The Fables of Aesop*, by R. Springs, is a large book of 143 Aesop fables illustrated by Frank Baber.

*The Leakey Family: Leaders in the Search for Human Origins*, by D. Willis is an excellent description of this famous family's work on our African origins. Suitable for intermediate readers, it could also be read to children beyond kindergarten.

There are several notable national programs that serve as public advocacy groups for Black and White children. In addition, every city and most communities have children's advocacy organizations that can provide excellent resources and information for classroom teachers. One program is the Children's Defense Fund (CDF), which has headquarters in Washington, D.C. This organization publishes an annual analysis regarding the status of children in the United States. It provides current data on children and families in crisis, childcare, child poverty, infant mortality, prenatal care, teen pregnancy, and related concerns. From available data, the CDF has devised a ranking system that reports the status of children and families on a state-by-state basis. The organization strives to keep the U.S. Congress and the executive branch of our government informed about child and family conditions on a national scale in an effort to influence national policy and encourage state as well as the federal government to be responsive to the needs of all children in the nation. In the 1990s the CDF organized The Black Community Crusade For Children, to inspire African American parents, educators, and professionals and others in the Black community to participate in education and action regarding the problems of Black children.

Another important organization the National Black Child Development Institution (NBCDI), is also headquartered in Washington, DC. Its mission is to "serve as a critical resource for improving the quality of life of African American children, youth, and families through direct services, public education programs, leadership training, and research." Founded in 1970, the NBCDI sponsors an annual conference attended by thousands of professionals as participants and presenters. Their primary focus is on early childhood.

It is essential that classroom teachers seek out materials and information from a variety of sources to enrich the curriculum by incorporating African American history in its proper places as a continuous process.

# REFERENCES

Aries, P. (1962). *Centuries of childhood.* New York: Knopf.

Babitt, I. (1919). *Rousseau and romanticism.* Boston: Houghton Mifflin.

Brubacher, J. S. (1966). *A history of the problems of education.* New York: McGraw-Hill.

Chilcoat, G. W. (1993). Teaching about the civil rights movement by using student-generated comic books. *Social Studies,* 84 (3), 113-118.

Curti, M. (1951). *The growth of American thought..* New York: Harper.

———. (1959). *The social ideas of American education.* Paterson, NJ: Littlefield.

Dewey, J. (1910). *The influence of Darwin on philosophy.* Bloomington, IN: Indiana University Press.

Dishon, D., & O'Leary, P. W. (1984). *A guidebook for cooperative learning.* Holmes Beach, FL: Learning Publications.

Erikson, E. (1950). *Childhood and society.* New York: W. W. Norton.

Froebel, F. (1899). *The education of man.* (Trans.: Josephine Jarvis) New York: Appleton.

Gesell, A. (1932). The Yale clinic of child development. *Childhood Education,* 8, 468-469.

Gesell, A., & Ilg, F. L. (1943). *Infant and child in the culture of today.* New York: Harper.

Hall, S. G. (1911). *Educational problems.* New York: Appleton.

Ichilov, O, & Shacham, M. (1994). Interethnic contacts with gifted, disadvantaged students: Effects on ethnic attitudes. Urban Education, 19 (3), 187-200.

Kohl, H. (1993). The myth of Rosa Parks the tired. Teaching about Rosa Parks and the Montgomery Bus Boycott. *Multicultural Education,* 1 (2), 6-10.

———. (1991). The politics of childrens' literature: The story of Roas Parks and the Montgomery bus boycott. *Journal of Education,* 173 (1) 35-50.

Reisner, E. H. (1930). *The evolution of the common school.* New York: Macmillan.

Sheehy, E. (1954). *The fives and sixes go to school.* New York: Henry Holt.

Stanford, G. (1977). *Developing effective classroom groups.* New York: Hart Publishing Company.

Thorndike, E. L. (1911). *Individuality.* Boston: Houghton-Mifflin.

# IX

# Summary

*I am the son of my father. I am father of my son. Son's father. Father's son. An interchangeability that is also dependence; the loss of one is the loss of both. I breathe into the space separating me from my son. I hope the silence will be filled for him as it is filled for me by hearing the nothing there is to say at this moment. I hope saying nothing is enough to grip the silence, twist it to our need. Which is holding on, not letting go. My breath in him. This temporary contact fallen into silence, into listening for the other's silence. Not because it is enough but because its all we have.*

—John Edgar Wideman

The family is the first and most important center of orientation for all children. How "family" is defined is the point of reference from which we can determine the extent to which the needs of children can be met. How relatives enact their family roles affect how children define their world. Infants require a caring and supportive environment created by adults who have the power and inclination to create such an environment, one where the infant's needs can be met. What these adults choose to call themselves is not as important as the environment they create for the child. The concepts *mother, father, brother, sister,* and so on are learned by the growing child as it becomes a part of society and interact with significant others in the community and in institutions to which its family is connected.

Children can feel accepted, loved and cared for in a variety of family settings. Some families might be structured nonconventionally but be quite conventional in providing for the needs of growing children. It is essential that children are provided opportunities to interact with others in an atmosphere of trust, cooperation, and a positive valuing of them as individuals. Such experiences enable children to develop a positive sense of self, to grow into mature reciprocal adults in their own right, and to pass on to *their* children similar opportunities. These generational respons-ibilities provide a pool of role models from which children can evaluate the world through their own behavior and the actions of significant others around them.

Families are imperfect, but adults should strive to provide an environment that is accepting, supporting, and caring. When children's interests begin to turn outward to the larger society, and as outsiders are included in children's experiences, the foundations built in the earlier years will enable children to cope with personal differences brought to their attention through taunts and comparisons made by others. Occasionally African American children will be reminded that their skin color is not the same as that of some other children. Some White children will be reminded that they live with two adults of the same gender, or a mother and a father of different races or religions. And children with uncommon names, or recent immigrants, will be made to feel different. The extent to which these children view their differences as deficits or become discouraged and reluctant will depend in part upon how they are reared. Early experiences that were accepting and supportive will provide a foundation of feelings of security with their present status. On the other hand, early experiences that fail to provide an appropriate environment can instill doubt in the minds of children regarding whatever differences are brought to their attention. Support systems during early growth are essential, but children also need supportive adults well into adolescence.

Contrary to popular wisdom, children *can* be raised by a single adult or by extended family members who participate in creating a positive envi-ronment. There are circumstances under which two-parent families and single-parent families are each dysfunctional. The most effective formula for the proper rearing of children is not always in the number of adults but in the quality of the living environment. Individuals cannot be fully protected from negative experiences, but they can be prepared to cope with experiences in the sense that they do not devalue their own role in an encounter; that is, they do not blame themselves when in fact they are blameless.

Our society continues to expand the ways it transmits information and to increase the speed with which that information can be transmitted. Our knowledge is increased and modified at a rate limited only by our own desire to be shut off from the media and from people. It has been reported that children spend more time watching television than they do in school. Consider that there is power inherent in the manner in which we —and our children— receive knowledge. Whether information comes from teachers, parents, peers, or strangers on a television screen, it inherits the power of the source. The printed word in books has more power and credibility than words printed in newspapers to describe an event. A television news program, with its live-action reporting, is more believable still, and thus it has more power, than for example, a TV commercial. For this reason, many products are now presented in what appears to be a serious "news talk show." Even though this comes after a printed disclaimer on the screen tells the viewing public that the show is commercial advertising, a large segment of the population is unable to detect the deception. Unfortunately, too many school teachers are in the category of the easily deceived. They are, therefore, unable to pass on to their students a sense of social and political awareness.

African American school children are taught that the early civilization known to have made critical contributions to our present-day Western society originated with the Greeks and Romans. The visual images that reinforce this information are images with which children cannot identify; thus they are images that deny Black children the opportunity to value their own image positively. The promotion of such Aryan omnipotence finds its way into all media images and pervades the marketplace. Such attitudes find their way into books and curriculum materials because they are so prevalent in the foundations of our institutions. Vivian Gussin Paley, in her book White Teacher, discusses an incident with a Black child in her classroom that illustrates this point.

Michelle, black and vivacious, pointed to a picture in a book I was reading to a small group and said, "I wished I looked like her." The "her" was a blond, pink-cheeked girl. I could have easily ignored this. Maybe Juli Ann, white and plain, wished she looked like the girl in the book too. When I was little, I know I would have wanted to look like her. But Michelle had a special obvious reason. I knew I must say something. "Michelle, I know how you feel. When I was little I also would have liked to look like this little girl. She doesn't look like anyone in my family, so I couldn't have looked like her. Sometimes, I wish I had smooth brown skin like yours. Then I could always be dark and pretty." Michelle looked down at her skin. So did everyone else. I don't know what she was thinking. But I knew the feelings that I had expressed were true, though I did not know it until I spoke. (Paley, 1979, pp. 12-13)

In radio and television news programs where "facts" are presented, "experts" are often called forth to add authenticity to a story. Experts who are consulted on nuclear physics, medicine, biophysics, and topics of an academic nature are usually White. Black experts are sought on issues of civil rights, segregation, teen pregnancy, delinquency, and the like. Growing and learning African American children are watching these depictions and are constructing their self-image. When Black adult images are presented on television, they are rarely more than entertainers on the light side of life. When people with whom African Americans can identify do appear, more often than not the program format is a presentation of the unusual or the exotic.

In many ways the German people have come face to face with the horror of the *Holocaust* in attempting to resolve its lingering effects by acknowledging responsibility. In the United States we have erected a permanent memorial in Washington, D.C., to inform each generation that the egregious acts of the Holocaust must never be allowed to happen again.

Martin Bernal (1990) wrote in *Black Athena*, that the "American colonies (had) twin policies of extermination of the Native Americans and the enslavement of African Blacks. (And) racism pervaded the thought of Locke, Hume and English thinkers." Yet, In the United States, neither our government nor our leaders have acknowledged in any permanent manner the more than 200 years of brutal treatment of African slaves in our country. Each year during the month of February, Black and White children are exposed to this insensitivity; but as Black History month closes, no acknowledgement comes forth, and no move toward resolution is made. We should not be surprised that when these children grow into adults, unsettled lingering issues result in discontent. We halfheartedly try to deal with them through school busing, affirmative action, and political correctness.

We have a competitive social and economic system that supports private initiative. African American children who do well in grade schools and universities, which almost always tout the Aryan model, can find a place of recognition for their achievements in society. Peers who have followed their same pathway will join them in regrouping. This new group can exist only by disengaging from African Americans in the larger society, except as consumers of their "products" that represent their success. Blacks in the lower-income residential areas are cut off from White and Black success models until they attain the financial requirements to "regroup" with those who have gone before them. The "left-behinds" in the African American ghetto are the children of the poor, the elderly, the poorly pensioned, the borderline mentally ill, and teens with children.

African Americans who have been able to negotiate the Aryan model successfully and earn a place for themselves in traditional institutions are being asked by organizations like the Children's Defense Fund, the National Urban League, and the NAACP to participate in the life of poor African American communities to help instill a sense of working for success, as someone probably did for them. There is a seductive will among "successful" African Americans to proclaim that they are "different" from those left behind, perhaps superior to them, despite the fact that they themselves have been admitted to a university because of a special program for minorities. Often their acknowledgement of special opportunities is pushed aside by denial.

Support for African Americans who for various reasons might find themselves rootless is embedded in Black history and mentioned by Frederick Douglass in his autobiography. "No young man starting in an untried field of usefulness, and needing support, could find that support in larger measure than I found it in William Whipper, Robert Purvis, William B. Powell, Nathan Johnson, Charles B. Ray, Thomas Downing, Theodore S. Wright or Charles S. Reason" (Douglass, 1982, p. 408).

Young African American adults who feel they have "made it" too often reject identifying with poor Blacks. They know how poor Blacks are condemned as unmotivated, uncaring, and unsuccessful by the group in which they themselves wish to maintain membership. A good example of this can often be found in city governments that have set up programs to assist the African American community. Initially, the programs are supervised by a White administrator who follows a set of guidelines that spell out traditional rules. Often these rules are so stringent that in order for the poor to receive grants, they must "out middle class the middle class." After a reasonable period of frustration, Black recipients may demand that the program change its leadership to enable a more "understanding" African American to be hired for the position.

After their demands are met, too often they find that the African American administrator has more conservative expectations than the White one did. The Black community's perception is often true because our nation's institutions and governments now have in place a selective system that will not permit African Americans to advance unless they live and work work in a White middle-class manner. Taking this cue, the Black administrator identifies more with the administrator who was asked to leave than with the people the program is designed to serve. This is only a small part of the general social process to which African American children and adults at all income levels are exposed.

What often happens to African American children in this process? They may identify with their roots and reject the messages of school and media, or they may accept those messages and reject images of neighborhood and home; or confused and frustrated, they may reject themselves.

A fourth-grade White teacher discussed one of her African American students with a group of colleagues in a graduate course on multicultural education. She explained that she had a very bright African American boy in the class, but she thought that he was a troubled child because he often appeared angry or sullen and could not look at her directly; rather, he always looked off to the side with an occasional glance in her direction. She knew he was smart because of selective things he did. He would complete only a part of an assignment, often the most difficult portion, as if to prove he could control his performance. "Was this a power thing?" she asked. She later remarked, "Maybe he just dislikes White people, so he seldom completes homework assignments." This teacher seemed sincere; she did a number of things with him in mind, like trying to develop an interesting topic of study, one that would provoke consistent responses to schoolwork.

It was during their first Black history month together that she informed her students they could design their own project.  Most students took the traditional approaches encouraged through school bulletin boards and the local media. This particular Black student chose to draw pictures of athletes for their in-class display. He insisted that he did not want his work to be displayed on the hallway bulletin board.  The teacher agreed because this was the first time that the child had shown an interest in a school project, and this one he would carry out on his own.

When his pictures were posted in the classroom, the Black child's artwork drew a great deal of attention from his classmates because the drawings depicted baseball players who were not among the most well known athletes.  After the students discussed their work in a class presentation, the teacher noticed that her "troubled" child started initiating several conversations with her, and she was pleased to pursue his questions to encourage the social interaction.   After a few days passed, one day when they were away from the others, he asked in a quiet tone what she thought was the *real* question of their interactions. "Miss Marshall, why is the president always White?"

The teacher was caught without an answer for that moment, but she gained tremendous insight into the social distance between herself and her student.  With this new perspective, the teacher's future planning could incorporate experiences that would enable this student to express his concerns about constructing a positive image of himself. Vivian Gussin, in *White Teacher,* described this phenomenon from her teaching experience.

As I watched and reacted to black children, I came to see a common need in every child. Anything a child feels is different about himself which cannot be referred to spontaneously, casually, naturally and uncritically by the teacher can become cause for anxiety and a obstacle to learning. (Paley, 1979, p. xv)

It is also true that classroom life involves the teacher's sense of self as a professional guiding the lives of children, and as an adult interacting with children as one would in family, in the community, and in other environments.

Paley also revealed that as a beginning teacher in a predominantly White school, she found it more comfortable to ignore racial diversity. "It was more comfortable to pretend the black child was white." It was also her view, that as a White teacher her inability to acknowledge and deal with racial differences early in her teaching career, "uncovered a serious flaw in my relationship with all children."

As professionals, we do not know the extent to which our own childhood growth and development might have contributed to who we are as professionals, parents, neighbors, or friends to others. Paley reported that it was only  as an adult, in a conversation with her own mother, that childhood  memories of feeling less than comfortable in school surfaced.

I was trying to explain how I felt being one of the few Jewish children in our elementary school, and I told her of my fears of being an outsider. She was astonished. She told me that more than a third of the school was Jewish, and insisted that I was a very confident child and proud of my heritage. It was difficult for her to accept my memories. I could see why I never told anyone how I felt when I was a child. Even now, I was feeling guilty. (Paley, 1979, p. 11)

African American children need  learning environments that respond to their sense of self,  that let them know that what they do is important. They also need a sense of their place in history, told accurately and told well. They need advocacy groups that actively pursue their interests and are persistent in calling attention to circumstances under which their needs are not met.

Too many African American children become trapped in a legal justice system because their combination of problems, such as abandonment, suspension from school, and inconsistent places of residence, are too complex for a single agency to handle alone. When agency services are not coordinated, which is often the case, the problems for such children become impossible for them to resolve. However, when children end up in court, the mere presence of an interested adult family member can mean the difference between going home or going to jail.

In their effort to retrieve some positive sense of self, all children who are negatively valued by their school will occasionally seek support from a group whose members have experienced similar rejections. Sometimes such groups are labeled "gangs," when in fact they are merely a  loosely knit support group.  The first step toward wanting to be in a gang is taken when children feel they cannot conform to the values inherent in the demands made upon them by the school.  This can manifest itself by children being placed in low-skilled reading groups because they have not quite figured out the phonetic code.  These are the times when such children might develop their own values, ones that will make them  feel important.  It should not surprise us that when children choose their own values, often they chose values contrary to the ones  preferred by teachers and schools. Thus a youngster might value being highly regarded for pushing a teacher or for serving time in jail.  The young person's  group might respect these acts of defiance against an institution that has the strong support of the society that, in their view, has shut them out.  The road to this final set of circumstances should be interrupted before our youth reach the point of intractability.

Too often the problems encountered by African American children are the subtle kind that emerge from teacher expectations and hidden racist attitudes. Paley (1979) remembered the first time Black children were admitted to a predominantly White school where she taught. She described the responses of some of her colleagues after two Black children were assigned to her classroom.

One by one the first week all the teachers came by to check out the two black children. That is not what they said they were doing, but that was what they were doing. Fred had quickly become part of an aggressive little group of seven. Every time someone walked in, these restless children could be found grabbing, yelling, arguing, pushing, and running. The six white children in the group received scant notice, but a comment was always made about Fred. "You've got your hands full with him." "Shouldn't he be in a special class?" Nothing was said about Valerie who had discovered the art corner the first day and hardly left the painting table for six weeks. Only Fred drew an immediate and consistent  response. He already had a reputation. Actually, John, Keith, Raymond,  David, Michael, and Denise behave just as Fred did. The differences were mainly color. (Paley, 1979,  pp. 6-7)

In the struggle among professionals for power and influence, it has become commonplace to publish the results of various studies depicting deficiencies among African American children and to describe their dysfunctional  families and neighborhoods.  Imagine the benefits that would accrue if resources provided to researchers and blue ribbon panels of various sorts were applied directly to solving  problems, as opposed to merely studying them hundreds of times.  Too often activities funded in the name of children and families are really intended for private gain or the benefit of an exclusive group.

The direction and intent of resources for programs like Head Start need a reexamination.  The true status and impact of such programs need to be better understood by the public. A great disparity exists between the benefits these programs are capable of providing and the resources appropriated to enable such programs to reach their maximum potential. The reluctance to fund such programs adequately is the result of an intermix of complex issues.  The popularized notion that African American children have limited I.Q.s and therefore cannot benefit fully from academic programs is laced with our reluctance to provide early care for the children of poor mothers.  Many members of the American scientific community have responded well to the faulty and sometimes fake investigations of intelligence that lead to a reporting  of Black negative-White positive results which have misguided public policy.  Often  it is still difficult for the facts to overtake the fancy. Very few of today's graduate students in the universities, for example, are aware of the falsifications in Sir Cyril Burt's studies that were reported up through the 1970s  and cited by Jensen and Herrnstein in support of their Black-White I.Q. articles.

Professor Alfred E. Mirsky of Rockefeller University  reminded us in 1971 that "when the scientist writes for the layman about race he has a responsibility not only to science but also to society, for that subject is socially and politically explosive. The scientist must adhere to standards of caution, distinguished between established fact, and willful fancy." African American children are always watching.

## REFERENCES

Bernal, M. (1990). *Black Athena.* New Jersey: Rutgers University Press.

Douglass, F. (1892). *Life and times of Frederick Douglass: Written by himself.* New York: Crowell-Collier Publishing Company. (Reprinted 1962)

Mirsky, A. E. (June 18, 1971). Science for laymen (Letter to editor). *The New York Times*, p. 36.

Paley, V. G. (1979). *White teacher.* Boston, MA: Harvard University Press.

Wideman, J. E. (1990). *Philadelphia fire.* New York: Henry Holt and Company.

# Selected Bibliography

Abubadika, M.I. (1972). *The education of Sonny Carson.* New York: W. W. Norton.

Achenbach, T. (1978). *Research in development psychology: Concepts, strategies, methods.* Riverside, NJ: The Free Press

Adler, M. J. (1982). *The Paideia proposal: An educational manifesto.* New York: Macmillan.

Ainsworth, M. (1979). *Patterns of attachment.* New York: Halstead Press.

Alba, R. D. (1990). *Ethnic identity; The transformation of White America.* New Haven, CT: Yale University Press.

Allen, K. E., Hart, B. M., Buell, J. S., Harris, F. R., & Wolf, M. M. (1964). Effect of social reinforcement on the isolate behavior of a nursery school child. *Child Development, 35,* 511-518.

Altshuler, A. A. (1970). *Community control: The black demand for participation in large American cities.* New York: Pegasus.

Ames, L. B., & Ilg, F. L. (1964). Gesell behavior tests as predictive of later grade placement. *Perceptual and Motor Skills, 19,* 719-722.

Anastasi, A. (1958). *Heredity, environment, and the question "how?"* Psychological Review, *65,* 167-208.

Anrig, G. R., Goertz, M. E., & McNeil, R. C. (1986). Teacher competency testing: Realities of supply and demand in this period of educational reform. *Journal of Negro Education, 55,* 316-325.

Antler, J. (1987). *Lucy Sprague Mitchell: The making of a modern woman.* New Haven: Yale University Press.

Apple, M. W. & Christian-Smith, L. K. (Eds.). (1991). *The politics of textbooks.* New York: Routledge.

Aptheker, H. (Ed.). (1973). *The collected published works of W. E. B. Du Bois* (38 Vols.). Millwood, NY: Kraus.

Assante, M. K. (1987). *The Afrocentric idea.* Philadelphia: Temple University Press.

Ausubel, D., & Sullivan, E. (1970). *Theory and problems of child development.* New

York: Grune & Startton.

Baer, D. (1976). An age-irrelevent concept of development. *Merrill Palmer Quarterly, 16,* 238-245.

Baldwin, J. (1963). *Notes of a native son.* New York: Dial Press.

Bandura, A. (1977). S*ocial learning theory.* Englewood Cliffs, NJ: Prentice-Hall.

———. (1969). *Principles of behavior modification.* New York: Holt, Rinehart & Winston.

Banks, J. A. (1988). *Multiethnic education: Theory and practice.* Boston: Allyn & Bacon.

Banks, J. A., & Grambs, J. D. (1972). *Black self-concept: Implications for education and social science.* New York: McGraw-Hill.

Bantock, G. H. (1965). *Education and values.* New York: Faber.

Barash, D. P. (1977). *Sociology and behavior.* New York: Elsevier.

Barbour, F. B. (1970). *The Black seventies.* Boston: Porter Sargent Publishers.

Barnes, E. J. (1980). The Black community as the source of positive self-concept for Black children: A theoretical perspective. In R. L. Jones (Ed.), *Black Psychology* (2nd ed.) New York: Harper & Row.

Bayley, N. (1955). On the growth of intelligence. *American Psychologist, 10,* 805-818.

Beard, R. (1969). *An outline of Piaget's developmental psychology.* New York: Basic Books.

Bereiter, C. (1972). An academic preschool for disadvantaged children: Conclusions from evaluation studies. In J. C. Stanley (Ed.), *Preschool programs for the disadvantaged.* Baltimore: Johns Hopkins University Press.

Bereiter, C., & Kurland, M. (1981). A constructive look at follow through results. *Interchange, 12,* 1-22.

Beswick, R. (1990). Racism in America's schools. *ERIC Digest Series,* EA 49.

Bettelheim, B. (1977). *The uses of enchantment.* New York: Random House.

Biber, B. (1984). *Early education and psychological development.* New Haven, CT: Yale University Press.

Bijou, S. (1968). Ages, stages, and the naturalization of human development. *American Psychologist, 23,* 419-427.

Billingsley, A. (1968). *Black families in White America.* Englewood Cliffs, NJ: Prentice-Hall.

Birnbrauer, J. S., Wolf, M. M., Kidder, J. D., & Tague, C. E. (1965). Classroom behavior of retarded pupils with token reinforcement. *Journal of Experimental Child Psychology, 2,* 219 - 235.

Blackstone, T. (1971). *A fair start: The provision of preschool education.* Cambridge, England: W. H. Heffer & Sons.

Blassinggame, J. W. (1972). *The slave community: Plantation life in the Antebellum South.* New York: Oxford University Press.

Blauner, B. (1989). *Black lives, White lives.* Berkeley: University of California Press.

Bloom, J. M. (1987). *Class, race, and the civil rights movement.* Bloomington: Indiana University Press.

Blum, J. M. (1978). *Pseudoscience and mental ability: The origins and fallacies of the IQ controversy.* New York: Monthly Review Press.

Bredekamp, S. (1987). *Developmentally appropriate practice in early childhood programs serving children from birth through age 8.* Washington, DC: National

Association for the Education of Young Children.

Bridges, K. (1933). A study of social development in early infancy. *Child Development, 4,* 36-49.

Brody, G. H., & Zimmerman, B. J. (1975). The effects of modeling and classroom organization on the personal space of third and fourth grade children. *American Educational Research Journal, 12* (2), 157-168.

Broman, S. H. (1975). *Preschool IQ: Prenatal and early developmental correlates.* Hillsdale, NJ: Lawrence Erlbaum Associates.

Bronfenbrenner, U. (1977). Toward an experimental psychology of human develop ment. *American Psychologist, 32,* 513-531.

Bronowski, J. (1973). *The ascent of man.* Boston: Little, Brown.

Bruce,T. (1984). A Froebelian looks at Montessori's work. *Early Child Development and Care, 14,* 75-84.

Bryant, D. M., & Clifford, R. M. (1992). 150 years of kindergarten: How far have we come? *Early Childhood Research Quarterly, 7,* 147-155.

Burrow, R. (1992). Some African American males' perspectives on the Black woman. *Western Journal of Black Studies, 16* (2), 64-73.

Bushel, D., Jr., Wrobel, P. A., & Michaelis, M. L. (1968). Applying "group contingencies" to the classroom study behavior of preschool children. *Journal of Applied Behavior Analysis, 1,* 55-61.

Caditz, J. (1976). *White liberals in transition.* New York: Halsted Press.

Callahan, R. (1982). *Education and the cult of efficiency.* Chicago: University of Chicago Press.

Campbell, A. (1971). *White attitudes toward Black people.* Ann Arbor, MI: ISR.

Case, R., & Bereiter, C. (1984). From behaviorism to cognitive behaviorism to cognitive development: Steps in the evolution of instructional design. *Instructional Science, 13,* 141-158.

Chase-Riboud, B. (1994). *The president's daughter.* New York: Crown Publishers.

Chattin-McNichols, J. P. (1981). The effects of Montessori school experience. *Young Children, 36,* 49-65.

Cheatham, H. E., & Stewart, J. B. (1990). *Black families: interdisciplinary perspectives.* NJ: Transaction Publishers.

Clark, K. (1965). *Dark ghetto: Dilemmas of social power.* New York: Harper & Row.

Clark, K. B., & Clark, M. (1947). Racial identification and preferences in Negro children. In T. M. Newcomb & E. L. Hartley (Eds.), *Readings in social psychology.* New York: Holt, Rinehart & Winston.

Clark, R. (1983). *Family life and school achievement: Why poor Black children succeed or fail.* Chicago: University of Chicago Press.

Cloward R. A., & Piven, F. F. (1974). *The politics of turmoil: Essays on poverty, race, and the urban crisis.* New York: Pantheon Books.

———. (1991). Race and the Democrats. *The Nation, 233 (20),* 737-740.

Coles, R. (1967). It's the same but it's different. In T. Parsons & K.B. Clark (Eds.), *The Negro American.* Boston: Beacon Press.

Conrad, E. E. (1974). *Peer tutoring: A cooperative learning experience.* Tucson: ACERD, University of Arizona.

Cowan, P. (1978). *Piaget: With feeling.* New York: Holt, Rinehart & Winston.

Cremin, L. (1961). *The transformation of the school: Progressivism in American education, 1876-1957.* New York: Knopf.

Cross, W. (1978). Black families and Black identity: A literature review. *Western Journal of Black Studies, 2,* 111-124.

Crouse, J., & Trusheim, D. (1988). *The case against the SAT.* Chicago: University of Chicago Press.

Cruickshank, D., & Kennedy, J. (1981). Beliefs about teaching in Montessori and non-Montessori preschool teachers. *Journal of Teacher Education, 32,* 41-44.

Cummings, S. (1977). Family socialization and fatalism among Black adolescents. *Journal of Negro Education, 46,* 62-75.

Darder, A. (1991). *Culture and power in the classroom.* Westport, CT: Bergin & Garvey.

Datan, & Reese, H. W. (1977). *Life span developmental psychology: Dialectical perspectives on experimental on experimental research.* New York: Academic Press.

Deasey, D. (1978). *Education under six.* New York: St. Martin's Press.

Debus, P. C. (1970). Effects of brief observation of model behavior on conceptual tempo of impulsive children. *Developmental Psychology, 2,* 22-32.

Deegan, M. J. (1988). Du Bois and the women of Hull House, 1895-1899. *American Sociologist, 19* (4), 301-311.

Denko, J. D. (1977). *Through the keyhole at gifted men and women: A study of 159 adults of high IQ.* Ann Arbor, MI: Published for Mensa Education and Research Foundation by University Microfilms International.

Derman-Sparks, L. (1989). *Anti-bias curriculum: Tools for empowering young children.* Washington, DC: National Association for the Education of Young Children.

Detlefsen, R. R. (1991). *Civil rights under Reagan.* San Francisco, CA: ICS Press.

Dewey, J. (1916). *Democracy and education.* New York: Macmillan.

DeWitt, K. (1992). The nation's schools learn a 4th R: Resegregation. *The New York Times,* January 19, p. E5.

DiBacco, T. V. (1987). Four Black Americans: How learning made a difference. *Learning, 15* (6), 46-47.

Di Leonardo, M. (1991). Racial fairy tales. *The Nation, 253 (20),* 752-754.

Diop, C. A. (1974). *The African origin of civilization: Myth or reality?* New York: Lawrence Hill.

Downs, A. (1973). *Opening up the suburbs: An urban strategy for America.* New Haven, CT: Yale University Press.

Dreyer, A. S., & Rigler, D. (1969). Cognitive performance in Montessori and nursery school children. *Journal of Educational Research, 62,* 411-416.

D'Souza, D. (1991). Illiberal education. *Atlantic Monthly, March,* pp. 51-79.

Dubanowski, R. A., & Parton, D. A. (1971). Imitative aggression in children as a function of observing a human model. *Developmental Psychology, 4,* 489.

Du Bois, W. E. B. (1962) *Black reconstruction in American 1860-1880: An essay toward a history of the part which Black folk played in the attempt to reconstruct democracy in America, 1860-1880.* New York: Atheneum. (Original work published 1935).

————. (1969). *The suppression of the African slave trade to the United States of America, 1638-1870, Baton Rouge, LA: Louisiana State University Press.* (Original work published 1896).

Dunn, F. (1993). The educational philosophies of Washington, Du Bois, and Houston: Laying the foundations for Afrocentrism and multiculturalism. *Journal of Negro education, 62* (1), 24-34.

Dupre, B. B. (1986). Problems regarding the survival of future Black teachers in education. *Journal of Negro Education, 55*, 56 - 66.

Edwards, A., & Polite, C. K. (1992). *Children of the dream.* New York: Doubleday.

Eitzen, D. S. (1975). Athletics in the status system of male adolescents: A replication of Coleman's "the adolescent society." *Adolescence, 10*, 267-276.

Ellis, S., Rogoff, B., & Cromer, C. (1981). Age segregation in children's social interactions. *Developmental Psychology, 17*, 399-407.

Erikson, E. (1968). *Identity: Youth in crisis.* New York: W. W. Norton.

Evans, B. (1981). *IQ and mental testing: An unnatural science and its social history.* Atlantic Highlands, NJ: Humanities Press.

Evans, E. (1983). Curriculum models and early childhood education. In B. Spodek (Ed.), *Handbook of research in early childhood education.* New York: Free Press.

Fagot, B. I. (1978). Reinforcing contingencies for sex-role behaviors: Effects of experience with children. *Child Development, 49*, 30-36.

Fancher, R.E. (1985). *The intelligence men: Makers of the IQ controversy.* New York: W.W. Norton.

Finch, M. (1981). *The NAACP: Its fight for justice.* Metuchen, NJ: Scarecrow Press.

Fiske, E. B. (1988). America's test mania. *The New York Times, Education Life,* April 10, pp. 16-20.

Foner, P. S. (1983). *History of Black Americans: From the emergence of the cotton kingdom to the eve of the compromise of 1850.* Westport, CT: Greenwood Press.

Ford, M. D. (1991). Defending the common school. *The Nation, 253 (20),* 748-752.

Fordham, S. (1988). Racelessness as a factor in Black students' school success: Pragmatic Strategy or Pyrrhic history? *Harvard Educational Review, 58*, 54-84.

———. (1991). Racelessness in private schools: Should we deconstruct the racial and cultural identity of African-American adolescents? *Teachers College Record, 92*, 470-484.

Fordham, S., & Ogbu, J. (1986). Black students' school success: Coping with the burden of 'acting White.' *The Urban Review, 18,* 176-206.

Forman, J. (1991). Saving affirmative action. *The Nation, 253 (20),* 746-748.

Formisano, R. (1991). *Boston against busing: Race, class, and ethnicity in the 1960s and 1970s.* Chapel Hill: University of North Carolina Press.

Frazier, E. F. (1963). *The Negro church in America.* Liverpool: University of Liverpool.

Friese, K. (1990). *Rosa Parks: The movement organizer.* NJ: Silver Burdett.

Froebel, F. (1889). *The education of man.* New York: D. Appleton. (Original work published 1826.)

Fry, E. B. (1971). Programmed instruction: An introduction. In C.E. Pitts (Ed.), *Operant conditioning in the classroom.* New York: Thomas Y. Crowell.

Gagne, R. M., & Briggs, L. J. (1974). *Principles of instructional design.* New York: Holt, Rinehart & Winston.

Gates, H. L. (1993). *Colored people.* New York: Alfred A. Knopf.

Genovese, E. D. (1972). *Roll Jordan roll: The world the slaves made.* New York: Pantheon.

Gerda, L. (1973). *Black women in White America.* New York: Vintage Press.

Gersten, R., & Carnine, D. (1984). Direct instruction mathematics: A longitudinal evaluation of low-income elementary school students. *Elementary School Journal, 84*, 395-407.

Geshuri, Y. (1975). Discriminative observational effects of observed reward and dependency. *Child Development, 46*, 550-554.

Gibson, M. A., & Ogbu, T. J. (1991). *Minority status and schooling: A comparative study of immigrant and involuntary minorities.* New York: Garland Publishing Company.

Gifford, B. R. (1986). Excellence and equity in teacher competency testing: A policy perspective. *Journal of Negro Education, 55*, 251-271.

Glasgow, D. (1980). *The Black underclass.* New York: Vintage Books.

Goings, K. W. (1990). *The NAACP comes of age: The defeat of judge John J. Parker.* Bloomington: Indiana University Press.

Goldman, J. (1981). The social participation of preschool children in same-age versus mixed-age groupings. *Child Development, 52*, 644-650.

Gollnick, D. M., & Chinn, P. C. (1983). *Multicultural education in a pluralistic society.* St. Louis: Mosby.

Goodenough, F. L. (1930). Inter-relationships in the behavior of young children. *Child Development, 1*, 29-47.

Goodlad, J. L. (1984). *A place called school: Prospects for the future.* New York: McGraw-Hill.

Goodykoontz, B. (1948). Recent history and present status of the education of young children. In N. B. Henry (Ed.), *The forty-sixth yearbook of the national study for the science of education: Part II. Early childhood education* (pp.1222-1236). Chicago: University of Chicago Press.

Gordon, T. A. (1978). The Black adolescent. In L. E. Gary (Ed.), *Mental health: A challenge to the Black community.* Philadelphia: Dorrance & Co.

Gottfried, A. E., & Katz, S. A. (1977). Influence of belief, race, and sex similarities between child observers and models on attitudes and observational learning. *Child Development, 48*, 1395-1400.

Gould, S. J. (1977). *Ever since Darwin.* New York: Norton.

———. (1979). *Transformations.* New York: Simon & Schuster.

———. (1980). *The panda's thumb.* New York: Norton.

Graziano, W., French, D., Brownell, C. A., & Hartup, W. W. (1976). Peer interactions in same-age versus mixed-age groupings in relation to chronological age and incentive condition. *Child Development, 47*, 707-714.

Green, D. S. & Smith, E. (1983). W. E. B. Du Bois and the concepts of race and class. *Phylon, 44* (4), 262-272.

Greenberg, P. (1987). Lucy Sprague Mitchell: A major missing link between early childhood education in the 1980s and progressive education in the 1890s - 1930s. *Young Children, 42* (5), 70-84.

———. (1990). Head Start—part of a multi-pronged anti-poverty effort for children and their families before the beginning: A participant's view. *Young Children, 45* (6), 40-52.

Hacker, A. (1992). *Two nations.* New York: Charles Scribner's Sons.

Hall, G. S., & Harrison, E. (1907). *The content of children's minds.* Boston: Ginn. (1924). The growth of the kindergarten in the United States. In International Kindergarten Union: Committee of Nineteen (Eds.), *Pioneers of the kindergarten in America.* New York: Century.

Harding, V. (1981). *There is a river: The Black struggle for freedom in America.* New York: Vintage.

Hauser, S. (1971). *Black and White identity formation.* New York: Wiley.

Herzog, A. (1978). *IQ 83.* New York: Simon & Schuster.

Hess, R. D. & Shipman, V. C. (1965). Early experience and the socialization of cognitive modes in children. *Child Development, 34,* 869-889.

Higginbotham, A. (1978). *In the matter of color, race and the American legal process: The colonial period.* New York: Oxford University Press.

Hill, P. S. (1987). The function of the kindergarten. *Young Children, 42* (5), 12-20.

Hill, R. (1971). *The strengths of Black families.* New York: Emerson Hall.

Hilliard, A. G., III. (1986). From hurdles to standards of quality in teacher testing. *Journal of Negro Education, 55,* 304-315.

Hochschild, J. L. (1984). *The new American dilemma: Liberal democracy and school desegregation.* New Haven, CT: Yale University Press.

Hoffmann, B. (1962). *The tyranny of testing.* New York: Crowell-Collier.

House, E., Glass, G., McClean, L. D., & Wood, C. T. (1978). No simple answer: Critique of the follow through evaluation. *Harvard Educational Review, 48,* 123-160.

Huber, T. & Kline, F. (1993). Attitude toward diversity: Can teacher education programs really make a difference? *Teacher Educator, 29* (1), 15-23.

Hughes, M. M. (May 1958). Teaching is interaction. *Elementary School Journal, 58,* 117-125.

Hunt, J. McVicker. (1961). *Intelligence and experience.* New York: Ronald.

Hunt, J., & Hunt, L. (1977). Racial inequality and self-image: Identity maintenance as identity diffusion. *Sociology and Social Research, 61,* 539-559.

Jenkins, A. (1982). *The psychology of the Afro-American.* New York: Pergamon.

Johnson, C. S. (1941). *Growing up in the Black belt: Negro youth in the rural south.* Washington, DC: American Council on Education.

Johnson, J., Koester, L., & Wanska, S. (1984). Preschoolers' social and task-oriented behaviors in multi-age small groups. *Child Study Journal, 14* (3), 237-249.

Joseph, A. (1977). *Intelligence, IQ, and race: When, how, and why they became associated.* San Francisco: R & E Associates.

Judd, D. R. (1991). Segregation forever? *The Nation, 233 (20),* 740-744.

Katznelson, I. (1973). *Black men, White cities.* New York: Oxford University Press.

Keller, M. F., & Carlson, S. M. (1974). The use of symbolic modeling to promote social skills in preschool children with low levels of social responsiveness. *Child Development, 45,* 912-919.

Kellogg, C. F. (1967). *NAACP: A history of the National Association for the Advancement of Colored People.* Baltimore: Johns Hopkins University Press.

Kilpatrick, W. E. (1914). *The Montessori system examined.* Boston: Houghton-Mifflin.

Kilson, M. (1981). Black social classes and intergenerational poverty. *The Public Interest, 64,* 58-78.

King, J. E., & Mitchell, C. A. (1990). *Black mothers to sons: Juxtaposing African American literature with social practice.* New York: Lang.

Kirp, D. L. (1982). *Just schools: The idea of racial equality in American education*. Berkeley: University of California Press.

Ladson-Billings, G. (1991). Beyond multicultural illiteracy. *Journal of Negro Education, 60* (2), 147-157.

Lazar, I. (1977). *The persistence of preschool effects: A long term follow up of fourteen infant and preschool experiments*. Washington, DC: Administration for Children, Youth, and Families.

Lee, C. C. (1984). Successful rural Black adolescents: A psychosocial profile. *Adolescence, 20*, 129-142.

Lefrancois, G. (1986). *Of children* (3rd ed.). Belmont, CA: Wadsworth.

Levitan, S. A. (1975). *Still a dream: The changing status of Blacks since 1960*. Cambridge, MA: Harvard University Press.

Liederman, S. H., & Liederman, G. F. (1974). Affective and cognitive consequences of polymatric infant care in the East African highlands. In A. D. Pick (Ed.), *Minnesota symposia on child psychology* (Vol. 8). Minneapolis: University of Minnesota Press.

Lightfoot, S. (1975). Families and schools: Creative conflict or dissonance? *Journal of Research and Development in Education, 9* (1), 34-44.

Lillard, P. P. (1973). *Montessori: A modern approach*. New York: Schocken Books.

Lindvall, C. H. & Bolvin, J. O. (1967). Programmed instruction in the schools. *Programmed instruction*. Chicago: University of Chicago Press.

Litwack, L., & Meier. (1988). *Black leaders of the nineteenth century*. Chicago: University of Illinois.

Locurto, C. M. (1991). *Sense and nonsense about IQ: The case for uniqueness*. New York: Praeger.

Lougee, M. D. (1979). Age relations and young children's social interactions. *Journal of Research and Development in Education, 13*, 32-41.

Lukas, J. A. (1985). *Common ground: A turbulent decade in the lives of three American families*. New York: Knopf.

MacLeod, J. (1987). *Ain't no makin' it*. Boulder, CO: Westview Press.

Mallory, N. J. & Goldsmith, N. A. (1990). Head Start works! Two Head Start veterans share their views. *Young Children, 45* (6), 36-40.

Massey, D. S. & Denton, N. A. (1993). *American apartheid*. Cambridge, MA: Harvard University Press.

Mbiti, J. S. (1970). *African religions and philosophies*. Garden City, NY: Anchor Books, Doubleday.

McMillen, N. R. (1989). *Dark journey*. Chicago: University of Illinois Press.

McPhail, I. P. (1987). Literacy as a liberating experience. *English Quarterly, 20* (1), 9-15.

McPherson, J. M. (1975). *The abolitionist legacy: From reconstruction to the NAACP*. Princeton, NJ: Princeton University Press.

Meier, A. & Rudwick, E. (1986). *Black history and the historical profession 1915-1980*. Urbana, IL: University of Illinois Press.

Meier, K., Stewart, J., & England, R. (1989). *Race, class and education: The politics of second-generation discrimination*. Madison: University of Wisconsin Press.

Mensh, E. (1991). *The IQ mythology: Class, race, gender, and inequality*. Carbondale: Southern Illinois University Press.

Meyer, L. A. (1984). Long-term academic effects of the direct instruction project follow through. *Elementary School Journal, 84,* 380-394.

Miller, L. B. & Bizzell, R. P. (1983). Long-term effects of four preschool programs: Sixth, seventh, and eighth grades. *Child Development, 54,* 727-741.

Miller, L. B. & Dyer, J. L. (1975). Four preschool programs: Their dimensions and effects. *Monographs of the Society for Research on Child Development,* (Serial No. 162), Nos. 5-6.

Milner, D. (1983). *Children and race.* Beverly Hills, CA: Sage.

Montague, A. (Ed.). (1975). *Race and IQ.* New York: Oxford University Press.

Mooney, C. J. (1991, Nov. 6). Study finds professors are still teaching the classics, sometimes in new ways. *Chronicle of Higher Education, 38* (2).

Moynihan, D. (1969). *Maximum feasible misunderstanding: Community action in the war on poverty.* New York: Free Press.

Murray, H. (1987). Du Bois and the Cold War. *Journal of Ethnic Studies,* 15 (3), 115-124.

Musick, J., & Householder, J. (1986). *Infant development: From theory to practice.* Belmont, CA: Wadsworth.

Myers, B., & Maurer, K. (1987). Teaching with less talking: Learning centers in the kindergarten. *Young Children, 42* (5), 20-27.

Nash, G. B. (1982). *Red, White and Black: The peoples of early America.* Englewood Cliffs, NJ: Prentice-Hall.

Nobles, W. (1974). African root and American fruit: The Black family. *Journal of Social and Behavioral Sciences, 20,* 66-77.

Noel, P. (1991). Black heart, White hunter. *The Village Voice, 36* (35), 37-41.

Oberle, W., Stowers, K., & Falk, W. (1978). Place of residence and the role model preferences of Black boys and girls. *Adolescence, 13,* 13 - 20.

Ogbu, J. U. (1981). Human competence: A cultural ecological perspective. *Child Development, 52* (2), 413-429.

———. (1983). Schooling the inner city. *Society, 21* (1), 75-79.

———. (1983). Status of schooling in plural societies. *Comparative Education Review, 27* (2), 198-190.

———. (1985). Research Currents: Cultural-ecological influences on minority school learning. *Language Arts, 62* (8), 860-869.

———. (1992). Adaptation to minority status and impact on school success. *Theory into Practice, 31* (4), 287-295.

———. (1992). Understanding cultural diversity and learning. *Educational Researcher, 21* (8), 5-14.

Orem, R. C. (1971). *Montessori today.* New York: Capricorn Books.

Orfield, G. (1978). *Why must we bus? Segregated schools and national policy.* Washington, DC: Brookings Institution.

Orr, E. W. (1987). *Twice as less: Black English and the performance of Black students in mathematics and science.* New York: W. W. Norton.

Papert, S. (1980). *Mindstorms: Children, computers, and powerful Ideas.* New York: Basic Books.

Parker, S. C., & Temple, A. (1925). *Unified kindergarten and first-grade teaching.* Boston: Ginn.

Parten, M. B. (1932). Social participation among children. *Journal of Abnormal and Social Psychology, 27,* 243-269.

Peeps, J. M. & Stephen, (1981). Northern philanthropy and the emergence of

Black higher education: Do gooders, compromisers, or co-conspirators? *Journal of Negro Education, 50* (3), 251-269.

Pendergast, R. (1969). Pre-reading skills development in Montessori and conventional nursery schools. *Elementary School Journal, 70,* 71-77.

Perlo, V. (1975). *Economics of racism U.S.A.* New York: International Publishers.

Perrone, V. (1991). *On standardized testing: A position paper.* Wheaton, MD: Association of Childhood Education International.

Perry, R., & Williams, P. (1991). Freedom of hate speech. *Tikkun,* July/August, pp. 55-57.

Pfeffer, P. F. (1990). *A. Philip Randolph, pioneer of the civil rights movement..* Baton Rouge, LA: Louisiana State University Press.

Piaget, J. (1932). *The origins of intelligence in children.* New York: International Universities Press.

————. (1970). *Science of education and the psychology of the child* (D. Coltman, Trans.). New York: Orion Press.

Piaget, J., & Inhelder, B. (1969). *The psychology of the child.* New York: Basic Books.

Piliawsky, M. (1984). Racial equality in the United States: From institutional racism to respectable racism. *Phylon, 45* (2), 134-143.

Piven, F. F. & Cloward, R.A. (1971). *Regulating the poor: The functions of public welfare.* New York: Pantheon Books.

————. (1977). *Poor people's movements: Why they succeed, how they fail.* New York: Pantheon Books.

————. (1982). *The new class war: Reagan's attack on the welfare state and its consequences.* New York: Pantheon Books.

Plato. (1945). *The republic of Plato* (F. M. Cornford, Trans.). New York: Oxford University Press.

Powell, D. (1989). *Families and early childhood programs.* Washington, DC: National Association for the Education of Young Children.

Rainwater, L. (1967). Crucible of identity: The Negro lower-class family. In T. Parsons & K. B. Clark (Eds.), *The Negro American.* Boston: Beacon Press.

Rambusch, N. W. (1962). *Learning how to learn.* Baltimore: Helicon Press.

Ravitch, D. (1983). *The troubled crusade: American education, 1945-1980.* New York: Basic Books.

————. (1990). Multiculturalism, e pluribus plures. *American Scholar, Summer,* pp. 337-354.

Record, W. (1964). *Race and radicalism: The NAACP and the Communist Party in conflict.* Ithaca, NY: Cornell University Press.

Reed, A. & Bond, J. (1991). Equality: Why we can't wait. *The Nation, 253(20),* 733-737.

Reuter, J., & Yunik, G. (1973). Social interaction in nursery schools. *Developmental Psychology, 9,* 319 - 325.

Rist, R. C. (1979). *Desegregated schools: Appraisals of an American experiment.* New York: Academic Press.

Ross, B. J. (1972). *J. E. Spingarn and the rise of the NAACP, 1911-1939.* New York: Atheneum.

Rousseau, J. J. (1947). L'Emile ou l'education. In O. E. Tellows and N. R. Tarrey (Eds.), *The age of enlightenment.* New York: F. S. Croft. (Original work published 1762.)

————. (1961). *Emile* (B. Foxley, Trans.). New York: E.P. Dutton. (Original work published 1762).

Sadler, J. E. (Ed.). (1969). *Comenius*. London: Collier-Macmillan.

Saltz, E., Dixon, D., & Johnson, J. (1977). Training disadvantaged preschoolers on various fantasy activities: Effect on cognitive functioning and impulse control. *Child Development, 48*, 367-380.

Sava, S. G. (1987). Development, not academics. *Young Children, 42* (5), 15.

Schmidt, P. (1992). Study shows a rise in the segregation of Hispanic students. *Education Week, 11* (17), 1, 19.

Scott, J. W. (1976). *The Black revolts: Racial stratification in the USA*. Cambridge, MA: Schenkman Publishing Company.

Searle, J. (1990). The storm over the university. *New York Review of Books,* December 6, pp. 34-41.

Seefelt, C. (1981). Social and emotional adjustment of first grade children with and without Montessori preschool experience. *Child Study Journal, 11*, 231-246.

Shapiro, M. S. (1983). *Child's garden*. University Park: Pennsylvania State University Press.

Sharp, E. (1972). *The IQ cult*. New York: Coward, McCann & Geoghegan.

Skinner, B. F. (1953). *Science and human behavior*. New York: Macmillan.

————. (1968). *The technology of teaching*. New York: Appleton-Century-Crofts.

Sleeter, C. E. & Grant, C. A. (1987). A analysis of multicultural education in the United States. *Harvard Educational Review, 57,* 421-444.

Smilansky, S. (1965). *The effects of socio-dramatic play on disadvantaged pre-school children*. New York: Wiley.

Smith, L. (1949). *Killers of the dream*. New York: W. W. Norton.

Smith, R. M. (1991). With justice for all. *The Nation, 253 (20),* 754-756.

Snyder, A. (1972). *Dauntless women in childhood education*. Washington, DC: Association for Childhood Education International.

Snyderman, M., & Rothman, S. (1988). *The IQ controversy, the media and public policy*. New Brunswick, NJ: Transaction Books.

Spencer, M., Brookins, G., and Allen, W. (1985). *Beginnings: The social and affective development of Black children*. Hillsdale, NJ: Lawrence Erlbaum.

Stallings, J. (with D. Kaskovitz). (1974). *Follow through classroom observation evaluation, 1972 - 73*. SRI Project URU 7370. Menlo Park, CA: Stanford Research Institute.

Standing, E. M. (1962). *The Montessori method: A revolution in education*. Fresno, CA: Academy Guild Press.

Staples, R. (1975). To be young, Black, and oppressed. *Black Scholar, 7*, 2-9.

Steele, S. (1990). *The content of our character*. New York: St. Martin's Press.

Steinberg, S. (1991). Occupational apartheid. *The Nation, 253 (20)*, 744-746.

Steiner, G. Y. (1976). *The children's cause*. Washington, DC: Brookings Institution.

Stewart, J. B. (1984). The legacy of W. E. B. Du Bois for contemporary Black studies. *Journal of Negro Education, 53* (3), 296-321.

Taylor, H. F. (1980). *The IQ game: A methodological inquiry into the heredity-environment controversy*. New Brunswick, NJ: Rutgers University Press.

Taylor, R. (1976). Psychosocial development among Black children and youth: A reexamination. *American Journal of Orthopsychiatry, 46,* 4-19.

Thomas, C. M. (1992). *Comparing theories of child development* (3rd ed.).

Belmont, CA: Wadsworth.

Traub, J. (1991). Separate and equal. *The Atlantic, 268* (3), 24-37.

Vose, C. E. (1959). *Caucasians only: The Supreme Court, the NAACP, and the restrictive covenant cases.* Berkeley: University of California Press.

Vygotsky, L. (1986). *Thought and language* (rev. ed.). Cambridge, MA: The MIT Press.

Watson, J. B. (1913). Psychology as the behaviorist views it. *Psychological Review, 20,* 158-177.

Watts, J. G. (1983). On reconsidering Park, Johnson Du Bois, Frazier and Reid: A reply to Benjamin Bowser's "The contribution of Blacks to sociological knowledge." *Phylon, 44* (4), 273-291.

Weber, E. (1969). *The kindergarten.* New York: Teachers College Press.

Weikart, D. (1971). *Early childhood special education for culturally different children.* Ypsilanti, MI: High Scope.

West, C. (1993). *Race matters.* Boston: Beacon Press.

White, J. M., Yussen, S. R., & Docherty, E. M. (1976). Performance of Montessori and traditionally schooled nursery children on tasks of seriation, classification, and conservation. *Contemporary Educational Psychology, 1,* 356-368.

Whiting, B. B., & Whiting, J. M. W. (1975). *Children of six cultures.* Cambridge, MA: Harvard University Press.

Wilkerson, I. (1991). One city's 30-year crusade for integration. *The New York Times,* December 30, pp. 1, 11.

Wilkinson, J.H. (1979). *From Brown to Bakke: The supreme court and school integration, 1954-1978.* New York: Oxford University Press.

Williams, C. (1987). *The destruction of Black civilization: Great issues of a race from 4500 B. C. to 2000 A. D.* Chicago, IL: Thirds World Press.

Williams, G. W. (1968). (1968). *History of the Negro race in America from 1619 to 1880: Negroes as slaves, as soldiers, and as citizens* (2 vols.). New York: Arno Press. (original work published 1892 & 1893).

Williams, L. R., & Fromberg, D. P. (Eds.). (1992). *Encyclopedia of early childhood education.* New York: Garland.

Williams, V. J. (1989). *From Caste to a minority.* Westport, CT: Greenwood Press.

Wilson, W. J. (1987). *The truly disadvantaged: The inner city, the underclass, and public policy.* Chicago: University of Chicago Press.

Wohlwill, J. F. (1973). *The study of behavioral development.* New York: Academic Press.

Wright, R. (1966). *Native son.* New York: Harper & Row.

Yarmolinsky, A., Liebman, L., & Schelling, C.S. (1986). *Race and schooling in the city.* Cambridge, MA: Harvard University Press.

Young, K. (1990). American concepts of infant development from 1955 to 1984: What the experts are telling parents. *Child Development, 61* (1), 17-28.

Zangrando, R. L. (1980). *The NAACP crusade against lynching, 1909-1950.* Philadelphia: Temple University Press.

Zigler, E., & Gordon, E. (1982). *Day care: Scientific and social policy issues.* Boston: Auburn House.

# Index

Yale University Clinic of Child
  Development, 193
YMCA for Blacks, 75

Zale, Jonathan, 53
Zambian, 153

**About the Author**

HARRY MORGAN is Professor of Early Childhood Education at West Georgia College. He is the author of *Social Work in Early Childhood Programs* (1975) and *The Learning Community* (1973).